Also by Bahia Abrams

The Other Half of My Soul

ALIEN AT HOME: DIVINE INTERVENTION

The Life of Elie Sutton

as told to Bahia Abrams

Sutco Publishing
New York, NY

www.ElieSutton.com
ElieSutton@aol.com
BahiaAbrams@aol.com

First Printing—March 2011

Library of Congress Control Number
2010943274

Sutton, Elie and Abrams, Bahia
Alien At Home: Divine Intervention

ISBN 978-0-615-40085-3

This story belongs to Elie Sutton. Bahia Abrams wrote it as it was revealed
to her. Certain events in this book have been compressed, expanded,
or chronologically rearranged to reflect the importance, meanings, and
perceptions held by Elie Sutton. In preparing this book, every effort was
made to ensure accuracy of the information.

Designed and printed by Albert Hakim - www.laserwave.com

To my wife, Tunie,
to my family,
and to the memory of my father, Selim Menashé Sutton,
whose relentless devotion to his family
serves as an inspiration for future generations.

~~~~~~~~~~

I considered my path, and my legs returned me to the guarding of Your law
—Psalm 119:59

ACKNOWLEDGMENTS

I am grateful to Bahia Brenda Abrams for agreeing to take on this project. Tenaciously, she left no stone unturned with her meticulous probing, writing and rewriting, and researching to ensure accuracy. Her commitment, patience, foresight and endless hours went far beyond my expectations. She captured my life story as no one else could have.

I thank my children and their spouses for their encouragement, and for reading and commenting on the manuscript as it was in progress. Their input was invaluable and their reflections were, at times, more precise and sensitive than mine.

I value the support from my wife, Tunie, and from so many in my community—my extended family and friends who championed me during this project, often inquiring and anxiously awaiting my book's publication.

– Elie Sutton

~~~~~~

Elie Sutton devoted countless hours to this project, making available his staff, speaking with me candidly and honestly, answering my questions with abounding detail. It is only because of Elie's brilliant mind and extraordinary memory that I was able to capture his story.

When we needed a professional editor to critique the manuscript, I could think of no one more competent than Derry Eynon, a colleague and journalism professor. His guidance went beyond the realm of normal editing and I thank him for his valuable contribution.

I greatly appreciate the meticulous support of Ran Balleza of Sutton Management who provided computer expertise, synchronized the book's pages, and prepared the pictures.

And finally, I thank my husband, Allan, for putting up with my many late nights as I was absorbed in writing Elie's story.

— Bahia Brenda Abrams

REFLECTIONS FROM ELIE SUTTON

I lay my family's miseries on the doorsteps of Arab governments that feed their populations with hatred for all infidels, particularly the Jews. I believe that the story of the Palestinian refugees is a scam of outlandish proportions. Arab leaders from five surrounding countries immediately attacked the newly created state of Israel. So confident were they of destroying the Jews, they refused to accept the two-state solution voted by the United Nations in November, 1947. In 1948, they wanted it all. Today, nothing has changed.

It was an easy sell to the Palestinians, and easy to incite them to flee their homes, regroup, and then return to obliterate every Jew in the land. So great was the assurance of a quick victory, the people bought into the scheme. Jewish leaders pleaded with their Arab counterparts to calm the populace, to work toward a peaceful resolve—but to no avail.

Those Palestinians who chose to remain in Israel, in their homes, and not join in the frenzy, lived to share in the prosperity of Israel. They have been afforded full citizenship with rights and social benefits, as well as the opportunity to become part of the Israeli government. Those who opted to believe the lies fed to them and join the maddening crowd, were transported into Lebanon and Transjordan where they were not given citizenship but, instead, put into refugee camps to be used as pawns for Israel's destruction. Today, most of these Palestinians still live in refugee camps under the control of Palestinian leaders who use public relations to propagate world sympathy for their cause. Conveniently, the world blames Israel for the Palestinian plight and ignores the fact that, compared to the Palestinians, a far greater number of Jews from Arab lands lost their businesses and their homes, with no right of return.

Israel today stands as a shining example of success, transforming a desert into a thriving democratic country; making world contributions in the advancement of science, medicine and technology; and committing a global presence to help wherever natural disasters strike.

ALIEN AT HOME: DIVINE INTERVENTION

ONE

A PEOPLE'S MOST PRECIOUS GIFT IS THEIR HISTORY

Halab, the city of my birth, is one of the oldest, continuously inhabited cities in the world. My people's presence in the Syrian city goes back thousands of years. According to legend, our patriarch Abraham, on his sojourn from Ur to Canaan, settled for a while in Aram Soba, the ancient name for Halab. Stories tell of Abraham sharing milk from his goats with the city's poor. The name Halab comes from the Arabic word *halib*, meaning milk. In later centuries, the Ottomans referred to it as Halep. And during the French Mandate after World War I, it came to be called Alep, then Aleppo.

Hebrews began to populate Aleppo as early as the reign of King David, around 1,000 BCE, when his general, Joab, entered the land. Because of its popular bazaars and its strategic location for trading, midway between the Mediterranean Sea and the Euphrates River, Aleppo became a thriving caravan route. Thus, for Jews, given their proclivity for being merchants, Aleppo became a desirable location to settle.

Over time, the Jewish population multiplied. Word spread of their righteousness and strict adherence to G-d's laws. They prospered and earned a prestigious position in the region.

In Bahsita, the section known today as the old city of Aleppo, Jews built the Great Synagogue. The Aleppo Codex, the oldest known copy of our Bible with cantillation marks, was, for centuries, housed there. Sadly, after World War II, anti-Zionist Muslims engaged in violent riots against the Jews, torching the Synagogue and destroying a large portion of the Codex.

* * *

By the fourth century of the Common Era, Christianity had taken hold in the Roman Empire, and by the seventh century, Islam was well rooted and growing stronger. Consequently, Syria found itself overrun alternately between the Byzantines and the Muslims. During this long period, the Jews established a tight-knit community of their own, faring better under Muslim rule than Christian domination.

Renowned scholars and great rabbis flocked to Aleppo, becoming an integral part of the cohesive Jewish community there. With much joy and fulfillment, they engaged in lively correspondence with their *Torah* peers in Baghdad, Cairo and Spain. Maimonides, the great twelfth-century scholar, wrote his famous *Guide to the Perplexed* as a letter to Yosef ben Yehudah ibn Shimon of Aleppo. Later, in a letter to the Jews of Lunel, France, Maimonides praised the breadth of scholarship and high religious standards of the Aleppian Jewish community.

By 1516, Aleppo, with a population of about fifty thousand, was absorbed into the Ottoman Empire when the sultan, Selim I, conquered the ruling Mamluk Empire that was then centered in Egypt. Under Ottoman rule, Aleppo was able to continue its position as a major city in northern Syria and a thriving center for trade, industry and commerce.

* * *

The seeds of my family tree can be traced back to the late fifteenth and early sixteenth centuries, the time following the Spanish

Inquisition. Fleeing from the harsh realities imposed by the Spanish throne and the Inquisitors—forced Catholic conversion or death by fire—my ancestors traveled east across the Mediterranean in search of safe haven.

Sultan Beyazid II, then ruler of the Ottoman Empire, took note of the Iberian Jews—their skilled innovations, and, in some cases, their smuggled money. Opening his lands to these refugees from Spain, the Sultan is reputed to have said about King Ferdinand's expulsion decree, "Can you call such a king wise and intelligent? He is impoverishing his country and enriching my kingdom."

Moreover, in the face of rising anti-Semitism in Italy, many Italian Jews, known as *Franj* or Francos, also were drawn to Aleppo. It took many years for the Spanish, Franco, and native Aleppian Jews to put aside their differences and meld into one people, one cohesive community, but when that happened, the unique culture of Jewish Aleppo blossomed.

By the end of the sixteenth century, with the rise of the Levant Company, a chartered import-export trading business, two things happened. Aleppo was thrust into the unparalleled position of being the focal point for European trade, and England had become the world's greatest power. With sole rights to importing spices, perfumes, and currants, and to exporting cotton and textiles, the Levant built warehouses and a factory in Aleppo. Jewish merchants, pleased with exponential growth in their businesses, thanked G-d for their blessings and new prosperity.

* * *

From 1516 until 1918, Syria was ruled by the Ottoman Empire as a district, not as a separate state. But during World War I, from 1914 to 1918, the Ottomans made a grave miscalculation, aligning themselves with Germany. In the end, Germany lost the war and the Ottoman Empire collapsed. The victorious Allied powers—England, France, and the United States—abolished the Ottoman Empire and quickly carved out their bounty, awarding control of Syria and Lebanon to France, and Iraq, Palestine, and Trans Jordan to England. The region to the north, what is now Turkey, was subsequently attacked by Greece. A Turkish army officer named Mustafa Kemal, who opposed surrender, led the Ottoman Turks to victory and independence. In 1923, under the Treaty of Lausanne, the land was declared the Republic of Turkey. Kemal became its first president. He instituted a Western style democracy, modernized the country, gave equal rights to all, and raised the education and economic levels of the people. Eventually, Kemal assumed the surname Atatürk, Father of the Turks, and is revered in Turkey to this day.

* * *

In 1922, the League of Nations granted the French a mandate over Syria and Lebanon. French rule was harsh, suppressing newspapers, political activities and civil rights. The financial management of Syria came under the control of French bankers and, next to Arabic, the French language became the second official language of the country. When the French stalled on their promise to frame a constitution for Syria, the people grew increasingly embittered and disillusioned. Incited by their leaders, massive Muslim uprisings against French rule erupted. A nationalistic fire, burning to achieve independence, enveloped Syrian Muslims.

Aleppo's population at that time was about 125,000. Muslims made up almost ninety percent of the population. Small pockets of Christians and Armenians comprised another five percent, and the Jewish community formed the last six percent.

As in ancient times, Aleppo's Jews were clannish. Although continuing to do business with the local Muslim merchants, they lived and socialized among themselves. Intermarriage was forbidden and anyone violating this boundary was excommunicated and mourned as if dead.

Dedicated to their beliefs and observances of religious law, they made Jewish education compulsory for all their male children. Attending synagogue regularly, observing the weekly sabbath and all Jewish holidays, holding firmly to kosher dietary laws spelled out in Leviticus—all these practices were routine for the Jews of Aleppo. Syrian culture, with its customs and traditions, also was deeply rooted in my people, and our heritage still lives on wherever we may be. We are one people, undivided, not only through our religion, but also through our food, music, celebrations, entertainment, business practices, language and mannerisms.

* * *

In 1925, the year of my birth, resistance to the French had become a full-scale revolt across Syria. The French tried ruthlessly to smother the rebellion with aerial bombardments of civilian areas and heavy armor in urban neighborhoods. Adding to this upheaval, the Balfour Declaration of 1917 that promised Zionists a home in Palestine, triggered a passionate rise in anti-Semitism throughout the Arab world. This hostile zealotry had taken on a life of its own and was not going away.

For a short time, in the earlier half of the 1930s, the country experienced a lull and hoped the worst was over, but the spirit of revolution smoldered underground. In 1936, it broke loose again when France reneged on a treaty guaranteeing Syria its independence.

* * *

Our immediate history had a strong impact on my childhood. I grew up in a tumultuous atmosphere fueled by anti-French antagonism and mounting hostility by the Arab population against all Jews. My father, Selim Menashé Sutton, a proud and humble man, watched the trouble spiral upward for many years. Driven to protect his family, to find a way to get us all out of Syria, he carefully deliberated how to do this while continuing to earn a living and provide for us. Above all else, he wanted to free his children from the oppressive, threatening existence in Syria. Whatever sacrifices my father had to make to protect our futures and shield us from danger, he would do.

Developing a well thought out strategy, my father planned to send off his sons, one by one, as soon as each of us was old enough to travel. Departure would come during our teen years, before we had a chance to meet someone and marry, before we became entranced by earnings from a job or a business. He would allow nothing to hinder our emigration, no distraction to sway his decision.

With money for our passage to somewhere, and a little extra in our pockets until we found work, my father prayed to G-d for the strength to enable him to implement his plan, and for each of us to make it on our own when our time arrived.

My father, Selim Menashé Sutton A"H

Great Synagogue "al-Kanisat al-Kabira"
housed the Aleppo Codex

Aleppo Codex - Scroll

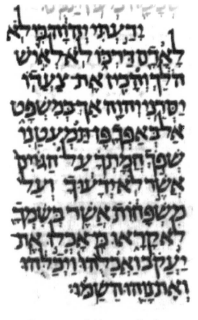

Portion of Aleppo Codex

TWO

The Syrian government recorded my name and religion, and a birth year of 1926. Nothing more. In Syria, no one celebrated birthdays, so a month and day were irrelevant. It took 80 years to learn that my life began on December 26, 1925.

On my eighth day of life, I had a *brit milah*, a ritual circumcision performed by a *mohel* from the Dayan family in Aleppo. This ancient rite, dating back five thousand years to the time of our patriarch Abraham, bound me in a covenant with G-d.

Family and friends came to our house to share in the joy of my birth. They celebrated the milestone with their presence, gifts and prayers, blessing me with a long life of Torah study, prosperity and many children. Syrian pastries and Turkish coffee were served. The guests lingered to socialize and engage in their favorite pastimes. In our apartment living room, the women played cards and the men played *tawleh* (backgammon).

* * *

I am the third son of Selim Menashé Sutton and Adele Laniado Sutton. My mother was promised to my father at the age of twelve. They married when she was sixteen and he was twenty-six. The match was considered substantial because both my parents came from respected families. Lineage always has been important to Syrian Jews, it is what has forged our identity and secured our future. Yet relative to the majority Muslim population surrounding us, the idea of lineage in our tight-knit community was ironic. In Aleppo, Jews were second-class citizens.

* * *

My *imee* (mother), in spite of her very limited education, was wise and caring. Yet in all family matters, she deferred to my father. She was the subservient wife. I do not remember my mother ever raising her voice to my father or confronting him on any issue. I also can't remember a time growing up when she was not pregnant or nursing.

Adele Laniado Sutton was one of eight children. She had three brothers and four sisters. My maternal grandparents were Haim and Farha Laniado. This was all the extended family we had and were very close with them.

My mother was always meticulously groomed. The few pieces of jewelry she had gave her much pleasure. When she and my father were first married, he presented her with a beautiful gold bracelet. She loved wearing it, along with her pearl necklace and gold wedding band.

To my mother, her children were the most important part of her life and she spent much time with us. I think her greatest joy was on special occasions when she had all of us dress up in our finest clothes and march off to the photographer's studio for family pictures.

Reflecting back, I realize now how much she had shaped my life. I took her for granted, something I regret. To this day, her words continue to resonate: *allah ma'ak*, the Arabic phrase meaning 'May G-d be with you.' Instinctively, the words flowed from her lips every time one of us left on a trip, especially for my father who traveled often on business.

* * *

Like my mother, my father also was one of eight children; four brothers and three sisters. His parents married in 1862. I never knew my paternal grandfather, Meir Menashé Sutton. He died before I was born. My paternal grandmother, Symbol Sasoon Sutton, died when I was seven, yet I remember her vividly. To me, she seemed very old, very aloof. Deep wrinkles lined her face, and all the time she wore a drab-colored headscarf tied under her chin. My paternal aunts and uncles left Aleppo when I was young, searching for a better economic life, or to get married, or to escape the escalating wrath of Muslim anti-Semitism. They settled in Palestine and the Americas.

My *ebee* (father) was bright and intuitive, disciplined and focused. There were times when we experienced his anger and knew when to reel ourselves in. His stoic demeanor masked the sensitivity and love I sometimes detected in him. When my father arrived at a decision, he stuck with it; no one and nothing could budge him.

Always earning a decent living, his responsibility for his wife and children was never in doubt. We were not rich, but we did live comfortably. Selim Menashé Sutton worked hard so that none of his children would have to.

With an outward charm, he flattered women and made friends easily. Everyone liked my father, especially my mother's family. Our Jewish community in Aleppo was an integral part of his life. He engaged in charitable giving, fundraising and helping wherever he was needed.

I know my father loved me. I know I loved him. I wish we had expressed those feelings to each other, just once. *I love you.* Three simple words that convey so much, yet for some, are so difficult to utter. The memory of my father is lodged in my mind; his presence is lodged in my heart.

* * *

I want to begin my story at the very foundation of my life, but I cannot. My mind only allows me to journey back to the age of three. So this is where I will embark.

My father was offered a three-year contract from the Turkish army to supply their soldiers with blankets and other bedding. With the help of our housekeeper and two of my uncles, my parents packed our belongings for the move from Aleppo, Syria to Mersin, Turkey. My brothers, Miro and Saleh, were sent outside to play catch ball. I stayed in the apartment to be near my parents.

* * *

We arrived in Mersin, a small city in southern Turkey near the border of northern Syria. Settling into a rented house, my father hired a Turkish woman to be our live-in maid. With three active sons, no running hot water, no refrigerator, no washing machine or dryer, and no convenience foods like we have today, my mother needed help.

My brother Miro attended kindergarten where he quickly picked up the Turkish language. Saleh and I were too young to go to school, so we stayed home learning Turkish from our maid and from the Turkish children with whom we played. Soon, the three of us were speaking Turkish more than Arabic. This did not sit well with my parents who wanted us to maintain our Arabic tongue. I think they counted the days until we could return to Aleppo, to reunite with our close extended family, our Jewish community and the familiarities of our lives.

During those three years in Turkey, one incident affected me so greatly that I never quite let go of its memory. I was around four years old. It had been a beautiful sunny day and the maid took me to the park to play. On our way home, while walking down a wide sidewalk, passing small shops, houses and apartments, a large procession of people approached. Marching along, they accompanied a horse-drawn open carriage with a fringe around the top. Excitedly, the maid swooped me into her arms, holding me up so I could see. "Look, Elie! Look! It's a funeral procession! They're carrying a dead body. The man in the coffin is dead."

The concept of the word *dead* was strange to me. My parents had never spoken of this. I stretched my neck, trying to get a glimpse. An open coffin, although at the time I did not know what a coffin was, lay in a rectangular space inside the carriage. A man, with his hands resting across his chest, was perfectly groomed—all dressed up with his hair neatly combed. He appeared to be in a deep sleep. I did not understand any of this. Disturbed, I gazed at the dead man, then stared down into the maid's face. Keeping in step with the procession, she continued to hold me high while rapidly explaining what 'being dead' means. I looked back at the well-groomed body. Feelings of anxiety took hold. "Is he Jewish?"

"No, Elie, he is not Jewish. Only Christian people dress up dead bodies."

"Do Jews get dead?" I was afraid to hear the answer.

"Yes, Jews die. Everybody dies . . . eventually."

All of this was beyond my grasp. "Take me home," I cried. "I don't like this." I needed to see my father and my mother. I needed to see Miro and Saleh. I wanted them near me so I would feel safe.

* * *

Sometime after that experience, I was awakened one night by my mother's loud moans. Then silence. I lay in bed with my eyes wide open.

My mother's cries began again and continued in intervals throughout the night. I was frightened. The experience with the dead man days earlier, haunted me. Visions of my mother dying, overwhelmed me. Then I heard scuffling outside the door. My brothers, with whom I shared the bedroom, sat up in their beds.

"Elie?"

"Yes, Miro . . . What?"

"Are you okay?"

"I'm scared for Imee."

The maid came into our room. She told us that soon there would be a new baby in the house and we should all try to get some sleep.

"I want to see Imee. I want to see Imee. I don't want her to be dead ... like that man." Clearly agitated, I began to cry.

"Your imee is going to be okay. She is having some pain and it hurts. But tomorrow the pain will go away and she will be better and you will have a new baby in your house. Your imee is not going to die. She will be okay." The maid tried to calm my fears.

The next afternoon, my brothers and I welcomed our sister Margo.

* * *

We returned to Aleppo in 1932, when I was six years old. I do not know if it was because my father's contract was not renewed or if my parents wanted to go home to our family and to our Jewish community. The Turkish maid did not return with us.

We moved into a modern apartment building in Jamalieh, a nice area in the new section of Aleppo, outside the old city of Bahsita. My mother was content because we had electricity and a new maid, and we lived close to my maternal grandparents. Our apartment had four bedrooms, an eat-in kitchen, a living room and one bathroom. Many

Jewish families resided in the building. A few Muslim families and some foreigners also lived there. They kept their distance from the Jews and we kept our distance from them. Still, we existed peacefully on the property.

The Jewish children formed close friendships, attending school together, playing catch ball, hide and seek, hanging out in each other's apartments and sometimes doing homework together. I went to school at the Talmud Torah, a Jewish elementary school for boys, located not far from our apartment. My brothers, our friends and I walked together to school.

In the classroom, we learned to read and write Hebrew so we could recite our prayers in synagogue and at home. We were immersed in Torah, the most revered and sacred book of my people. Like a sponge, I absorbed the first five books of our Bible—from the Creation of the world to the death of Moses. What captivated me most was the first book, the Book of Genesis. The stories, the characters, and the plots gripped me like I was reading the finest novel. We also studied the Talmud, the collection of ancient rabbinic oral laws, with Rashi's commentaries guiding us through the difficult passages.

Yet for the Talmud Torah to be an accredited school, the full load of Judaic studies was not enough. The state required instruction beyond our Jewish curriculum. We had to learn not only mathematics and geography but also French and Arabic languages, literature and history.

In addition to this demanding schedule, religion consumed a great deal of our lives. Our family kept strictly to the tenets of orthodox Judaism. We ate only kosher food, both inside and outside our home. Early every morning, my father chanted his prayers in Hebrew, sometimes in the synagogue and sometimes at home. He donned his *tallit*, prayer shawl. He lay *tefillin*, a pair of small black leather boxes that store pieces of parchment inscribed with passages from the Torah. Wrapping the straps of the tefillin to his arm and to his forehead, he prayed, praising G-d and proclaiming his faith and devotion to Him. In the early evenings, he would go to the synagogue for more prayers, combining *Mincha* (afternoon prayers) and *Ma'ariv* (evening prayers) into one service. My brothers and I were taught that when each one of us reached the time of our Bar Mitzvah, this daily ritual would be a requirement, a condition of our Jewish life.

On Friday evenings and Saturday mornings, we attended synagogue for weekly sabbath services. When my mother and sister attended with us, they sat in the balcony with the other females, separated from the men. My brothers and I sat with our father in the main sanctuary, immersing ourselves in prayer, swaying to the melodic chanting of the cantor.

Jews have many holidays. We celebrated every one. Always lavish meals, always our family together, always sharing with my grandparents, aunts, uncles, and cousins, and always much time spent in the synagogue. During the holidays of Rosh Hashanah, Passover and Sukkot, men, accompanied by their older children, would make short visits to relatives and friends, extending holiday greetings. All of the social calls were usually scheduled on one day, and at each stop, we were served a homemade sweet, a compote and Turkish coffee.

To get a sense of how deeply religion was rooted in my life, I'll share the Jewish holidays we celebrated each year. In early fall, our first holiday of Rosh Hashanah ushered in a ten-day period of self-examination, repentance and supplication, marking the beginning of the Jewish year. Then came Yom Kippur, the Day of Atonement, our day of fasting. *On Rosh Hashanah it is written and on Yom Kippur it is sealed: How many shall leave this world and how many shall be born into it;*

who shall rest and who shall wander; who shall be at peace and who shall be tormented . . . .

Sukkot arrived on the heels of our high holidays, bringing in nine days of joy, proclaiming the beginning of the fall harvest and commemorating the forty years of wandering in the desert after the Exodus from Egypt. Shemini Atzeret marked the conclusion of the fall harvest. In synagogue on Simchat Torah, we read the final verses of Deuteronomy and then the first verses of Genesis, followed by singing and dancing around our Torah. In early winter, during the eight days of Chanukah, we lit the candles of the Menorah and celebrated the rededication of the Second Temple in Jerusalem.

By late winter, we heralded in Purim, our most fun holiday. It honored yet another rescue of the Jewish people. Our heroine, Queen Esther, the Jewish wife of the Persian King Ahasuerus, intervened to save her people from annihilation by the king's chief adviser, Haman. In costumes and noisy groggers, we would go to synagogue to hear the rabbi read *The Book of Esther*.

Then, for eight days in early spring, the much anticipated holiday of Passover arrived. With our extended family at our large seder table, we engaged in liturgy, prayers, songs, and rituals, recounting the story of the ancient Exodus of the Israelites from generations of slavery in Egypt to freedom in the Promised Land of Israel. Our Passover diet for the week required an abstention from eating any leavened foods, especially bread.

The Omer, lasting forty-nine days, is the bridge between Passover and the final holiday of the Jewish year, Shavuot. The first thirty-three days of the Omer marked a time of no engagements, no weddings, no Bar Mitzvahs, no celebrations of any kind. It was a period of mourning for 24,000 Jewish students who had perished from a plague. On the thirty-third day, we celebrated Lag ba-Omer and resumed all celebrations and happy occasions.

Shavuot, coming fifty days after the end of Passover, honored the anniversary of Moses receiving the Ten Commandments at Mt. Sinai as well as the reaping of the first fruits of spring. In addition to these holidays, we observed several fast days throughout the year.

In early fall, the cycle of holidays would begin again. I tell you this to understand the full extent of how my education and my religion occupied my life.

* * *

Still residing in our apartment, three more brothers were born—Rafoul, whom we called Fillé and eventually Ralph; then Joseph, whom we called Basha and eventually Joe; and then Morris. Our family was outgrowing its living space. We needed to move.

My father's two single brothers, my uncles Hillel and Abraham, had built a large house in Jamalieh, not far from our apartment and near to my grandparents. Their business was failing and no job prospects were in sight. Moreover, anti-Semitism was furiously on the rise. Zionism was the cause. The Muslims viewed the Jews as a fast-approaching plague.

Looking at the future before them, my uncles decided that their best option was to leave Syria while they still could easily get out. They wanted to build a new life in Palestine, but they had no money. Approaching my father, they asked him to consider buying their house. A deal was made. To this day, I do not know the arrangements. My uncles Hillel and Abraham emigrated to Palestine and we moved to our new home.

* * *

The two-story house sat on the corner of a main street in Jamalieh. Its exterior was of Jerusalem limestone. Six steps led to a small porch and the front door. The rectangular-shaped main floor consisted of a large entrance foyer and living room surrounded by three rooms on each side. Our bedrooms faced the street. In the back of the house was a big kitchen plus one bathroom and one toilet for our entire household. There were two outdoor courtyards. One was accessible from the dining room and the other from the foyer and living room. The lower floor was equivalent to a large unfinished basement, which we used for storage. In our new home, in an upscale, modern section of Aleppo, we had no refrigerator, no freezer, no washing machine, no dryer, no running hot water and no central heating system. In the winter, each room was warmed by charcoal-burning trays. We bathed once or twice a week, using boiled water to fill the bathtub. In this house, we felt safe. Robberies and attacks in the area were relatively uncommon.

* * *

Aleppo, as well as the capital Damascus, had a low standard of living and the laws of Syria were strongly influenced by Islam and its holy book, the Qur'an. Local authorities were inefficient, backward and corrupt. The bureaucracy was prone to bribery. Human rights were easily compromised and women were treated as second-class citizens. Many wore veils in public. At times, suspected criminals were condemned with no trial and executed by hanging in the square. Municipal record keeping was sporadic and useless.

In my city, Jews had to keep a low profile. We learned how to avoid, at all costs, any contact with the local police. In public, we were never to wear a yarmulke or any clothing that displayed our Judaism. A Jewish star or any symbolic jewelry worn around our neck was to always be tucked under our shirt, kept invisible. Still, no matter how low-key and inconspicuous our practices were, everyone knew who was a Jew and who was a Muslim.

In time, my father made a decision. Sitting us around the table, he announced that there was no future for his children in Syria. "As soon as each of my sons is old enough, he will leave. One by one, each of you, on your own, will make a new life for yourself, a life away from the uncertainties, threats, and instability of living among Muslims. Here in Aleppo and in all of Syria, life will get worse for Jews."

I was a mere adolescent and had not yet had my Bar Mitzvah. *What was my father saying?* I could barely grasp his words. "But, Ebee, when . . . when?"

"I cannot tell you when. When the right time comes, I will know it."

"Why can't we all leave together? Our family . . . together?"

"No, Elie, we cannot all leave together. I have a business here and a family to support. And you will need money when you leave, plus enough to get you through until you find work. If I don't have my business, if we all leave together with no job prospects for me, no easy way to start up my business again, then what do we do? How can we survive? I will not have my family living in poverty, begging in a foreign land. Do you hear what I am telling you, Elie?"

I hung my head and nodded. My world as I knew it would some day be snatched from me. When, I did not know.

Assuring us that it was not going to happen tomorrow, or next month, or even next year, my father suggested we continue with our lives, our schooling, our friends. As always with his decisions, my mother was in full support. When my father was determined, there was no turning back.

* * *

My mother's younger brother came to live with us in our new house. My uncle Reuben, who was single, was diagnosed with tuberculosis. It seemed that having his own private bedroom in our home was more therapeutic for him than remaining in his own residence with my grandparents.

Although my parents had concerns about us being in such close contact to this illness, their hearts were too big to turn my uncle away. I think if they had been more aware of the consequences of their generosity, they may have limited our family's exposure. Much later, my brother Saleh contracted the disease—but more about that in another chapter.

* * *

After successfully completing my elementary school years at the Talmud Torah, I could choose between two private schools to continue my education. The Alliance Française was one. Headquartered in France, this Jewish school had many branches throughout the Middle East and North Africa. The required curriculum included the study of Hebrew and other courses relating to our religion, subjects I had already fulfilled at the Talmud Torah.

The other school was the Lycée Français, a French secular school that had an expanded curriculum reaching the equivalent level of an American college. The teachers were French born or French educated. The curriculum was taught in French and emphasized the sciences; geography; global history; mathematics, including algebra, geometry, and calculus; and a full comprehension of reading and writing in the French language. Moreover, as part of the government mandated curriculum, Arabic courses were included in the program of study. I chose the Lycée Français. It is the school from which I graduated.

There were also government subsidized schools which emphasized an Arabic curriculum and were attended mostly by Muslim students. A minimal level of education was taught in those public institutions, and attending public school was not compulsory. Moreover, a sizable portion of the population lived in the interior of the country, on farms or in villages where schools did not exist. Illiteracy in Syria was widespread, a generally accepted norm.

Still, all schools, private and public, had one thing in common— no importance was placed on music, arts and sports. Musical instruments were almost non-existent. There was no instruction on drawing or painting. And only occasionally did students play soccer, but it was never part of any curriculum. At the Lycée, we had one basketball court for the entire high school.

My classes at the Lycée were mixed, boys and girls. I had to adjust to this change, which was so unlike the boys-only Talmud Torah I had attended. Student dating was not encouraged; it went against the customs of our time. Co-ed social interaction occurred only on special occasions. Parties were sometimes arranged by adults and the music came out of a record player. Dancing was strictly supervised.

* * *

After our high holidays in the fall, I began my secondary education with a heavy heart. The weight of my father's decision played on my mind and I could not let go of the image I had constructed. *Leaving my family and my home. Leaving my city. Leaving my community and my friends. Leaving my school. Going off to some unknown country, with unknown people, speaking an unknown language. All alone. Never to come back.* The prospect of being isolated as a virtual orphan in some distant place in the world frightened me. Not knowing when, intensified my anxiety. By now, I knew I wanted to become a doctor. Would I ever be able to pursue that goal? I decided that 'yes I would,' no matter what obstacles confronted me.

* * *

Coming home from school, watching my mother kneading the dough and preparing it for the communal ovens for baking, comforted me. The communal ovens, capable of reaching the high temperatures needed to bake the flat Syrian breads for our Sabbath meals, somehow assured me that I was not being forced to leave, at least not yet. Sometimes, when doing my homework, I subtly observed my mother and the maids preparing big pots of food, also to be sent to the communal ovens for cooking. My mother's role was the same as with all Syrian women—cooking, cleaning, caring for her family. I clung to these small periods of time when life was not so threatening.

Why must a dark cloud hang over the Jews? We knew we were different. In the synagogue, we were careful not to be too loud, lest our voices be heard on the outside. Ceremonies such as blowing the shofar on the high holidays or celebrating the merriment of Purim were conducted so as not to disturb the Muslims. Our ways and our religion were scorned, mocked and ridiculed. The heat of hatred against the Jews rose and fell with the climate. In Aleppo, it was definitely on the rise.

* * *

My first profound experience with what it meant to be a Jew living in a Muslim land occurred when I was twelve, just after we returned from summer vacation. Two weeks before Yom Kippur, my father and grandfather came home with their arms loaded with squawking hens and roosters. They took the chickens to our basement and left them there. My brothers, my sister, Margo, and I had two weeks to play with these birds. The maid was responsible for feeding them with grains, fattening them up, preparing them for the annual *kaparot* ceremony. For two weeks, the sounds of the noisy creatures resonated upstairs into our living quarters. Through the Rosh Hashanah holiday, during the nights, in the mornings, we heard *Cluck, cluck and cocka doodle doooo*. This was fun for my siblings and me, and for awhile my spirits lifted. However, I knew the chickens were doomed and my mother and her helpers would be plucking feathers, cleaning and cooking the birds for our evening Yom Kippur meal, the meal preceding our twenty-five-hour fast, and just before attending Kol Nidre services at synagogue.

* * *

A few days before Yom Kippur, my maternal grandfather came by our house. "Elie, are you ready to go?"

I could hardly contain my excitement. This year was my turn, my first time to accompany my grandfather. I felt so special. My wide smile, stretching from ear to ear, showed my joy. Descending the steps to the basement, we gathered up the hens and roosters, securing each one with the equivalent of a leash. We could not afford to lose any of them.

Outside, the weather on that fall day was welcoming. Under a clear, blue sky, a gentle breeze cooled the hot rays of the sun, and I could detect a faint outline of the moon as it lingered in the heavens from the night before. On this day, we would symbolically transfer our sins and the sins of our family members onto another object—a chicken.

As we started on our way, I detected a twinkle in my grandfather's eyes. His grin beamed down upon me. I wanted to say, 'I love you, Jidaw.' I wanted to thank him for choosing me this year. I wanted to tell him how grateful I was for being able to share holidays with him and my grandmother. But I felt awkward. Unable to put my feelings into words, I said nothing.

The kaparot ceremony was held in an open field a mile from our house. We clung to the chickens, sometimes stopping to put them down, giving our arms a rest while securing their leashes. As we walked along, we passed apartment buildings, houses with courtyards, the big mosque, the bakery where we sent our dough to be baked, our synagogue, and the Talmud Torah where I had went to school. Crossing streets, we dodged a horse and buggy, a bicycle, four trams and a car.

The wide pasture soon came into view. "Look, Jidaw! Look!"

My grandfather's expression showed his joy. Firmly grasping the chickens, we picked up our pace. Men and boys crowded onto the field, standing in line, waiting their turns. Loud squawks from the chickens echoed in the air. We got into the queue.

Our turn came. The *shochet* (specially trained Jewish ritual slaughterer) examined each of our chickens, checking that they were healthy and blemish-free. Once the creatures passed inspection, feathers were plucked from their necks to make it smooth for the sharp knife to do its job.

Our rabbi led us through the ancient ceremony, a practice carried down from biblical times. Each hen and rooster was circled over our heads three times. The life of a chicken in exchange for purifying a human soul, for G-d's forgiveness of our sins. My grandfather provided the names of our family members. Roosters were sacrificed for the males and hens were sacrificed for the females.

One by one, the shochet thrust a quick slash to each chicken's neck, then threw the birds to the ground. For several seconds, the chickens danced around disjointedly, spilling their blood before falling lifeless.

* * *

Gathering the dead poultry in our arms, we began the trek back home where our chickens would be prepared for our holiday meal.

"Thank you, Jidaw. Thank you for such a wonderful day. I'm so happy to have . . ." Suddenly, a young Muslim man startled me from behind. Giving me a hard push, he threw me off balance, snatched the chickens from my arms, and dashed off. It all happened so quickly, there was no time to react. I felt sure he did this because I was a Jew. Feeling helpless and humiliated in front of my grandfather, I began to cry. "I'm sorry, Jidaw. I'm sorry for not holding on tighter."

With his arms filled with dead chickens, he tried to comfort me. "It's okay, Elie. It's okay. Things happen for a reason. This is in *Hashem's* plan. This was not your fault." He placed two chickens in my arms. "Here, these are getting too heavy for me. I need help carrying them home."

"But Jidaw, what if . . .?"

"I trust you. Tonight, a special prayer to Hashem for keeping us safe . . . yes?" A tender smile warmed his face. "Let's go home."

I nodded, "Yes, Jidaw." Then, " Jidaw?"

"What?"

"It's because I'm Jewish that he took the chickens. He wouldn't snatch chickens from another Muslim." Tears streamed down my cheeks. "Why do they hate us so? Why, Jidaw? Why?"

Our house in Aleppo

My family in our backyard; from left: Morris, Edgar, Adele, Selim, Joe and Ralph

THREE

LIFE IS A SUCCESSION OF LESSONS WHICH MUST BE LIVED
TO BE UNDERSTOOD—RALPH WALDO EMERSON

Being a Jew living in Syria was not a good thing. With no letup in the Muslim stance on anti-Semitism, I began to realize that my father's resolve to send each of us away had been a difficult choice, but a choice that held merit. My mother was resigned to supporting my father with his plan and accepting such a fate for her sons. Bringing children into the world, raising them, watching them leave—this had to be heart wrenching for my parents who did not know if they would ever see us again.

* * *

Sometime during my twelfth year of life, I had my Bar Mitzvah. One of the rabbis, a teacher from the Talmud Torah elementary school that I had attended, coached me through my portion of the Haftorah reading, prepared me in the melodies of the *pizmonim* and instructed me on the tones of the *maqam*.

Arriving at the synagogue on a Thursday morning, wearing my new tailor-made suit and my hair neatly combed, I was ready. On my wrist was a new, stylish watch, the standard Bar Mitzvah gift for most boys. On my finger was a ring with a blue sapphire stone, meant to ward off the 'evil eye.' Standing on the bimah, I looked out at my family, at my father. I wanted them to be proud.

Today, I would become a man. I would wear tefillin for the first time. I would be called to the Torah to chant my assigned *parasha*, my segment of the weekly reading from *The Five Books of Moses*. I now would be counted into a *minyan,* a minimum of ten men coming together to pray to Hashem. This ritual marked my rite of passage, formalizing my responsibilities to my religion and to my G-d.

Like my father, I would, from now on, lay tefillin for morning prayers, and pray again in the late afternoons and early evenings. Every day of my life, in Hebrew, I would recite prayers praising our G-d. My training at the Talmud Torah school prepared me for all of this.

It was preferable that I attend communal prayers at the shul, but my father did allow for a little flexibility when schedules conflicted and we could not attend synagogue. At those times, my father, my brothers and I prayed at home. Missing prayers was not ever acceptable. Moreover, on the Sabbath and on holidays, there were additional prayers to our recitations. In accordance with our tradition, I adhered to every ritual and held sacred the laws of our Torah.

Following my Bar Mitzvah ceremony at the synagogue, family and friends came to our house. Spread across our large dining room table was a wide array of hors d'oeuvres and Viennese pastries. The guests helped themselves to Turkish coffee and the homemade delicacies. Tables were set up in the living room for the men to play backgammon and for the women to have their card games.

* * *

My parents were definitely stoic and we children were definitely not spoiled. Like most families in our community, my father's role was to support our family and make decisions—not to dispense affection. My mother's role was to support my father in his decisions and to make sure her family's needs were met. And like most women in the community, my mother got dressed up for her routine card games with lady friends. Rarely, did she permit anything or anyone to interfere with this diversion.

To help my mother with the household chores, we always had at least one, but most times two live-in maids. With so many children to care for and no appliances or hot water, helpers lessened the heavy burden on my mother. But my parents were cautious of who they brought into our house. Once, there was a tragedy involving a Muslim maid who worked for a family in our Jewish community. Their young daughter died mysteriously. Foul play was suspected, although never proven. After that incident, my parents closely screened who they hired, who they could trust. "Only Jewish women," my father asserted. On this issue, like so many others issues, he was uncompromising. So, in our house, we grew up with Jewish maids, uneducated women who came from poor families. My father gave them a job, a place to live, and insisted we treat them decently. In turn, they helped with the laundry— hand washing the clothes, hanging them to dry and ironing them. They kept our large house clean, served the meals and assisted my mother with the cooking and baking.

* * *

My father was a wholesale textile merchant, the sole owner of his business. His workplace was located on the ground floor inside a *khan*, a compound of many business establishments. A large guarded portal kept the complex secure. Furthermore, each individual concern had a heavy door that could be bolted for additional protection, especially when a business was closed. My father rented three connecting rooms at the khan. One room was set aside to be his office, where he did his own bookkeeping. The two larger rooms served as his warehouse. Bolts and bales of fabrics in many different varieties and qualities filled the storage space.

Salesmen earned their money through commissions. They would solicit buyers for the fabrics and bring them to the office to meet with my father. Many times, I watched the wrangling. The buyer would fake disinterest, showing his readiness to walk out because he was not getting the price he expected. The salesman would then pull him back, even blocking the exit if necessary. This performance sometimes went on for hours until a deal was made. Sales were on credit and sealed with a handshake; sometimes a promissory note was signed. My father expected payment in thirty to sixty days.

Often, I stopped at my father's office during my days off from school. Since it was an hour's walk from our house, I usually took the public trams which ran frequently and the fare was cheap. Almost no one owned a car. Bicycles were scarce and horse-drawn carriages operated as taxis. In the office, I would run insignificant errands for my father. I also took naps on top of piled-up goods, the only place I could lie down in the middle of the day and sleep. I loved it.

Then there was the entertainment, which for me was the best part of my office visits. Witnessing the negotiating process between salesmen, buyers and my father never failed to amuse me. It was a sport that I learned well. Later, in my adult life, when I had businesses of my own, I played the game quite successfully.

At times, when inventory needed to be replenished, Selim Menashé Sutton traveled to Beirut, Lebanon, to buy stocks of fabrics from various importers. A busy harbor, Beirut was the the port of entry for goods from all over the world, most notably from China and Japan. My father skillfully negotiated large purchases of differing materials, then had his orders shipped by freight train or truck to his warehouse in Aleppo. On these buying trips, my father always closed his office. He was not comfortable trusting the salesmen to run the business.

My father made a good living and we lived well, two facts he felt compelled to repeatedly remind us of. "We are a large family," he would say. "There is always plenty of food in our house. All of you wear nice clothes. You go to good schools. You have money for the things you want. You spend summer vacations in the mountains." At this point, he would pause, hoping we were digesting his words. "And this big house . . . do you think it runs on its own? It takes money to maintain it. I work hard every day so we can afford this comfortable life."

* * *

For sure, I did not spend all my free time in my father's workplace. Sometimes I chose to be with friends. My social boundaries were strict. The Muslims did not associate with us, and we did not socialize with them. My friends were Sephardic Jews like myself. On days off from school, we hung out together. The social connections, even on a casual level, filled a need. Friends were important. They were my digression, indirectly easing the heavy burden I put on myself.

Because access to sport activities was not readily available to us, we found other things to do. My friends and I roamed. From souq to souq, from marketplace to marketplace, we passed our time. One place sold coffee beans, rice and spices. We took pleasure in sniffing the scents of pepper, oregano, and cinnamon. Another souq sold all kinds of fresh vegetables. Still another housed butcher shops and tanneries. When we wandered through the fabric shops with their colorful displays of materials, I often would speculate on which, if any, had purchased their goods from my father.

Strolling through the covered bazaars, we inevitably would stop to buy charcoal-broiled corn or chestnuts, all readily available from the busy vendors. What I loved most was the ice cream. In Aleppo, we could get the most delicious ice cream. Never, since I left Aleppo, have I been able to find ice cream that good. Mmmm . . . in my memory, I can still savor the soft, cold taste on my tongue.

The souq was an exciting place to be. People came from all over—from the city, the villages and the farmlands. Peddlers arrived with their donkeys loaded down with merchandise. Everywhere, one could hear the loud wrangling from buyers and sellers. Haggling was not exclusive to my father's office. It was a national pastime. The Aleppian people thrived on it.

I liked the fact that, on these enjoyable afternoons, I did not have to rush home for dinner. The only times my family ate together was on the weekly shabbats and on Jewish holidays; then, our presence was mandatory. But on all other evenings, we ate separately. Accommodating our varying schedules simplified life for all of us. Whatever time each of us was ready for a meal, the maid was ready to serve it.

* * *

One day, when walking home from school with my friends, something terrifying happened. Our normal route took us past a water-pumping station. There were many public water-pumping stations around the city because some homes did not have running water. A crowd had been gathering around the station. Grisly sounds echoed through the air. Curious to see what was going on, my friends and I edged our way toward the front. Two Muslim men were engaged in a fierce argument. Pretty soon, the argument escalated into a bloodthirsty fight. Horrified, I wanted to leave.

"No, Elie. Stay. We all want to watch," one of my friends said.

"But what if . . ."

"Come on, Elie. This is exciting. We're all staying to watch," another friend coaxed.

I looked around. Masses of people now converged and more were coming. They were all male Muslims, mostly adults. It would have been a struggle for me to make my way out. Moreover, I did not want to be seen as a spoilsport by my friends. So I stayed.

The two men were going at it, punching, kicking, scratching. Blood oozed from their faces, their noses, their mouths. The audience was absorbed, apparently enjoying the spectacle. They did nothing to stop it. They only gawked. My friends and I, what could we do without jeopardizing our own lives? Although it was difficult for me to watch, my curiosity did get the best of me. Then I saw one of the combatants leave and the other stagger to the ground. I thought the melee might be over, but it wasn't. The man on the ground struggled to get up. Nobody offered to help. Within minutes, the man who had left, returned with a butcher knife. Like a savage, he stabbed his adversary over and over again, stopping only when the loser, soaked in his own blood, gasped for his last breath. Swiftly, the attacker fled the scene.

The police arrived, but it was too late to stop the havoc or thwart the killing. Quickly, the people dispersed. In silence, my friends and I left the site. I headed home.

This horrifying event was one I wished I had not witnessed and I tried to sort out how such things happen. What causes humans to become so angry that they lose all sense of right or wrong? Is anger so powerful an emotion that one cannot help but succumb to its destructive force? Later, I heard that the murderer was caught, news that offered me little consolation.

When I related this incident to my father, he responded, "If the Muslims do this to their own people, just think of what they are capable of doing to us Jews. Things will not get better in Syria. Now, do you understand why each of you must leave?"

"But with my family . . ." I tried to reason.

"No, Elie. One by one. Each of you. This is my plan. It is the best I can give to my children."

Entrance to the khan - my father's office and storeroom

My brother Joe at main entrance to khan,
during a visit to Syria in the year 2000

FOUR

IT IS IN OUR LIVES AND NOT IN OUR WORDS
THAT OUR RELIGION MUST BE READ—THOMAS JEFFERSON

At home, we all spoke Arabic. It was our everyday language. At school at the Lycée, we spoke French. Hebrew was mandatory for praying and religious instruction.

* * *

I was riddled with anxiety about my future and felt the weight of the world on my shoulders. My teachers noticed my pensive, somber nature. Joking, smiling and laughing had all but disappeared from my demeanor. I feared being wrong or doing anything that might be perceived as improper. I could not tolerate triviality or insincere social convention. I avoided anyone with extreme attitudes or excessive behaviors. Two things saved me from myself. First were my studies. I was a serious and excellent student. Second, I had an overwhelming desire to go to medical school and become a practicing doctor so I could heal people. My medical training would forever be in my brain. No one could take that knowledge from me and I always would be able to earn a living because the need for doctors is constant. Moreover, I wanted to be held in high esteem and feel good about myself. For these reasons, I was driven to attain my goal.

The Latin proverb, *virtue stands in the middle*, had a significant impact on me. Throughout my years at the Lycée, this maxim served as a guideline to help bolster my outlook, otherwise depression might easily have taken hold.

At the Lycée, our Jewish student body was forced to join various nationalistic groups and attend many of the meetings. The gatherings served as a venue to promote beliefs that foreigners caused Syria's problems, especially the Jews of Palestine who wanted their own state. The message could not be more clear. The Jews of the world are undesirable waste, and we Jews of Syria are inferior and should no longer assume Syria to be our home. Syria would never again count on the Jews to be productive citizens or be part of the country's future. We saw our roots being yanked from under us.

My friends and classmates regularly discussed our fate and agreed that it would be a sham for any of us to consider a future in Syria. We had to leave the country. Life as we knew it must eventually come to an end. My father was right. I had to come to grips with his decision.

* * *

In the Mediterranean region, Aleppo's climate was predictable. Winters, although cold, were rarely freezing. Snow fell on occasion, but it rained far more than it snowed. Spring was beautiful with moderate temperatures and little precipitation. Summers were dry and hot, lasting from May through September. I cannot remember rainfall during those months. Most of the wet weather in Aleppo occurred in the fall, beginning around the Jewish holiday of Sukkot.

During the summer months, schools throughout Syria were not in session, so summer time was synonymous with vacation time and my family headed to the higher grounds of Lebanon where temperatures were twenty to thirty degrees lower than in Aleppo. We would pack up, board a train, and in three hours would be in the mountainous region known as the Switzerland of the Middle East. Most every summer, my father rented a house in one of the many small villages, though not necessarily always in the same village. Numerous families from our Jewish community in Aleppo joined us in these mountains, as well as Jewish families from Beirut who sought to escape the city's heat and humidity. Thus, the Lebanese and Syrian Jews mingled, becoming a cohesive unit during the summers.

We rented furnished houses owned mostly by Christians and Druze, and since the kitchens in these non-Jewish houses were not in accordance with Jewish kosher laws, we had to make the kitchens kosher. I remember my mother and the two maids taking out all the pots and pans, dishes, and cutlery and separating them into two piles—some to be used strictly for dairy and some strictly for meat. Then they would dip them in boiling water to kosher everything.

Thanks to the large summer influx of Jews into the Lebanese highlands, there were synagogues and rabbis, as well as easy access to kosher foods. Our religion was portable. We could take it with us and adhere to our traditions wherever we were. My father, like most men in our community, worked during the week, so time with family in the mountains was on the weekends. Normally, he arrived Thursday or Friday and returned to Aleppo on Monday mornings.

Our summers in the mountains were less hectic than life in Aleppo, and I was happy there. I always welcomed the long lull from school.

Lebanese society, with its Western leaning culture, embraced a more open and accepting mindset than did Syria. I loved the rugged, yet graceful and majestic mountains where we rented a house, as well as the beautiful beaches on the Mediterranean and the exciting city of Beirut. For entertainment, my friends and I went to surrounding villages and visited relatives and friends. We hung out in the cafés, picnicked, and played soccer, cards and backgammon. Trains, buses and car services provided daily commutes to and from Beirut and the beaches. I secretly wished we could have remained in Lebanon permanently.

* * *

By the end of the summer, we left Lebanon and returned home in time to prepare for Rosh Hashanah and Yom Kippur. I did not look forward to my return to school after the holidays because of the anti-Semitism I knew would confront me, but I did want to get back to my studies and be another year closer to realizing my dream of medical school.

* * *

In the fall of 1939, Yom Kippur, the holiest of our holidays, fell on Saturday, September 23. Because this occurred simultaneously with our sabbath day, an additional level of sanctity and spirituality illuminated our observance. I walked with my family to our nearby shul. A gentle breeze ruffled in the early morning air as clouds began to form overhead. We approached the simple structure, faced with Jerusalem stone. A wide courtyard separated the building from the Talmud Torah Yeshivah that I attended before going on to the Lycée. A big gate and a caretaker kept the property secure.

As we entered the synagogue through the large wooden door, my mother and my sister quickly proceeded to the second floor where a balcony-like section was reserved for the women. The area was set back and a *mechitzah*, a curtain, kept the women secluded. My father, my brothers and I took our seats together on the main level. The men around us already were into the service. Some glanced up, smiled and nodded, then went back to their *machzors*, prayer books.

Everyone in the congregation held our rabbi in the highest esteem. He was the faithful transmitter of G-d's words, spelled out in the Torah. He was our authority on Jewish law and we followed his dictates without question.

On this holy morning as the Ark was opened, revealing the three Torahs before us, we stood to honor the sacred teachings passed down from Hashem. We remained standing for quite some time, swaying to the mellifluous tones of the cantor. When the Ark was closed, we took our seats. Everyone was intently engaged in prayer. I held in my hand my machzor, the book passed down to me from my father's father. Suddenly, an angry outburst reverberated around the room, jolting my concentration. I lifted my eyes toward the blaring sounds. At the front, a member of our congregation, red-faced and sweating, waved his fist at our beloved *hacham*, rabbi. The rabbi quietly tried to calm the man. The more gentle the rabbi's words, the louder the man became.

In disbelief, I yanked at my father's sleeve, "What is he doing?"

"Pay no attention, Elie . . ."

"But, Ebee, look what he's doing. He's yelling at the rabbi. Someone needs to stop him."

"Quiet, Elie. Focus on your prayers," my father muttered with annoyance.

"But he's yelling at the rabbi. Why isn't anyone helping the rabbi?" I continued to keep my voice low.

"Elie, I think the rabbi can handle the situation." He looked at me sternly.

"But . . ."

"The man is overwrought. He doesn't know what he's doing. Now, shhhhh," my father snapped. I detected his anger brewing. "Learn from his mistake!"

"Such a terrible sin. Surely he will suffer some awful punishment for this. Do you know what will happen to him?"

"Stop it, Elie!"

My father clenched his teeth and the muscles in his face tensed. I knew I should say no more. This was not the time to test my father.

* * *

At 4:45 in the morning on September 1, 1939, the giant guns of the German battleship Schleswig-Holstein opened up, firing upon the Polish city of Danzig. Day after day, the German Luftwaffe attacked one Polish city after another. Then, on September 17, Stalin's Red Army crossed Poland's eastern border to assist their Nazi ally. Although Poland, France and England declared war on Germany, the Polish people were left to defend themselves.

The French army, reputed to be the finest in the world, stood aside and did nothing. They chose to take refuge behind the Maginot Line, a broad fortification of concrete and steel spread along the French-German border. The British, following the policies of Prime Minister Neville Chamberlain, were equally inactive.

On September 23, 1939, as I sat with my family in the synagogue on Yom Kippur day, the German Army went on a rampage in Drobin, Poland, coercing the town's rabbi to sweep the marketplace, destroying Jewish businesses, stripping Jewish houses, and forcing the Jews to wear armbands with a yellow star. When the Germans demanded an unrealistic sum of money that the Jews could not pay, the Germans killed many of them and sent the rest to concentration camps as slave labor.

* * *

After our high holidays in the fall of 1939, I entered my second year at the Lycée. Facing more anti-Semitic attacks, escalated by Hitler's triumphs across Europe and the Grand Mufti's successes in stirring up the Muslim populace against the Jews, I found myself dreading the daily sneers from my non-Jewish classmates. I felt like an alien in my own country. I wanted to flee this environment, escape from Syria. I wished my family and I could just leave. But that was not to happen. My father's decision was firm.

My only salvation was to finish my homework in the evenings and walk with my friends to the coffee house. That was my distraction from the mounting pressures scarring my self esteem. There, my friends chattered and joked, but I usually said nothing.

A block from my home were two coffee houses diagonally across from each other. Except in the winter time when the cafés were closed, my friends and I hung out there in the evenings after we finished our homework. Both coffee houses each accommodated more than one hundred people. Each had a large street-level rectangular room with windows lining all four sides. Men, young and old, frequented the cafés. Women were not forbidden entry, but they normally did not venture out of their homes alone.

Upon entering the café, we paid a cover charge once we chose a table and sat down. Waiters served pastries, ice cream, light food and coffee. Men played either backgammon, a variety of card games, or billiards with three balls—not the fifteen-ball game we are familiar with in America. My friends and I could usually be found at the pool table or playing solo or bridge. Sometimes my father came to the coffee house to socialize and play backgammon with other Jewish men, but his work kept him from doing this too often.

Almost everyone smoked cigarettes or a *narguile*—a water pipe with a mouthpiece filled with tobacco and burned by charcoal. Inevitably, the room was saturated with smoke. My mother never needed to ask where I spent the evening. She knew by the smell of my clothes.

My grandparents lived across the street from the two coffee houses. I loved my grandparents and often I went to their house to visit. They were my sounding board. I talked to them about the anti-Semitism at school and about my father's decision to send each of us away. They listened and offered me pastries and coffee.

* * *

Thursday, November 2, 1939, marked the twenty-second anniversary of the Balfour Declaration. Jews all over the Muslim world knew better than to venture outdoors. We stayed inside our homes behind bolted doors. This year, my father's determination to emigrate his sons took on greater urgency.

In a formal statement of British policy, Foreign Secretary Arthur James Balfour had given to Lord Walter Rothschild a letter spelling out the terms of a national homeland in Palestine for the Jewish people. Rothschild, an active Zionist, worked together with his close friend, Chaim Weizmann, later the first president of Israel, to pursue the dream of a Jewish homeland. The letter of Declaration, on November 2, 1917, set in motion both a strong message of hope to Jews everywhere and a brutal wave of anti-Zionism/anti-Semitism attacks on Jews throughout the Arab world. From the time of that British precept, every November second marked a surge in the ongoing violence against Jews in Muslim lands. Men, women and children were spat upon, beaten, imprisoned and sometimes killed just for being Jewish. We knew to remain in our homes and out of sight.

Britain, which was responsible for the mandate, soon acknowledged the rights of Arab countries to stand in solidarity with the Palestinian-Arab cause. As an increasing emphasis and greater need was placed on the value of Middle-Eastern oil, Britain became the linchpin of their own national politics.

* * *

On a Saturday afternoon in January 1940, after services at the synagogue and a lunch of leftovers from the festive shabbat dinner the night before, my father, my brothers and I sat at the dining room table to study the parasha, the Torah portion of the week. Outside, the weather was cold and drizzly. Hours passed. Soon night crept in. My mother went into labor. My father sent a helper to fetch the midwife. By midnight, we had another brother. We called him Edgar. I now had six brothers and one sister. Edgar was the last of my parents eight children.

* * *

War raged everywhere. Germany at one end of the globe and Japan at the other were each on a course of world domination and there could be only one victor. I prayed for Germany to fail in its goal of an earth comprised only of an Aryan race. I prayed for it not to be a world without Jews.

In our geography class at school, we followed the movements of world events. On a large map, we recorded Hitler's progression with head pins. It seemed like every day we advanced the head pins from one city to the next.

At home, the radio was on more than it was off. My father's ear was glued to the news broadcasts. I think he tried not to alarm us. I know he wanted to protect us for as long as he could. But world events were not a secret. In time, my father realized that we all knew what was going on.

By June 1940, France surrendered to the Germans on condition that Paris remain untouched and be declared an open city. The seat of French government was relocated to Vichy in the south of France under the leadership of General Phillipe Pétain, who was a national hero.

Meanwhile, General Charles de Gaulle fled to England with a small group of loyal followers known as the Free French. Joining with the Allied forces, he became a significant and reliable source for military strategies and his support base grew exponentially.

With the Vichy government now in charge, the balance of power in the Middle East shifted. French Vichy authorities assumed greater control over Syria than Paris had under the French Mandate. In Iraq, the Grand Mufti of Jerusalem issued a *fatwa*, a ruling proclaiming a holy war, giving Muslims a free ticket to kill Jews at whim, anywhere in the Muslim world. They could torture us, beat us, and incinerate our homes, businesses and synagogues. All Jews felt the heat rising. The Muslims in Syria hated us, but they also hated the French and did not want to be ruled by outsiders.

* * *

My father had four brothers. Two emigrated to Palestine after they sold us their house. The other two had left for the United States many years before, settling in Brooklyn, New York, where a growing community of Syrian Jews had taken root. My American uncles were married, had families, started businesses and lived comfortably. Occasionally, my father and his brothers corresponded.

One day in early summer of 1940, my father received a reply to a letter he wrote to his brother Joe who had a successful business importing table linens, bed linens and handkerchiefs. Uncle Joe had an office in Shanghai, China. His employees there were responsible for buying products in various stages of development, supervising the entire manufacturing process and loading the finished goods onto a freighter destined for the port of New York.

Uncle Joe accepted my father's offer to employ one of his sons and asked my father to arrange transportation to Shanghai for him. With war raging across the world, Japan, with it's imperial ambitions in the Far East, was advancing deeper into China. The timing could not have been more imperfect. It was not safe for anyone to travel. Still, my father was determined. Without informing his brother, Selim Menashé Sutton decided to send not one, but two of his sons to Shanghai. Perhaps he believed that Miro and Saleh together stood a better chance of staying afloat. I will never know.

My father announced the news. "Miro and Saleh will leave for Shanghai, China, as soon as it can be arranged."

I felt the blood drain from my head. For a moment, blackness confronted my vision and I thought I would falter. Panic and anger bubbled up within me and my body quivered. After my two older brothers, then who? Me, the third son. I am next. Why did my father wait so long? Why didn't he save enough money to get all of us out of Syria together? I was afraid for Miro, who was not yet nineteen, and Saleh, who just turned seventeen. To be out on their own, confronting uncertainties and a war of cruel and gruesome dimensions, was not fair. I also was worried about my own future.

* * *

I convinced myself I could control my fate. My determination to go to medical school and become a doctor was as strong as my father's determination to get us safely out of Syria. I concentrated on my schoolwork. I was smart. My grades were exceptional. I could do it. No Shanghai for me.

*Clockwise: Sutton family in Aleppo—Selim, Saleh, Adele,
Joe, Ralph, Morris and Edgar*

Brother Joe, father Selim and mother Adele in Beirut

FIVE

The timing to send Miro and Saleh to Shanghai could not have been worse. A great conflict between Japan and America was on the verge of exploding. As each vied for economic control in the Far East, Japan's military might grew wider and stronger. Japan's imperialist policies were strategically aimed to dominate China and secure its vast raw material reserves. Simultaneously, the Chinese believed strongly in nationalism and self determination, yet its weak army was no match for the Japanese.

In 1937, Japan captured the famous Marco Polo Bridge, located just outside of Beijing. This strike on the longest ancient stone bridge in northern China set in motion the Second Sino-Japanese War. Casualties mounted on both sides, month after month as one battle followed another.

Frustrated by their own losses, Japan decided to retaliate, ordering their Imperial Air Force to conduct massive air bombing raids on civilian targets in every major city of unoccupied China. The attack left millions of civilians dead, injured or homeless. By 1940, the Chinese Army launched a full-scale counter-offensive, but its limited experience in modern warfare and sub-standard weaponry were no match for the Japanese.

The city of Shanghai, where Miro and Saleh were going, was known for its thriving cotton industry and abundance of cotton mills. As Japanese dominance grew in the region, Shanghai's cotton production tumbled and non-Japanese trade relations deteriorated. Yet, Shanghai did hold its status as an open city. If you could get there, you were welcome to stay. No questions asked. No visa. No papers of any kind were required. European Jews fleeing the Nazis found sanctuary in Shanghai, despite Japan's alliance with Germany. Japan sensed a certain indebtedness to Jews that dated back to 1905 when an American Jewish banker, Jacob Schiff, financially supported Japan during its 1905 war with Russia.

* * *

Like all children in our Jewish community in Aleppo, we led sheltered lives. We were not spoiled, but rather protected from the harshness of the outside world. My father, like all fathers in our Jewish community in Aleppo, was strict. My siblings and I always knew to obey him, never to challenge him. When he entered a room, we stood. When we walked, my father stepped out first. We followed behind. Only on occasion when he took our hand, did we walk alongside him. My father's word was law. His decisions were set in concrete. Selim Menashé Sutton demanded our respect and he received it.

* * *

For Miro and Saleh, their time had come. I do not believe they were aware of the potential dangers in Shanghai. And I suspect that my Uncle Joe did not bargain for two employees arriving together. Nevertheless, they booked their trip. Following is the story my brother Miro told to me many years later:

We were on holiday from school when Dad told Saleh and me that we would be going to Shanghai to work for Uncle Joe. From there, he gave us hope that we could eventually make it to the United States . . . to New York. We knew nothing of Uncle Joe's business. The only information we were given was that he was married, had a family, lived in America, in Brooklyn, New York; he was Dad's older brother, and he would meet us when the boat reached Shanghai. Never were we told that Uncle Joe had asked for only one of us. We had no idea what would be expected of us when we arrived. And I don't think Uncle Joe knew how young Saleh and I were.

Dad, Saleh and I left Aleppo and went to Palestine where we spent several days visiting relatives. From there, we boarded a train to Port Sa'id. As the train crossed the Sinai, the conductor approached us, "Your tickets and papers." He waited until all three of us took out the documents, then glanced through them. "You don't have the correct papers to get into Egypt." Abruptly, he pulled the cord, stopping the train. "Get off the train. We cannot take you any further." On the documents, the conductor noted our religion; it was enough evidence to support his action.

Unsettled about being forced out in the middle of the desert, we began to walk. Not long after, we spotted a small village in the distance and thanked G-d. Reaching the tiny community, Dad was able to engage a driver and for a token of money, he agreed to take us to Port Sa'id. We had not gone far when a sandstorm blew up, covering both the road and the car. We had to turn back. In the village, Dad found a man who agreed to put us up for the night. Dad gave him some money and he led us to what looked like a barn with a few makeshift mattresses on the floor. This is where we slept, or at least tried to sleep.

By morning, the desert was calm and the road was passable. Dad engaged another man to take us to Port Sa'id. When we arrived,

Dad thanked the driver and paid him. We found our way to the dock, but we missed our boat. We had to wait another two weeks for the next ship destined for Shanghai to come in. Dad rented a hotel room for us. We said our 'goodbyes' and Dad returned to Aleppo. That was it. No advice. No guidance. We were now on our own.

Saleh, always the adventurous one in our family, was energized. "Finally, on our own," he said. "Finally we can do whatever we want. Father isn't here to control us."

Because I was more apprehensive than Saleh, his confidence and excitement were reassuring. Port Sa'id was a quiet place with not much to do, except when an occasional boat docked at the pier and passengers disembarked. Then the town came alive. Stores opened and traders did what they love best—noisy haggling with customers. But we had to be careful. We didn't have a lot of money to spend. What Dad gave us had to stretch to Shanghai.

Finally, our ship came in. It was a large boat called Conté Biancamano. We boarded, then checked out our cabin. It wasn't as bad as we had anticipated. In fact, it was pretty comfortable. Our difficulty came at mealtimes. Italian cuisine was served to the passengers, mostly Jews fleeing Hitler and Stalin. The food looked and smelled delicious. If only we could have eaten it. Every day, it took discipline and willpower to keep to our kosher dietary laws. We passed on those wonderful meals and restricted ourselves. However, we didn't go hungry. We filled up on whatever bread and cheese and fruit were offered.

When we reached Bombay, traders in their little dinghies lined up alongside the boat, selling all kinds of goods. Some peddled a variety of fruits. We bought lots, including over one hundred bananas. We thought we could store them in our cabin where we believed they would stay fresh. We were not aware of the short shelf life of bananas.

After thirty days at sea, we arrived in Shanghai. Having never met Uncle Joe, I had sent him a telegram with the name of the ship and the cabin number. When the ship docked in Shanghai Harbor, Uncle Joe came on board. Saleh and I spotted him right away because his resemblance to our father was so strong. He looked us over, but said nothing. I detected by his expression that he was not elated to have two of us, two nephews under his responsibility. This was not the agreement he had made with Dad. He had expected only for me to work for him in Shanghai, not Saleh.

In an uncomfortable silence, Uncle Joe took us to the YMCA. We checked into two small rooms while he stayed next door at the Park Hotel. But the next day, Uncle Joe softened, showing his warmth and generosity. We felt everything would be okay.

A week after we arrived, Uncle Joe announced that he must return to New York, to his family and to his business headquarters. "I have to decide quickly what your roles will be in the company here in China," he explained. Thinking Saleh to be the older, he said, "I'm sending you to Swatow to meet with an agent who represents our company, Sutton and Husney. I'm hoping to establish a lucrative operation there, especially since the cotton mills in Shanghai are in decline." He pulled out a map and gave Saleh some background. "Swatow is a busy port city in the Tropics, several hundred miles south of Shanghai. It is a transport hub and distribution center for exporting." Uncle Joe pointed to Shanghai on the map. Saleh nodded as he studied the route Uncle Joe was tracing down the east coast from the East China Sea to the South China Sea. His finger stopped at Swatow. "Saleh, I'm sorry you'll have to make another long journey so soon after arriving, but I'm giving you the opportunity to set up and manage a vital office for us. My staff will book your passage. A boat leaves in two days."

I looked at Saleh, feeling bad for him. What choice did he have? His eyes told me this was not what he envisioned. I wondered how, alone at age 17, he could handle that kind of responsibility and if he could cope. But I said nothing. I don't think Saleh fully understood what was expected of him or the unknown environment he would confront.

I stayed, working for Uncle Joe in the Shanghai office, trying to help salvage his business there. For me, at least there were Jews in Shanghai—and some were Syrian. Shanghai had a cohesive community of foreigners and a social life. But Swatow? What could there be for Saleh in Swatow?

Because of the war, I had very little contact with our family in Aleppo. The Red Cross was in charge of the mail. I was allowed a maximum of twenty-five words sent via Switzerland, a six-month undertaking. Then it took another six months for a twenty-five-word letter from Dad to get back to me. Telephones were scarce and our family never owned one anyway. Telegrams were very expensive and were only allowed for emergencies in Syria. Airmail letters were unreliable and subject to government censorships. My contact with Saleh was minimal, so I had no idea what went on in Swatow.

Within months of Saleh's departure, he was back in Shanghai— weak, pale, thin, and coughing up blood. I took him to a doctor. Saleh had tuberculosis.

I sent Dad an emergency telegram. It was decided that Saleh should return to Aleppo for medical treatment. Mom and Dad wanted him home. They were worried.

I thought about Uncle Reuben who came to live with us when we moved into our house. I remembered that he had tuberculosis and Mom and Dad gave him his own private room, but I know they were concerned about all of us being exposed.

Could it be that Saleh contracted tuberculosis from Uncle Reuben? Could the bacteria have been lying dormant for so long? Or was it in Swatow that Saleh was stricken? I guess we'll never know the answer.

SS Conté Biancamano carrying Miro and Saleh to Shanghai

Miro (Mike)

Saleh

*My father's brother
Uncle Joe Sutton*

SIX

MY SON, HEED THE DISCIPLINE OF YOUR FATHER, AND DO NOT
FORSAKE THE TEACHING OF YOUR MOTHER—PROVERBS 1:8

Occasionally my friends and I hung around the French Military Officers Club located not far from our house. It had two tennis courts, and if we were lucky they would let us serve as ball boys. In rare instances, we were even allowed to pick up a racket and play.

One afternoon in the spring of 1942, after leaving the Officers Club with my friends, I remember feeling quite low. Since Miro and Saleh's departure, I had felt a void in our house, in our family. Now Saleh was coming home, sick. Miro was alone in Shanghai. Did my father understand what he was doing? Had he reached his decision without thinking through all of the possible consequences? In my head, I questioned his actions, but I kept those thoughts to myself, never daring to challenge him.

I feared for my own future. I was next. Where would I be sent?

* * *

For Saleh, the trip back to Aleppo was riddled with complications. The war with its mounting battles and occupations around the globe made getting a visa next to impossible. Reserving transportation was made difficult by over bookings and long delays. I watched my parents' anxieties heighten with each passing day. They wanted Saleh home. They wanted to give him the care he needed to get better.

Finally, we received word that Saleh had obtained a visa. He was on his way home.

* * *

Once again, my father made the harrowing trip to Port Sa'id and met Saleh when the boat docked. At home, all of us saw how very sick Saleh was. A continuous fever rendered him lethargic and he only wanted to sleep. Coughing spasms shook his skeletal frame and sharp pains stabbed into his chest. Sometimes I sat with him and watched as he spit up blood. When my mother brought food to him, he refused to eat. My poor brother, I was not sure he would survive. Seeing him in this condition intensified my compulsion to study medicine. I now knew how much I wanted to help people be well. I was committed to becoming a doctor.

After making inquiries, my parents learned that Saleh could be cured, but it would take a long, regimented course of medicines, plus rest and the proper environment. His immune system was so fragile that any germ easily could invade his body and bring on death.

My father found a good sanitarium. It was in a remote mountainous area in Lebanon where the climate was favorable to his recovery. Saleh was put under strict medical supervision. If he had remained and completed his course of treatment, he would have been cured. But Saleh had no tolerance for isolation and no patience to wait out the recovery time.

After a few weeks in the sanitarium, Saleh began to feel better and made the decision to leave. The medical staff tried to reason with him. The doctors explained to my father that if Saleh did not complete the full regimen, he would relapse, possibly die, and surely infect others, especially family members. But nothing would change Saleh's mind. In that respect, he was like my father.

Memories of Saleh before he left for China flashed in front of me—young, handsome, popular, a vibrant teenager who never sat in one place for too long. He loved adventure and everyone wanted to be his friend. Now Saleh was different. Would he ever be himself again?

* * *

Years ago, when my father made the determination to export his sons, he also established a policy of never allowing his sons to earn a living in Syria. He did not want any of us to be tied to that land.

So when Saleh came home from the sanitarium, there was no work for him to do. He was forced to pass his time leisurely and paid little attention to the medical advice he was given. My parents attended to his every need and secured the best medical care they could afford. In the house, he was given a private bedroom overlooking the street so he could interact with his visiting friends. He was even given a second-hand car, paid for by our father—something almost unheard of.

Still, I sensed a restlessness in Saleh. His energy level was on the rise and he could not tolerate being confined. My parents were not happy to see him waver from his prescribed medical regimen, but Saleh's health did seem to slowly improve.

* * *

While World War II engulfed the globe, we continued to follow the unfolding events, but it was the presence of the Vichy in Syria that concerned us most. Under Hitler's command, the French Vichy government maintained its occupation, breathing down our necks, making life exceedingly difficult for us. All the Jews in our community were frightened. The prospect of our future following the same destiny as the Jews in Europe alarmed us. Anti-Semitism's ugly head grew stronger by the day while Muslim riots against French occupation went unabated. For protection, we took to spending more time in the house.

Our once spirited existence transformed into dreariness. There were shortages, especially of life's essentials. Everything seemed to be rationed and people were forced to stand in lines for hours to receive their daily allocations. However, my father would not allow any of us to stoop to that level. He said, "Anything that can be bought with money is cheap—if you have the cash." He was willing to pay inflated prices on the black market to get us what we needed. Slowly, I watched humility and anguish take its toll on my father and wondered if he silently questioned his own decisions.

I continued at the Lycée, getting closer to graduation and my goal of medical school. Summers still spelled vacation time and we maintained our ritual of sojourning to the mountains of Lebanon.

* * *

By 1944, the tides were turning in favor of the Allies, thanks to a number of miscalculated actions by the Germans. Despite a pact with Stalin, Hitler betrayed his friend and attacked Russia. Fierce Russian resistance and harsh Russian winters brought defeat upon the Germans on the Russian front. Then, of necessity, Russia joined America and England to become a formidable power against the Nazis. By June, the Allies mounted a massive offense, landing on the beaches of Normandy in France. This began the liberation of Western Europe. In Italy, the people revolted against Mussolini and executed him. They then joined the Allies. Hitler faced his end.

Monitoring changing events, Syria's Muslims could taste their independence. For so many years, the War had diverted their attention and stifled their nationalistic zeal. Now that France was liberated and the Vichy were history, the Syrians were determined to take their country back. Their bottled-up passions erupted in relentless mass hysteria all over Syria and the people were determined to get the French out of their country.

* * *

In April 1945, shortly after Passover, I witnessed another brutal murder. Our house was situated on a main thoroughfare. Public trams traveled parallel to our house, making daily runs, picking up and dropping off passengers. A newly-built Sunni mosque across the street from our house held prayers five times a day, seven days a week. One specific Friday afternoon, men went inside the mosque for *juma*, congregational sabbath prayers. The imam of this mosque had a penchant for inciting his congregants.

I was sitting with Saleh by the window in his room. We observed the men coming out of the mosque. Simultaneously, a tram pulled up at the stop by our house. A soldier in a French uniform stepped down from the vehicle. A maddening crowd spotted him and went wild.

I ran to get our family. "Hurry. Hurry. Come see. Come see." We huddled together by the window, watching the violent scene. A gang of Muslims that just left the mosque lunged at the soldier, striking him on all sides. They punched him, pounded him and stabbed him with knives until he was dead.

"My G-d, my G-d," my mother cried. "What will become of us?" Seeing my mother in such a state, frightened my sister Margo, and she clung to my mother.

I detected pain in my father's eyes. How much longer could he continue to protect his family from this savagery? Edgar was still a toddler and we shielded him from the window, but our mother's tears sent him into a panic.

With my siblings close by, Saleh uttered, "Let's hope those Muslims don't climb the steps to our house."

I shuddered. My skin erupted in goosebumps. My heart pounded so aggressively, I thought it would leap from my chest. For a while, I sat frozen, fearing they would soon come to attack us because we were Jews. Then we saw the police approach and the crowd quickly disperse.

Afterward, the incident played over and over in my mind. If only I could have helped the soldier. My insides ached for the trooper. What a horrible way to die. Days later, I heard that the soldier was not French, but a local Muslim working for the French army. No one ever was held responsible.

In May, just before the end of the school year, we learned that two French teachers from the Lycée were brutally murdered. The episode was kept hushed and so we never knew the details of how it happened, but we did know why. Then, during that last week of school, the announcement came. The Lycée in Aleppo was closing its doors. No longer could it risk the safety of its staff.

How could this happen? I had one more year left to graduate. One more year of credits before entering medical school. I will not let my dream die. I convinced myself that I could control my own fate.

* * *

The war in Europe ended in May 1945. Berlin had fallen to the Russians, Germany surrendered to the Allies. Japan was on the verge of defeat. President Harry Truman's authorization to drop the atomic bomb crippled Japan, bringing its aggressive actions to a halt. By August 1945, Japan's dominance in Asia was no more. The Japanese left China.

In Syria, the French had lost all command. Muslim mania to get the French out of the country reached uncontrollable dimensions. Everything hinting of French was wiped out. At schools, instruction in French was disallowed. French words were removed from street signs and store banners. All that was French in Syria was no more.

* * *

I learned that the Lycée operated a school in Beirut and was accepting students in the fall. It followed the same curriculum as my Lycée in Aleppo. My hopes soared.

Often, my father went to Beirut on business. He knew the city and had many contacts there. I cautiously approached him about the Lycée. Initially, he was reluctant, but he did not say *no*. I believed I could convince him. This was so important to me. "YES." I could enroll in the Lycée in Beirut and live there, near the school, during that year. I was euphoric.

My father arranged for me to stay with the Levis, a Sephardic family living on the top floor of a four-story walkup. I had my own room and a kosher breakfast every morning. The Levis shared an open terrace with the Krooks, an Ashkenazie family living on the same floor. The Krooks ran a successful, fancy appetizer store on the ground level. The building was in a bustling business district of downtown Beirut and within close walking distance of my school. For my other kosher meals, my father contracted with a nearby, family-run hotel, a place he often stayed during his business trips to Beirut.

My elation soared higher when my closest friend, Ezra, and two other classmates, Rahmo and Moshe, all from Aleppo, enrolled in the Lycée in Beirut. Quickly, we became a solid foursome. I was sure I now had control of my life. There was no limit as to what I could accomplish.

* * *

Beirut is a city with a prime location on the Mediterranean coastline. At the time, it was more cosmopolitan than any place in Syria and more cultivated than anywhere else in the Middle East. Its culture and its society boasted a strong Western influence. Beirut had superior academies of higher learning, multi-national corporations, big financial institutions, fancy hotels, private beaches, sport clubs, gambling casinos, world-class entertainment and wonderful international cuisine. Beirut, the 'Paris of the Middle East,' was a resort for the nouveaux riche and for the Saudis, Kuwaitis and others from the Gulf States who came flush with cash. People flocked to Beirut, enriching not only its night life but also its economy.

During my family's many summer sojourns to the Lebanese mountains, my friends and I would take day trips to Beirut. Now I was living there, basking in the society.

The Jewish-Lebanese community, although half the size of the Syrian community, profited from not only a higher standard of living but also from many organized activities. With a Jewish youth club, sport recreation and social pastimes, Ezra, Rahmo, Moshe, and I took advantage of amenities unknown to us in Syria. We also went on organized ski trips in the Lebanese mountains and took swimming lessons at the St. George Hotel. And the Jews in Lebanon were more lenient about their religious observances. We liked everything here.

You might think at this point that our lives were carefree and full of fun, but I assure you there was another side: our studies. We had to keep our grades up and take our education seriously. Ezra, Rahmo and I had the same determination to be doctors. Moshe pursued a career in business. Our teachers encouraged and supported our ambitions, indicating that we were more than qualified to pursue medical school.

To me, studying medicine was like learning a new language. Confident that my excellent memory and recall for facts would serve me well, I was enthusiastic about the future.

* * *

Nearing graduation in the spring of 1946, Ezra, Rahmo and I, guided by our teachers, set about applying to medical schools. We were all accepted. Rahmo opted to attend the Faculté Francaise de Médecine in Beirut to remain near his family. Ezra and I were accepted to the well-known Université De Montpellier in Montpellier, France. This famous school on the Mediterranean coast is the oldest medical school in continuous existence in the western world.

I cannot describe in words the passions aroused in me. My dream was on its way to becoming reality. All I needed to confirm my acceptance was to send a deposit for the tuition and make my travel arrangements. I could not wait to tell my father. His son was going to be a doctor. How proud he would be.

* * *

Excitedly, I handed the enrollment forms to my father. I studied his grim expression. When he shook his head, I knew.

"I'm sorry, Elie, you can't go to medical school," he said.

I felt my pulse sink. My father's words sliced through me like a sharp blade carving out my insides. "Ebee . . . what are you saying? I don't understand. I thought you would be proud . . ."

"I said you can't go to medical school. It's not possible."

This can't be happening. I've come so far. I can't stop now. My eyes filled with tears, but I would not allow myself to cry. "Why . . . why?"

"Elie, let's sit down and talk this through."

I loved my father. I respected him. But 'let's sit down and talk this through' did not mean he and I would have a dialogue. It meant that he would make the decision, he would dictate my next move in life and I would nod politely and reply, 'Yes, Ebee.'

Downhearted, I sat on the chair in the living room. My father sat on the sofa across from me. He began, "Six years of war. France, like most of Europe, is in ruins. Their economies are shattered. It would take six, maybe eight years to complete your schooling and become a doctor. Eight years before you could start earning a living.

"Elie, I care about you. You're my son. But I have six more sons and a daughter and a wife, your mother. I have done my best to give all of you a good life. To support you in a good style. You never had to work a day in your life . . ."

"Maybe that's the problem . . ."

"Do not interrupt your father!"

"Yes, Ebee. I'm sorry."

He went on, "I have had a decent business and worked hard to give you all that you want and need."

He's repeating himself, I thought.

"But I'm not rich. The future for our family, for all Jews is at risk. Syria is a hotbed. Muslims rise up against the Jews like they rose up against the French . . . except worse. Israel, the Zionist movement, the Balfour Declaration have given Muslims in the Middle East an excuse."

I detected my father's anguish and the difficulty he had talking to me. In a round about way, he was saying he was defeated. My heart softened and I felt badly for him. In silence, I waited.

He continued, "Elie, I'm not a rich man. We have lived comfortably over the years, but I am not rich. I can't afford to pay for your medical school. I can't afford to financially support you for the next six or eight years. I don't know if I will even have a business next year." He stopped, barely able to look at me.

I wanted to say something. I hoped we could find a solution, a way to change this verdict. But I knew my father had already made his decision.

"Elie, you will join your brother Miro in Shanghai. We will begin to make arrangements right away. Your travel. Your visa . . . Once there, you will be on your own to make your own decisions and choose what is best for you, just as Miro is doing. I can do no more."

SEVEN

Saleh announced he was ready for another trip to Shanghai. To me, it was obvious that Saleh had been conditioned over the years. Ingrained in his psyche was my father's plan—get out of Syria at any cost. I was concerned for Saleh's health and afraid he might suffer a relapse, so I tried talking with him.

"In China, there's disease and shortages of food and medicine. If you go back and get sick again, then what, Saleh?"

Saleh would not listen to any of this. "Elie, you're not telling me anything I don't already know. But this is my life. And when I think of my future, I know it won't be as long-lasting as yours. So I'm going to live for as long as I can. I'm not about to sit around and shrivel up." Saleh had the same stubbornness as my father. Once he made up his mind, he stood firm until he got his way; and most times, he did get his way. Saleh was spoiled.

At some level, my father knew Saleh was not up to the long journey, but what could he do? Insisting Saleh remain in Aleppo, watching him wither away, was not an option. That would have been a disservice to him. So my father approved Saleh's request to go to Shanghai with me.

I found consolation in Saleh's determination and was glad he wanted to come with me. I had been dreading this venture into the unknown by myself and I feared making the long trip alone.

* * *

Summer arrived and my father rented a big house in Falougha, Lebanon, a quaint mountain-resort town. In the back of my mind, I questioned my father's priorities, not only about money but also about keeping our family in Syria far too long. There was enough money for all of our summer vacations, for all the things he believed we should have or wanted to have. He always had reasons why we could not leave Syria as a family.

And now this. Medical school. My life as a doctor. My hopes and dreams snatched from me. He did not have the money, he said. Was I upset? Was I disappointed? Yes, I was. This decision would haunt me the rest of my life.

* * *

Rationally, I knew that dwelling on my distress was not wise. The decision was made and it was over. So with my brother Saleh, I turned my attention to the journey to Shanghai.

My brother Miro had been in Shanghai for five years. All that time, he lived under Japanese occupation. During the war, Japan sided with Nazi Germany, so its relationship with America was more than hostile. In Shanghai, all Americans and certain foreign residents were taken prisoner and sent to concentration camps. My brother was fortunate; he had Syrian nationality. And since Syria had been under French mandate and the Vichy French had allied with Germany, my brother was safe. But Miro's business activities suffered and our correspondence with him had been sporadic. Only now that the war was over could we hope for a quick reply to our letter. We asked Miro about living conditions and business prospects in Shanghai, and we wanted to alert him of our plans.

While Saleh and I waited to hear from Miro, we began our quest for travel to Shanghai. We did not join our family in Falougha right away. Instead, we remained in Syria, focused on getting our passports. In my most vivid imagination, I could not have envisioned the bureaucratic complexities that confronted us.

It began the day Saleh and I weaved through the narrow cobblestone alleyways leading to the main part of town. We then crossed a small bridge extending over a stretch of water and reached a small island. A small government building stood before us. We entered and made our way to the passport office. A man gave each of us an application form. Saleh and I went home, taking our time to carefully coordinate our information as we filled in the documents.

Returning the next day with our applications in hand, the same man quietly looked over the forms and shook his head. "I'm sorry, but neither of you qualify for a passport."

Saleh and I looked at each other. We knew why. We were Jews, and Jews were not looked upon as kindly as Muslims were. And although we were not foolish enough to indicate permanent emigration, the man assessed the situation and concluded that we had no intention of returning to Syria.

Our astute father, who anticipated the possibility of rejection, had given us extra cash to be used for bribes. Discreetly, we handed money to the man. Inconspicuously, he put the cash in his pocket.

"It will take some time," he said.

Another man appeared. "Is there a problem?" He took the forms and looked them over. Without making eye contact, he said, "Come back next month and we'll see what we can do."

Saleh and I were not going to let this opportunity pass us by, so we cautiously slipped some money to this man as well. "We will have to send these applications to Damascus. We are not authorized to approve them. Come back in a month," he said.

A month! We had to do something. "When will you send them to Damascus?" I asked.

The man pretended to study the papers, but said nothing. I pulled out more money. He took it. "Jews wanting to leave the country . . . how long do you intend to be away?"

Several more days of interrogations, bribes, delays and referrals followed. Finally, they agreed to forward the papers to Damascus within the week. Our father instructed us to go to the capital and expedite the process. In Damascus, we were confronted with a litany of questions; some insignificant and some about our return trip. Rehearsing our answers beforehand, Saleh and I responded to each inquiry. We were polite, we bribed and we probed into the reasons for further delays.

Meanwhile, Moise Dweck, a member of our Jewish community, heard of our plans and approached us, asking to join us on our trip to Shanghai. Moise was five years older than me. He came from a middle-class working family, not as comfortable as we were. Moise was warm, sociable, bright and he had a patron. His cousin Tony Shayo, a well-off merchant in Shanghai, was sponsoring his trip and had a job waiting for him. Quickly, Moise began the process of obtaining a passport. We warned him of the pitfalls.

Finally, all of our passports were approved in Damascus and sent back to Aleppo. Moise, Saleh and I were overjoyed to have them in our possession. Our trip to Shanghai was now a reality and the three of us began making plans for our journey when a letter from Miro arrived. Anxiously, Saleh and I waited for our father to open it. The news was grim. *Do not come to Shanghai*, he wrote. *The future is bleak, at best. Business opportunities are meager. There is nothing for you here.* He went on to tell us that he was exploring how to get out of China and relocate to America.

Miro's letter was unsettling, but Saleh and I were not going to let it discourage us. We had come so far. A few more difficulties would not deter us. Proceeding moment by moment, we chose to face any obstacles in Shanghai when we arrived.

* * *

Our travel schedule included a train from Aleppo to Beirut, a plane from Beirut to Cairo, and then to Shanghai by air. For Moise, Saleh and me, it seemed straightforward enough, and Saleh's previous trip to Shanghai five years earlier boosted our confidence. I did not understand that Saleh had traveled by boat, one boat during wartime —a journey that could not compare with the unchartered waters ahead of us. Adding to this, we failed to recognize our own immaturity and lack of experience.

* * *

Saleh and I spent the balance of the summer vacationing in Falougha with our family. I knew this would be my last summer with them. I reflected on my life, on my parents and on my siblings. We were a good, close family with high morals and strong ethics. We learned about the importance of honesty and fair treatment of others, and G-d was a powerful force in our lives. Although I had no concept of what I would face in Shanghai, I believed that if Saleh and I were separated, for whatever reason, I could make my way. I had no choice. I had to.

* * *

Our family returned to Aleppo in early September to prepare for the high holidays of Rosh Hashanah and Yom Kippur. The nine days of Sukkot quickly followed. Then we celebrated Shemini Atzeret and Simchat Torah. Upon conclusion of our fall holidays, we had a special family shabbat meal with grandparents, aunts, uncles, and cousins. All the foods that Saleh and I favored were served.

On Sunday afternoon, a going-away party was given in our honor, holding to a long Syrian custom in our community for those about to travel far. Family and friends came with a variety of gifts and wooden boxes filled with homemade pastries. They offered all kinds of advice, encouragement, and wishes for a safe and blessed trip.

The following day, Monday, October 21, 1946, we were ready to depart. My suitcase held my clothes, gifts and pastries. My tallit, tefillin and siddur used for daily worship and for shabbat and holidays lay between my belongings, keeping them safe from damage. My brothers lined up to say goodbye before they left for school. I suspect some of them wished they could join Saleh and me, though some may have been just as happy to remain in familiar territory. Raffoul, now fourteen, would be the next to leave. I gave him a hug, although I'm not sure he knew what to do with it. Then there were Joe, Morris and my youngest sibling, Edgar who was only six. We said our goodbyes and they went off to school.

Margo stood quietly, waiting her turn. With tears spilling down her cheeks, she hugged me. "I'm going to miss you, Elie. Thank you for taking me to see the doctors in Palestine." Margo had a condition called *elephantiasis*, a parasitic infection that caused swelling and disfigurement to her foot. When I was sixteen and she was twelve, we traveled together to Palestine so she could receive better medical care.

My mother cried. "Allah ma'ak. Allah ma'ak." G-d be with you, she repeated over and over.

"Thank you, Imee . . for everything. I'll miss you, but let's not say goodbye. We'll see each other again. I know we will."

* * *

It was time to leave. With passports in hand and U.S. dollars in our pockets, we were ready.

My father accompanied Moise, Saleh and me on the train from Aleppo to Beirut. In Beirut, we stayed the night at the same hotel where I had my meals when I was a student at the Lycée. The next morning, we followed my father from travel agency to travel agency until finally we were able to book flights to Cairo. Inquiries about travel beyond Egypt were not answered. We were told that we had to wait until we arrived in Cairo to make further provisions.

All the while, my father appeared cheerful and optimistic about the future. He chatted away as if he were attending a social function, hiding his true feelings from us.

* * *

Escorting us to the airport in Beirut, my father waited until we checked in and everything was okay. He walked us to the gate and wished Moise well. Then, with resignation, he hugged Saleh, making him promise to take care of himself. This was a second goodbye for the two of them.

It was my turn. I noticed that my father had difficulty looking at me. *Does he really know the impact of his decision on me? Instead of being on my way to medical school in France, I'm on my way to Shanghai, China. How is this possible? How was he able to weigh these two options? I hoped to make him proud, hoped he would want me to be a doctor as much as I wanted it for myself.* I think my father felt he had failed me, that's why it was so hard for him to look at me. I reached out my arms to hug him. "Goodbye, Ebee."

For a moment, he responded to my hug, then briskly pulled away. I caught his eye and wanted to thank him for all he did for me over the years. I wanted to say, 'I love you, Ebee.' In that instant, I realized how very much I loved my father, how much he meant to me, how much he did for me. He set an example for me to follow and taught me how to live my life. I forced him to look at me, "It's okay, Ebee. It's okay," I said, hoping to put his mind at rest. His eyes filled with tears. Quickly, he turned away, heading toward the main terminal. "Ebee," I called out to him. He turned back. Our eyes held and I knew. I would never see my father again.

My family posing for a photograph; seated: my parents Adele and Selim
Standing clockwise: Morris, Joe, Ralph, Margo and Edgar

Old street in Aleppo with tram, horses and buggies

EIGHT

LIFE'S CHALLENGES ARE NOT SUPPOSED TO PARALYZE YOU,
THEY ARE SUPPOSED TO HELP YOU DISCOVER WHO YOU ARE
—BERNICE JOHNSON REAGON

In our minds, Cairo was the jewel of the Orient, the land of the Great Sphinx of Giza, the Great Pyramid, the city of a thousand minarets, the melting pot of ancient and modern Egyptian civilization, the bread basket of the Middle East. And flowing through Cairo is a segment of the Nile River that predictably overflows its banks every year, keeping the soil fertile.

Moise, Saleh and I had planned to check into a hotel, book our flights to Shanghai with a travel agent, spend a few days sightseeing, then be on our way. Absorbed with optimism and confidence, we were not prepared for what was ahead.

On arrival, we looked forward to stepping out into an exciting, modern city—a city like Beirut, but more so. Instead, we found Cairo to be a shabby, dirty, and overpopulated city with an unmistakable abundance of poverty. Cairo also was subject to periodic sandstorms that blew in from the vast surrounding desert.

With our luggage intact, we took a taxi to the old, upscale and majestic Shepheard Hotel in downtown Cairo where we were fortunate to have booked reservations; one room for Moise and one room for Saleh and me. Expecting to stay just a few days in this hotel where politicians, wealthy businessmen and the higher echelons of society lodged, we settled into our rooms, then went out for something to eat.

Tired after a long day, we returned to the hotel, ready for a good night's sleep. As we walked through the grand lobby, we passed guests sitting around in small groups, engaged in open discussions about politics and world events. Finding their dialogues interesting, we unobtrusively listened in on the conversations. Over the many weeks that we were unwillingly confined to Cairo, this became a favorite and educational pastime for us.

Through our eavesdropping, I learned about the conduct of Egypt's King Faruq. The people hated him. In 1936, at the age of sixteen, he inherited the throne from his father. Eventually he married, had three daughters and divorced his wife for not producing a son. Despite his enormous wealth, he turned into a kleptomaniac and a highly-skilled pickpocket, and came to be known as 'the thief of Cairo.' Addicted to fine cuisine, he became grossly overweight, topping three-hundred pounds. Faruq also had an obsession for beautiful women, demanding their company whether they were married or not. But King Faruq's worst behavior was his insensitivity and indifference toward the welfare of his people and his country.

I reflected on the nationalistic spirit that gripped Syria during the French occupation and how strongly the Syrians wanted the French out. Now, a similar nationalistic spirit was rising in Egypt. Cairo was on the verge of a major uprising. Egyptians hungered for a coup. This was not a place where we wanted to linger.

* * *

On our first full day in Cairo, we rose early, ate breakfast and set out to book our flights to Shanghai. This did not happen. After several attempts over many days, we grew accustomed to getting around Cairo on foot. If we had to go an extra long distance, we took a taxi. Never did we ride the trams where multitudes of people jammed inside each public vehicle, squeezing into seats, pushing against each other for standing room, hanging dangerously off the doorsteps. Our priority was not to live precariously, but rather to secure our travel to Shanghai as soon as possible.

Our strong expectations were quickly shattered when we discovered that getting a flight out of Cairo was not going to be a simple task. Major obstacles awaited us. First, we were Jews in an ever-growing anti-Semitic Muslim world. Second, only two airlines flew the Cairo-Far East route—Pan American Airways and KLM Dutch Airlines. Both airlines used the reliable DC-4 craft, a small, forty-two passenger plane requiring several refueling stops. Although Cairo was a refueling stop and airplane seats could be gained or lost, we were not optimistic. Diplomats, their families and military personnel, all holdovers from World War II, were given priority seating, making it nearly impossible for us to book a flight. Third, the refueling stop after Cairo was Basra, Iraq. Iraq required every foreigner to show a visa, even if a passenger was just traveling through and not going to deplane. We had our visas, but only to enter and exit Egypt, not to enter and exit Iraq. Our plans did not include a touchdown in Basra. We had believed we would go directly to Shanghai from Cairo.

* * *

Desperate to move on as quickly as possible, we found our way to the Iraqi Consulate in Cairo. We diligently filled out the applications requesting transit visas and handed them to the clerk. Politely, we were told to return later in the week. "Your visas will be ready for you then," the man assured us.

The image of Shanghai came into view. We were excited. We also were infused with a false sense of hope.

By the end of the week, we made a second visit to the Iraqi Consulate. Approaching the same clerk, we knew instinctively by the somber look on his face that something was not right.

"I'm sorry," he said. "We had to refer your request to Baghdad." He lowered his eyes so as not to look at us directly. "Your passports . . . they indicate that all of you are Jews."

Despair. That is the only word to describe how we felt. What would we do now? Where could we go? Certainly not back to Syria. Should we try to find jobs and support ourselves? How do we live? For Saleh and I, we could not keep asking our father for more and more money. I thought about medical school. My dream. My aspiration. Instead, I was stuck in Cairo.

I begged, "Please . . . Please. Isn't there anything you can do to help us? We will not get off the plane in Basra . . ."

"Come back in a few weeks. Baghdad will make a decision then," the man replied.

"A few weeks! How long is a few weeks?" I asked. "Three? Four? More? Never?" I wanted an answer that I knew we would not get.

Moise, Saleh and I looked at each other. To bribe him would have cost a lot. Even by pooling our money, we could not possibly come up with enough. This path went nowhere. We had to find a different strategy. Downhearted, we took a taxi back to the hotel.

Back in the lobby, we leisurely sipped coffee and kept our eyes and ears open, hoping to latch onto someone who could help us, believing that someone with influence would hear of our plight and be willing to help. But that was not to happen, at least not yet. People seemed more interested in discussing King Faruq and the future of Egypt than in exploring the future of three Jews from Aleppo who wanted to go to Shanghai.

* * *

From the beginning, we were naive about the requirements and obstacles of world travel. But now that we were enlightened, we decided that together we would defy the odds stacked against us. Somehow, some way, we would reach Shanghai. Moise, Saleh and I strived to maintain a positive attitude, remaining tenaciously focused on our goal, praying for a miracle. This was not easy. We were jobless and running out of money, but I knew that there was no turning back. For me, I could not go home. This was not an option.

The only way to obtain airline tickets was through securing transit visas. If we could get such visas, we could land in Basra, even if we were Jews. Saleh and I wrote a letter to our father explaining the problems we faced and asking for more money. How much longer we would be detained in Cairo, we did not know. Fortunately, Moise was able to loan us some money until we heard from our father. In ten-day's time, American Travelers Cheques arrived at the hotel. Our father came through for us. Saleh and I paid Moise what we owed him. Shortly thereafter, we received a letter from our father.

Elie and Saleh — Your family hopes you are both safe and well. Saleh, we worry about you. We do not want you to get sick again. Elie, please look after your brother. I am sorry about your difficult situation. I spoke to many in our community, hoping for some advice. Elie, do you remember your literature professor at the Lycée, Iztaz

(Professor) Sibikh? He is now the Syrian ambassador to Egypt. His office is in Cairo. I urge you to call and set up a meeting with him right away. Keep me informed of the outcome. I will not be able to support you and Saleh forever. Things are not going well. But I will send you additional money as you need it, at least until you get to Shanghai. — Ebee

I read the letter to Saleh and Moise. My father's reference about things not going well indicated government censorship, restraining him from elaborating on the deterioration in Syria.

"Do you really think the ambassador will help?" Moise asked.

"I don't know," I responded. "I remember the man being stern. Indifferent. A very strict professor. But we have to try."

Saleh put his hands together as if in prayer, then rolled his eyes. "I hope the ambassador has favorable memories of you," he jested.

* * *

The three of us took a cab to the Syrian Embassy. At the front desk, I identified myself and asked for an appointment.

"The ambassador is a very busy man," said the young office worker in an attempt to brush us away.

When we refused to leave, he asked us to wait. Several minutes later he returned. The ambassador will see you next week.

Next week, we thought. Time seemed to be going nowhere for us. We had become beggars, grateful for any bits of crumbs thrown our way. "We should at least be grateful we got an appointment," I said meekly. Depression tugged at our sleeves, but we did not allow it to take hold.

* * *

On the day of our appointment with the ambassador, we arrived at the Syrian Embassy with time to spare. The three of us agreed to keep any optimism in check. If we were to be disappointed, we didn't want the letdown to overwhelm us.

The ambassador invited us into his office. With an abundance of Arab hospitality, he offered us coffee and sweet delicacies. We exchanged pleasantries and reminisced about our days at the Lycée. Then, sensing an opening, we explained our situation. In silence, he sat and listened, appearing indifferent to our needs. I knew the man was brilliant. It was clear he understood our travel plans. He also was aware that we had no intentions of returning to Syria, although that was never spoken. The man could easily have helped us. He certainly was in a powerful position to do so.

I observed his facial expressions and body language. I watched as he skillfully subdued his pleasure. He was in control and chose to let us flounder in Cairo or return to Syria. Moise, Saleh, and I looked at each other. We hoped that maybe his heart would soften, but that was a delusion.

The ambassador stood, accompanied us to the door, and said, "I wish you well. Come back and visit us when you return from China . . . Goodbye."

That was it. No hint of our being invited back. No mention of him looking into it. Nothing. We left with crushed spirits. What kept us from becoming completely unraveled was the fact that we had each other. Three Aleppian Jews with the same dilemma and identical mission. Our bond to each other grew evermore solid.

Instead of taking a taxi, we walked back to the hotel. On the street, we met some local people and stopped to chat with them. They were friendly and asked where we were from, detecting the difference in our Arabic dialect. Telling them of our plight, they recommended that we frequent a café named Groppi where members of the Jewish community spent late afternoons and evenings.

That night, we went to Groppi's. The famous patisserie and chocolaterie located in Soliman Pacha Square was exquisitely adorned with crystal chandeliers, artistic mosaics and elegant marble floors. Café regulars were the créme of society. Everyone who was anyone went to Groppi's to indulge in the most delicious desserts, to enjoy the evening entertainment and to socialize with the elite.

Groppi's soon became our mainstay. Every day, we lingered there for hours, befriending the local Jews and looking for leads from the well-connected—anything that might move us out of Cairo and into Shanghai.

* * *

During this time, Saleh and I never missed our daily prayers. In the mornings, we put on tefillin and prayed in our hotel room. I do not know what Moise did. His family was not as religious as ours and we were not in his room to see. In the early evenings, before dinner, Saleh and I returned to our room to recite Mincha and Ma'ariv prayers. Sometimes Moise would join us. On Friday nights and Saturdays, our Sabbath, Moise followed our lead. We found a neighborhood synagogue to attend and never let a day pass without praying to G-d. And we were also careful about the food we ate, always keeping to our kosher dietary laws.

* * *

On one particular evening, we lingered at Groppi's until quite late, socializing with the locals, hoping to lift our melancholy. At closing time, as we headed toward the door, a man approached us. On a piece of paper, he slipped us the name of a prominent Iraqi businessman, a Jew named Kamal Tawfik who often visited Cairo. He was in Cairo, staying at the Shepheard Hotel. Surprise, elation, encouragement, new expectations—our emotions soared. We were incredibly grateful for the information and profusely thanked our benefactor.

The next day, instead of hanging out at Groppi's, we approached the hotel desk and asked for Mister Tawfik's room number. We contacted him and requested a meeting. He came down to the lobby, greeting us with a warm smile. We explained our predicament. He responded reassuringly.

"I have many contacts in the Iraqi government. I can secure your transit visas quickly. Possibly in two weeks. Be patient. It will happen."

We thought this man was sent from G-d. This was the miracle for which we prayed. From the goodness of his heart, this Iraqi Jew was going to help us without asking anything in return. We were touched by his benevolence.

"I will be in Cairo for a while on business. When Baghdad approves your visas, I will let you know. Then all three of you must return to the Consulate Office to have your passports stamped."

"We are extremely grateful and will never forget you. May G-d bless you for your kindness."

Humbly, he bowed his head. "I am glad I could be of help. I wish you all a safe journey."

* * *

Our prospects for reaching Shanghai took on new life. Only one more hurdle to conquer. Even with our visas, how could we purchase airline tickets without money? We never expected to be in Cairo this long, nor to spend so much money before arriving in Shanghai.

Again, we contacted our families, first giving them the good news, then asking for more money. It took almost two weeks for our letters to reach home and to receive a response. During that time, we went daily to the travel agents and airline offices. We hounded them, refusing to accept a negative reply.

* * *

Our money from home arrived in the form of American Travelers Cheques. Kamal Tawfik informed us of Baghdad's approval of our transit visas. The Consulate Office stamped our passports. KLM reserved three seats for us. We felt the weight of the world lifting off our shoulders.

Our travel itinerary included refueling stopovers in Basra and Karachi before ending in Calcutta. We were told to visit the office of China National Airlines to book our flight from Calcutta to Shanghai.

* * *

With four days left before our departure, we could relax. Everything finally fell into place. With the pressure off, we moved sightseeing to the top of our list and visited the Great Pyramid and Great Sphinx, the Egyptian Museum of Cairo, the 1200-year-old Ben Ezra Synagogue where the Cairo Genizah was stored, and a modern and upscale district of Heliopolis with many foreign embassies and fancy homes and manicured gardens.

* * *

On Monday, December 16, 1946, two months after leaving Aleppo, we boarded the first leg of our flight to the Far East. Stop one: Basra, Iraq.

Old Shepheard Hotel in Cairo

Groppi's Café

Great Sphinx of Giza

NINE

DESPAIR IS A CHEAP EXCUSE FOR AVOIDING ONE'S PURPOSE IN
LIFE. A SENSE OF PURPOSE IS THE BEST WAY TO AVOID DESPAIR
—REBBE MENACHEM MENDEL SCHNEERSON

Through the small window, I looked out at the vast desert below. Sand seemed to cover the earth. It was not a place where I wanted us to be. As the plane touched down in Basra, I tensed. "Please, G-d," I prayed, "watch over us. Help us make it out of here without incident."

The hatch opened and the steps were set down. Everyone waited in their seats. Three Iraqi men in uniform, I did not know if they were police or military, boarded the plane and began to check everyone's passports. One of them approached us. My heart pounded from fear. For an instant, I glanced at Moise and Saleh. I sensed they were uneasy, too. We were foreign Jews on Iraqi soil. Anything could happen. Being detained could cost us our lives. This was not Cairo.

I watched as four people were allowed to deplane. The rest of us did not move from our seats. The aircraft sat on the tarmac for what seemed like hours. Four new passengers boarded. Two hours after our landing, we were in the sky again heading toward Karachi. Whew! Moise, Saleh, and I breathed a sigh of relief.

* * *

In Karachi, we could not technically set foot in the city, but after inspection of our documents, we were allowed to deplane and stretch our legs in a transit lounge. Within an hour, we were on our way to Calcutta, India, our final stop with KLM Airlines.

* * *

We landed in Calcutta in late afternoon. Passing through immigration formalities was easy. India was still part of the British Commonwealth and Calcutta had a British governor.

We hoped our layover in Calcutta would be short. We were anxious to get to Shanghai and settle into our new life. From the airport, we took a bus into town and to our hotel. It was December and the weather was very hot and very humid. We were in the Tropics. Looking out open windows of the bus, we passed sights that jolted us into a reality we had never known. Shabby tents housed large families. Squatters and homeless people, unkempt and dressed in dirty rags, slept on the ground. Smoke percolating from stalls where food was cooking sent repugnant fumes into the air. Sacred cows wandered aimlessly through the streets. Large crowds gathered around posters of Mahatma Gandhi, the Great Soul who was leading India to inde-pendence through non-violent practices.

* * *

Given the poverty of Calcutta, our hotel accommodations were lavish. After a good night's sleep and an abundant breakfast in the morning, we visited the offices of China National Airlines. We hoped to book our flights and leave Calcutta as soon as possible.

"All flights on China National Airlines are suspended indefinitely," the man at the desk told to us in English.

Taken aback, we inquired about the reason. The man hesitated. We pushed for an answer. "Last week, two of our planes traveling the same route you want to take now were involved in separate crashes. Catastrophic accidents. Many people were killed. We are awaiting the results of independent investigations which could take several weeks. That is all I know, that is all I can tell you."

The three of us looked at each other. We were drained, frustrated, angry. Two months in Cairo and now this. We did not know anyone in Calcutta. Communicating with our families would be a lengthy process, if we could contact them at all. This place clearly was not Cairo. In Cairo we spoke the same language and ate familiar foods. There was a Jewish community and a synagogue. We could interact with people. But this? We walked the streets with cows and witnessed multitudes living in squalor. Everything was alien. We felt beaten. Perhaps Shanghai was not meant to be. The signs certainly were there. If I did not have Saleh and Moise with me, if my father had sent me out on my own, I do not know what I would have done. None of us wanted to be detained in this G-d forsaken place and none of us wanted to risk our lives traveling with such an accident-prone airline. Two undesirable alternatives. What a dilemma!

* * *

On the third day of our stay, an excruciating pain awakened me in the early morning. My head felt like it was on the verge of exploding. I lay in bed hoping it would stop. I debated whether or not to wake Saleh. When I could take the agony no longer, I called out to my brother.

"You have a toothache," he said. Saleh went downstairs to inquire at the hotel's front desk about getting help. They recommended a British dentist nearby.

I had never been to a doctor or a dentist in my life. In Syria, there was no such thing as going for medical checkups or dental cleanings. One sought medical help only in a crisis, and until Saleh had come home ill with tuberculosis, I cannot remember anyone in my family making use of a doctor or a dentist. Illnesses and pains were handled with chicken soup, chamomile tea and hot or cold compresses. A cut was cleaned with alcohol and bandaged. More serious ailments were handled by those knowledgable in home-made medications and natural healing. For a toothache, one good shot of *arak* worked wonders. (Arak is a colorless, highly potent, fiery anise-flavored alcoholic drink that is distilled from fermented grapes.) There also was the very popular cod liver oil, prized for its nutritional value. My two youngest brothers, Morris and Edgar, were given this foul smelling, foul tasting supplement every day.

Now in a strange city, stricken with intense pain, sitting in a dentist's chair for the first time, I was anxious and tense. The dentist examined my mouth. "Well, first, I can see that your teeth have been neglected. I suggest you begin taking better care of them. Second, the only way to alleviate your pain is to extract the tooth that is giving you the problem. The pain will not go away on its own, I can guarantee you that." He spoke slowly and calmly, recognizing my limited comprehension of English.

As best I could, I tried to explain to the dentist that Moise, Saleh and I were in Calcutta for only a short time. He urged me to visit a dentist to evaluate my mouth once I reached Shanghai. He also recommended that I see him one more time. "If you are still in Calcutta three or four days from now, let me check you again, just to make sure no infection develops. In the meantime, here are some aspirins. If you experience any more pain, take two of these. They will help ease your discomfort." He smiled reassuringly, "I think the worst is over for you, but as a precaution, do try to come back." I thanked the man and paid him.

Four days later, I visited the dentist again. "Everything is healing nicely. I am glad you followed my directions," he nodded approvingly.

* * *

More than a week had passed and we were still in Calcutta. There was not much to do and no one beside ourselves with whom to talk. There were no cafés or hotel lobbies in which to hang out and socialize. Sightseeing was non-existent, unless we wanted to go into the slums. This overpopulated city with intense poverty, where sacred cows had first rights to roam the streets freely, was clogged with heavy traffic and sweltering in heat. Besides this, Calcutta still was recuperating from the "Great Calcutta Killing," the massive Hindu-Muslim riots of August 1946 that left 4,000 dead and 100,000 homeless. Our impulse to get out of this intolerable place grew more compelling by the hour.

Yet, not all was gloom. The three of us found strength in our daily worship and our strong connection to G-d. We were confident He would learn of our plight and answer our prayers. Fortunately, it was not difficult to remain faithful to our kosher dietary laws. We took most of our meals at the hotel. Breakfast consisted of bread, butter, and eggs. For lunch and dinner, we ate rice and vegetables flavored with curry and/or chutney, which was quite good. We stayed away from pork, ham, meat, chicken, lard and fish. Our religion played a prominent role in our lives.

To keep from getting bored out of our minds, we attended the cinema several times. The British brought English-dialogue movies to the screen with Hindi subtitles. Since we spoke little English, and definitely no Hindi, we did not understand much, but got the gist by piecing together the actors' movements. Before each show began, everyone in attendance was required to rise and sing the British National Anthem of G-d Save The King.

Feeling no allegiance to the British or to their royalty, we found this quite disturbing. We resented the British for their treatment of the Jews in Palestine. They occupied the territory, attempted to sabotage the Jewish struggle for a homeland, and threw their support to the Arab-Palestinian fight.

Moise, Saleh and I remained in our seats, sensing the strong glares of disapproval. Knowing we were foreigners in a foreign land, we concluded it would be unwise to bring attention to ourselves and jeopardize our eventual departure, so we stood.

After two weeks in Calcutta, we received word that flights to Shanghai would resume in three days. We could barely contain ourselves by the news. Rushing to the office of China National Airlines, we booked our seats. Safety risk or not, we were leaving.

* * *

Although elated to finally be departing Calcutta, Moise, Saleh and I were frightened about flying such a vulnerable airline. We questioned whether or not we would reach Shanghai alive.

Our first refueling stop was Chongqing, China, headquarters during World War II to The Flying Tigers who, under General Claire Chennault, kept supplies flowing to American and Chinese troops fighting the Japanese. This large industrial metropolis on the Yangtze River was the first inland commercial port opened to foreigners.

Our journey to Chongqing was scary. The plane rose and fell like a roller coaster. My stomach turned, somersaulting many times. The three of us clutched the armrests and closed our eyes, praying to G-d not to make these our final moments.

A Frenchman sitting in our row, spoke to us in his native tongue, "I see you are a bit uneasy. Is this your first time flying over these mountains?"

The three of us nodded. "Oui," we answered in unison.

Sympathetic to our fear, the gentleman tried to offer us solace. "The turbulence is coming from the mountains . . . the Himalayas below us," he explained. "This is a common winter occurrence called 'mountain wave.' We have been flying north into China. We are no longer in the Tropics and this is January. The winter jet stream is now at a lower altitude and the air mass in the 'mountain wave' flows up and down like ocean waves." He smiled, "I have taken this route often . . . for business. Everything will be okay. The plane will not crash."

I wished I could have believed him. Half an hour later, we landed safely in Chongqing where we had to stay overnight before the next leg of our flight. The airline put us up in a hotel.

* * *

In Chongqing, I had my first exposure to spoken Chinese. Hearing the language made me laugh, something I had not done in a long time. The words and tones sounded like birds singing.

Airline personnel directed us to our rooms. *This cannot be*, I thought. *No one should have to stay in such a dungeon.* It was unclean, unkempt, dingy. The bed linens were threadbare and stained. "This is not fit for a beggar," I said to Saleh and Moise.

"So what shall we do, Elie? Be glad this is not our final destination. Stay focused on Shanghai. For one night, we can tolerate it."

Instantly, I grasped what Moise was saying. We were not there to stay. We were on our way to Shanghai.

"You know what our problem is?" Saleh facetiously asked. "We are all spoiled." He turned to look at me. "Maybe this room was meant to bring us down a notch."

Surprised to hear this from Saleh, who was the most spoiled of all my siblings, I did not respond, but I knew he was right. Until now, we had lived well, despite our travel plans going awry and our money diminishing.

* * *

The next morning, we were on our way to Nanking, the capital located on the Yangtze River Delta. The city was remembered all over China for the Nanking Massacre of 1937, when the Japanese invaded the city and slaughtered 350,000 Chinese and brutally raped 25,000 women. In 1949, with the capture of Beijing, the Communists changed China's capital city from Nanking to Beijing.

Nanking was our last stop before Shanghai. We wanted to update our family in Aleppo and alert our brother of our expected arrival time in Shanghai. Unfortunately, this was not possible. Communications were limited and inadequate. We hoped Miro received our telegram notifying him of our flight schedule, sent before we left Calcutta.

In Nanking, everyone waited on the tarmac for the plane to refuel. The passengers gathered on one side. We watched the pilot call a meeting with his crew and the ground maintenance people. All appeared routine at first, but we soon discovered there was a problem. We were told that the plane was carrying excessive weight and some passengers needed to leave their luggage behind to be put on a later flight. Walking over to us, the captain announced, "We are less than 200 miles from Shanghai. For many of you, this has been a harrowing journey. My job is to assure your safety on this last leg of your trip."

For the first time since our odyssey began, Moise, Saleh and I felt relaxed and confident. The pilot was American and we were ecstatic.

"For your own protection, I am asking for volunteers to lighten the load on the aircraft. How many of you can help us by leaving your luggage here, now? I will personally guarantee that your belongings will arrive on a later flight." The captain waited. We all stood silently. "Nobody?" he appealed. None of us responded to his request. He waited longer. His eyes scanned each of us, imploring us, one by one. Still, not one passenger came forward. "Okay, then let's get out of here." Exasperated, he signaled to the crew to begin the boarding process.

At this point, the desire to reach Shanghai with our belongings intact was a greater motivation than was concern for our safety.

TEN

EXPERIENCE IS NOT WHAT HAPPENS TO A MAN, IT IS WHAT
MAN DOES WITH WHAT HAPPENS TO HIM—ALDOUS HUXLEY

On January 9, 1947, Shanghai came into view. So far, so good, I thought. The plane had not crashed. The extra weight did not kill any of us. I was glad we did not leave our belongings in Nanking. My ears popped as the plane began to descend. When it hit the ground with a thud, I thanked G-d that the plane was intact and we were safe.

At the airport, a committee of three strangers, Tony Shayo, Henri Baladi and Johnny Elias, all older than I, welcomed us. Tony Shayo, Moise's cousin and sponsor, was a single, wealthy Syrian-Jewish businessman living in Shanghai. Henri Baladi, an import/export merchant representing his family living in Beirut, was born in Syria, not Jewish and not married. Johnny Elias, a Sephardic Jew, was a Shanghai native whose parents emigrated from Iraq. Henri and Johnny were good friends of my brother Miro.

When Miro first arrived in Shanghai, everyone called him Mike. The name stuck and Mike is the name he is still known by to this day. So from here on, I will refer to my oldest brother as Mike, not Miro.

* * *

After retrieving our luggage, we went out into the damp, raw January weather. Although the temperature was above freezing, the moisture in the air was so heavy that it chilled our bones. Moise and

Tony bid goodbye to us and left in a very nice car driven by a Chinese chauffeur. Moise would be living with and working for his cousin who planned to take Moise under his wing and guide him through life in Shanghai. I did not see much of Moise after we left the airport. To be honest, I was envious because Moise was on his way to a new life, a better life, the kind of life my father had envisioned for us. Anxiety over our farewell took hold, leaving me with my feelings and thoughts in confusion. Saleh and I had traveled with Moise for the past three months and I thought we had developed a tight bond.

My brother Mike and I did not have a strong connection. When he left for Shanghai, I was twelve years old, just an adolescent. Still, he was my brother, my blood. After seven years of living apart, I so much looked forward to seeing him. So when he did not meet Saleh and me at the airport, I felt cheated, disappointed. Instead of being grateful that Mike cared enough to send his two good friends to look after Saleh and me, I thought: *Two strangers to greet us. How could he do this? Mike is the one I want to tell about our family back in Aleppo and about our three-month ordeal.* But Mike was in Manila on a business trip. I did not understand that he could not hang around Shanghai indefinitely waiting for us. Even we were not sure when we would reach Shanghai. Our three-month journey had been tenuous and unpredictable.

Henri Baladi and Johnny Elias took us to our new home at the YMCA in the International Settlement.

* * *

In 1947, Shanghai was a major city of six million people, including 100,000 foreigners. Today, in 2010, Shanghai, with a population of 20 million, is one of the world's largest ports. Situated on China's central eastern coast at the mouth of the Yangtze River, it borders the East China Sea. Its land is flat and many rivers, lakes, canals and streams weave through and around the region.

For years, Shanghai was separated into three distinct jurisdictions: the French Quarter, which was governed by the French; the International Settlement, which was administered jointly by the British and the Americans; and Hongkew, which fell into Japanese hands during World War II before being returned to Chinese authority after the War.

Hongkew, had a population of almost two million, mostly poor Chinese. It was where 20,000 Jews fled to escape Hitler and Nazi Europe during World War II. The Hongkew jurisdiction was the only place on earth that offered unconditional safe haven to Jews. No passports, no visas were required and no questions were asked. Jewish refugees arriving in Hongkew were assigned to live in what was known as the Shanghai Ghetto. Enduring squalid conditions and always in fear of being deported, the Jews survived with the native Chinese who openly relieved themselves into the Soochow Creek while others lowered buckets into the creek to scoop up water for cooking and washing. The Jews witnessed leftover food and other garbage thrown into the streets and were subjected to widespread diseases, including tuberculosis. On August 21, 1941, pressured by Hitler, the Japanese government closed Hongkew to further Jewish immigration. On February 28, 1943, the Japanese moved Jews into a one-square-mile refugee camp and imposed curfews, food rationing and tight policing. Still, the Japanese were less barbaric toward the Jews than they were toward the Chinese.

Outside of the substandard district of Hongkew, Shanghai looked vastly different. The International Settlement and the French Quarter were where the affluent foreigners lived. The White Russians came to Shanghai years before, escaping the Bolshevik Revolution and the Red Army. Sephardic Jews immigrated to the city to escape military conscription by the Ottoman Empire and to seek better lives. Jews and Christians from Great Britain, France, Italy, Portugal and the United States came to Shanghai in pursuit of favorable business opportunities. By the time I arrived in early 1947, these foreigners had been living in Shanghai for a long time, some for over 100 years. They had set down strong roots. Families prospered and they lived well. Moreover, companies from around the world, including American firms, ventured into Shanghai to expand their bases.

The French Quarter was upscale with palatial homes, opulent apartments, manicured lawns, social and sports clubs and immaculate streets. Professionals, foreign elites and diplomats lived in this district. Residents employed Chinese servants, called coolies, to be chauffeurs, cooks, maids, nannies, grounds keepers and much more.

The International Settlement was equally impressive with lavish homes and apartments, large department stores, fancy shopping, deluxe hotels, elegant office buildings, international banks, flourishing businesses and Chinese servants.

Throughout Shanghai, it was not unusual to see Chinese beggars roaming the streets and skillful pickpockets plying their trade. Bargaining was as prevalent here as it was in Aleppo. People haggled over everything. Getting around the city was easy. Beside walking, there were private automobiles, streetcars, buses, electric trolleys, rickshaws and bicycles.

Winters were cold and damp with strong northerly winds blowing down from Siberia, yet it rarely snowed. Summers were always hot, humid and sticky with occasional downpours and thunderstorms. The best seasons were spring and fall when the weather was at its finest.

* * *

The YMCA in the International Settlement became my home. It was a handsome-looking, nine-story structure situated on a main thoroughfare across the street from a park, a big playground and a race course. Part of the American network of the Young Men's Christian Association, the facility was known everywhere in Shanghai as the "Foreign Y." Membership was exclusive to visiting foreigners, resident immigrants and transients. Mike was living at the Y. Saleh had lived there for a short time when he arrived the first time, before Uncle Joe sent him to Swatow. There was another Y in Shanghai. I was never inside it; it was for the native Chinese.

On the ground floor, inside the entranceway of the Foreign Y, was a large café. This was a gathering place where light meals and snacks were offered to the general public. Also on this level were retail stores, bowling alleys, a large gym, a basketball court, showers, men's locker rooms and the only indoor swimming pool in the city. The second floor housed the administrative offices. The third floor had a formal dining room and a very large lounge. The lounge was the hub for all Foreign Y social activities. In this room, we enjoyed concerts, watched the latest international movies, attended lectures and danced with those of the opposite sex. The fourth through the ninth floors were the sleeping quarters and were off limits to females. The philosophy of the Foreign Y was to promote brotherhood, harmony and understanding through mutual respect and friendships that were guided in a serene, supervised atmosphere. There was no proselytizing and no strong emphasis on religion.

Given that I had no income and no job prospects on the horizon, and knowing that I would have to depend on my father's support for G-d knows how long, I was grateful that the cost for these living quarters was reasonable and affordable. I knew my father's business was sinking and I did not want to burden him more than necessary.

* * *

Although my room was tiny, barely enough space for me, a bed and my things, everything was immaculate and I was grateful to finally be settled in the city that my father had chosen for me. Saleh also had his own tiny room. It was next door and identical to mine.

Trying to sleep the first night in Shanghai was difficult. My mind raced with overwhelming thoughts of isolation in this new land while at the same time attempting to sort out the past months.

* * *

In the morning, Johnny Elias came by to pick us up. We had breakfast in the café, then went to Mike's office. A sign on the door in English read *Sutton and Husney Importers and Exporters*. A tall, attractive, red-haired Russian girl named Vera showed us around. She was born in Shanghai and spoke fluent English. Vera explained Mike's business trip to Manila and said he would return in a few weeks. This news did not make me happy. In fact, it filled me with more anxiety.

With a prod from Johnny, Vera described in detail the business of *Sutton and Husney*, which was headquartered in New York. The company imported embroidered sheets and pillowcases, tablecloths and hand-kerchiefs for sales and distribution throughout the United States. The Shanghai office filled orders received from New York and supervised the manufacturing, quality control, assembling and packaging, and the overseas shipping. Payment was by a letter of credit, a document issued by a New York bank guaranteeing payment to the exporter through a bank in China that had a relationship with the New York bank.

As I listened to Vera, I noticed the lack of activity in the office and asked her about it. "How is the business doing?"

"Not good," she responded. "The War hurt us. It's been a slow turnaround."

Johnny stepped in to expand upon the situation in China. "Although the United States emerged victorious from World War II, it now has another war to fight—the war against communism. America infused large sums of money into the Chinese treasury but it seems our corrupt leader, Chiang Kai-shek, and his inner circle of unscrupulous elites are now dangling, soon to be dropped from power. Mao Tse-Tung, a communist who was influenced by Marxist Russia, has a strong base and a strong following in northern China. His power and support are growing rapidly. Communism is at our doorstep and we are worried that China may soon go to Mao Tse-Tung and the Communist Party. If that happens, we will all be out of business."

Quietly, I digested this information and reflected on Mike's advice about this not being a good time to come to Shanghai.

Vera smiled, resuming where Johnny left off. "There is lack of confidence in the present Chinese government and our local currency is eroding. The Central Bank of China set the exchange rate for foreign transactions unrealistically low. Prices for raw materials spiral upward to keep pace with the money depreciation." She paused, giving us a chance to digest the information. "Can you understand the grim situation we are up against?" Looking directly at me, as if this was not a lesson for Saleh but only for me, Vera said, "Mike wanted you to have this education, to understand what lies ahead."

And this is better than going to medical school? I asked myself. I questioned my father's lack of research and guidance before sending me here and I had reservations about his wisdom in allowing Saleh to return to Shanghai.

My brother began to cough. Vera brought him a glass of water. I grew concerned. The whole time we were traveling, Saleh seemed okay. I did not see any signs of his tuberculosis recurring and I hoped he had been cured. Now with a coughing spell suddenly erupting, my uneasiness about this trip escalated. I looked at Saleh, "Are you okay?"

"I'm fine, Elie," he answered defensively.

* * *

Within days of settling into the Y and spending time in the Sutton and Husney office, we were taken for lunch to the Rose and Leaf Club, a private business association exclusive to its members and their guests. The Club was only open for lunch and through the late afternoon. Here we were exposed to many new faces, men who had businesses in Shanghai.

Johnny introduced me to many permanent residents who were part of the Sephardic community in Shanghai, several of whom Saleh knew. Many of these Jews had emigrated with their families more than 100 years earlier, during the silk-trade period. They became financially successful, owning real estate, shipbuilding and transportation enterprises. They also were generous philanthropists, looking after those less fortunate.

During my long stay in Shanghai, the Rose and Leaf Club became a routine place for me to socialize and do business. At times, I saw Moise there. Our interactions were cordial and I was always happy to see him, but the bond we shared on our journey had weakened.

Living at the Y was a positive experience. Everyone there was eager to develop new relationships. I became friendly with many people of Russian descent as well as with Americans, Canadians, Europeans and Indians. English was the universal language spoken among this heterogeneous group. I relished in how quickly I absorbed the language and increased my fluency. The little English I had learned at the Lycée gave me a base from which to start.

* * *

Johnny Elias became our mentor and was very kind to us. One Sunday shortly after we arrived in Shanghai, he invited Saleh and me to his house for a party to celebrate the birthday of his Russian girlfriend, Valia. Saleh was not feeling well and chose to remain at the Y.

When I arrived, Johnny's family and friends, and Valia and her sister Luba were there. All had already begun toasting the occasion with vodka. The custom of celebrating, included repeating "bottoms up" before downing each shot. Wanting to be part of the merriment, I joined in. My first drink was delicious, sweet and smooth going down. I drank another, then another, not understanding vodka's effects.

"Slow down, Elie. Stop and get something to eat or you'll get sick. Vodka should only be consumed with food," they warned.

"No, no, I'm fine," I replied. "This stuff is delicious. I like it." I poured myself another shot, and then another.

"Elie, enough! There's plenty of food. Go get something to eat!" Johnny argued.

"Maybe later. Right now, I'm fine. And I'm not hungry." Stubbornly, I refused to listen, thinking I knew what was best.

After a time, I began to feel queasy. Then I started to vomit. Barely able to hold my head up, I vomited for 24 hours. Johnny would not let me go home. He gave me a place to stay and looked after me. When the retching finally stopped, a pounding headache took its place.

"Now you know what a hangover is," said Johnny. "I hope you learned a good lesson." He had the servant give me fresh bread and butter to eat. When he saw that I could tolerate some food, he sent me back to the Y.

* * *

More than a month passed. It was late February and things were not going well. Mike had returned from Manila and was too busy to make time for me. He was winding down his life in Shanghai, making plans to close the Shanghai office of Sutton and Husney and preparing to leave for America. Mike was able to secure a visitor's visa and was going to work as a consultant for Uncle Joe at the Sutton and Husney office in New York. I was devastated.

I could not comprehend the situation from Mike's view. He had been in Shanghai for almost seven years, whereas I only recently arrived. Business prospects were grim and the political future of China was, at best, volatile. The only reason for Mike to stay was because I wanted him to. Saleh was getting sicker by the day. I needed Mike to help me take care of our brother. I needed Mike to teach me how to survive and how to earn a living in Shanghai. Abandonment is not what a brother is supposed to do.

I reflected on all that we had shared in Aleppo—the weekly shabbats, the Jewish holidays, our family, our home. I hoped that counted for something. I did not see what was best for Mike. My own apprehension clouded my vision and I refused to recognize that Mike was not doing this to hurt Saleh or me, but rather to grab onto a dream that might never come his way again. All I knew was that I was furious.

I wrote a letter to my brother expressing my anger and slipped it under his door, two rooms down the hall from mine at the Y. I did not have the courage to confront him verbally. In the letter, I recounted our 10,000-mile journey to Shanghai, only to arrive in a place with no job and no income and no brother to greet us. I admonished him for his absence and desertion, and for not caring enough to offer guidance on how to survive in Shanghai. I was too proud to plead with him, to ask him to reconsider staying for another week or two to hold my hand, to show me, to teach me. Only my rage was in the letter. I hoped for a compassionate response. I did not get it. Mike left and I hurt beyond all recognition.

* * *

March 7, 1947 was the holiday of Purim, a time for celebration and merriment. I was depressed. Mike was gone. Saleh was very sick.

Severe coughing drained Saleh's energy. A low-grade fever weakened him even more. He spit up blood, lost weight and neglected to eat. The doctor said if he did not get proper care, he would die. Saleh regretted leaving Aleppo and wanted to go home. I knew the damp climate of Shanghai was not conducive to his recovery. I wrote to my father.

Saleh is coming home. His tuberculosis has returned and he is very sick. I hope he can survive the journey back to Aleppo. I am sorry to ask again, but I need more money. What you sent last month is almost depleted and with Mike gone, I have no family to turn to except you. I pray that you, Imee, my brothers and sister are well . . . . Elie

* * *

Winter turned to spring. Mike had settled in New York. Saleh was back in Aleppo. And I continued my daily prayers.

Friday, April 4, 1947, it was not only the Jewish sabbath but also the first night of Passover in Shanghai. At home in Aleppo, I always looked forward to the yearly seders with family and relatives. This year it was different. This night, I was alone. No family. No friends. No one with whom to drink the four cups of wine. No one with whom to share the Haggadah reading. For the first time in my life, there was no telling of the story of the Exodus from Egypt, no joyous singing and no Passover meal. I missed my mother's cooking. I missed my family. Tony Shayo, Moise's cousin, had a big seder with family and friends, but I was not invited. Was I forgotten or left out on purpose? My heart was heavy. Emptiness and sadness overtook me. Tears welled in my eyes, trickled down my cheeks and I cried.

My father never prepared me for this. Did he think I could just pick up my life in Aleppo and transplant it in Shanghai? For this, was I denied a career in medicine? I thought about how much money my father had already spent since October when Saleh and I left. I also questioned my father's wisdom in not addressing the issue of religion before we emigrated. Did he honestly think I could maintain our strict level of observance, or was this part of the sacrifice?

A friend at the Y noticed my low spirits and asked what was wrong. When I told him about Passover and the first time missing a seder, he said, "Come Elie, let's both of us get something to eat at a fancy restaurant. My treat."

* * *

I knew the time had come for me to confront reality on many fronts. I was alone in Shanghai. Learning to make it on my own was my responsibility; I must quit asking my father for money. I worried about contracting tuberculosis; it is so highly contagious and I was in such close proximity to Saleh. Continuing to hold a grudge against Mike was wrong; I had no right to interfere with decisions about his life. Mike needed to make it on his own just as I now had to do.

My fathers words proliferated my mind, the words he spoke when I tried to convince him to let me go to medical school instead of to Shanghai. *"Elie, once you are in Shanghai, you will be on your own to make your own decisions and choose what is best for you, just as Miro is doing. I can do no more."*

For me, there would be no more insecurities, no more constraints and, except for my daily prayers, no more religious obligations. A new life was out there for me and I was determined to find it.

Luba and me out on a date

Friends at the "Y"

International Settlement - Shanghai

YMCA - International Settlement

ELEVEN

THE BRICKS HAVE FALLEN, BUT WE WILL REBUILD WITH
HEWN STONES; THE SYCAMORES ARE CUT DOWN,
BUT CEDARS WILL WE PUT IN THEIR PLACE—ISAIAH 9:9

By mid-April 1947, my odyssey had begun. I was determined to move from desolation to purpose. I went to the Rose and Leaf Club and actively mixed with the businessmen. Something good was coming my way. I could feel it. I could make it happen.

Two businessmen living in Shanghai who had been members of the Syrian-Jewish community in Aleppo were looking for someone to manage their office. Joe Nasser and Moises Shamah had an importing business and were successful in obtaining many government licenses to import household goods needed to fill the shortages created by World War II. But China's economic stagnation and political uncertainty slowed the sale of their large inventory and they wanted to dissolve their declining operation in Shanghai and grow their business elsewhere.

Meanwhile, The Chinese population on the mainland, though poor, needed someplace to safeguard whatever assets they had. This created a big demand for gold bullion, which was available in bars of differing weights. Gold was a negotiable commodity and Nasser and Shamah preferred to be in this business.

Knowing that I was looking for work, Nasser and Shamah approached me. Although I was young, had never worked a day in my life, and had no training or experience in business matters, they believed

I could be trusted. All three of us came from the same Jewish community in Aleppo and they knew my family. Nasser and Shamah offered me the job of office manager, working from their showroom at the Liza Building, a fancy skyscraper in the downtown section of the International Settlement. My responsibilities included supervising a staff of sales people, overseeing the accounting department and controlling the sale of inventory. I was given a one-year contract to sell all their inventory, turn it into cash and transfer the money to Hong Kong, a place free of government restrictions.

The opportunity to be immersed in the business world and to earn my own money, heightened my self esteem and boosted my courage. But even more so, I no longer had to burden my father. This is what Selim Menashé Sutton hoped, for each of his sons to find their way in the world. I knew his business was failing because of the escalating anti-Semitism in Syria. Now I could relieve him of his responsibility to me. I was overjoyed.

Carefully, I planned how best to succeed, vowing to do an exceptional job for Nasser and Shamah. They took a big chance on me and I was not going to let them down. My first action was to develop a good rapport with the sales manager, who proved to be adaptable and open to my proposals. With authorization from Nasser and Shamah, I was able to offer him and the staff generous severance packages if we reached our goal at the end of the one year period.

* * *

During this time, my social life at the Y soared. The staff often planned many activities that attracted the residents living there. I attended cultural programs, concerts, movies, dances, lectures and debates. Through these gatherings, I expanded my circle of friends.

I also continued to foster my business friendships at the Rose and Leaf Club and nurture relationships with my compatriots from Syria. Schooling and religion which had consumed my life in Aleppo were now replaced by work and socializing in Shanghai. I was very busy and I loved every minute.

* * *

Although I was totally devoted to doing the very best job for Nasser and Shamah, I also was aware that I had a one-year contract and the end was approaching. I began to put out feelers through my business and social contacts. I needed to secure other means of income to continue supporting myself in my newly-acquired lifestyle.

At the beginning of 1948, I was still managing the liquidation for Nasser and Shamah. My brother Mike, now settled and working in New York, started corresponding with me, carefully guiding me in the ways of the exporting business for hand-embroidered linens, his line of work when he lived in Shanghai. Slowly, my anger toward Mike dissipated and our relationship bloomed.

By April of 1948, Nasser and Shamah officially closed. The office in the Liza building had some leftover lease time I could use, so I remained in the office pursuing my own business as a buying agent. From New York, Mike sent me orders to fill, which I greatly appreciated. I also developed a few clients of my own through contacts with importers who came to Shanghai on buying trips.

About this same time, I was invited to a business meeting by Sam Hedaya who had come to Shanghai on a buying trip. He and two of his brothers owned Hedaya Import of New York, a well-established company with an excellent reputation. Learning of my new business venture and of my success at Nasser and Shamah, he asked me to manage their Shanghai office and work exclusively for them. I was flattered by such a tempting offer and told him so, but I did not accept the proposal. Instead, I took a calculated risk, explaining to him that it would not be wise for me to put all of my eggs in one basket and chance losing the business I already had cultivated. Sam Hedaya responded with a compromise. This time I accepted, adding Hedaya Import of New York to my roster of clients.

I took over the Hedaya operation in Shanghai, hired staff, ran the division as my own, and moved all of my undertakings into the Hedaya offices. This endeavor proved to be hugely successful and eventually stretched beyond our business dealings. Unbeknown to me at the time, Sam Hedaya would urge me to take out his niece Tunie Sultan, who later became my wife.

Things happened so quickly for me that there was no downtime between the successful closure of Nasser and Shamah and starting up my own company. Everything fell into place so smoothly, so seamlessly, so perfectly. I had business from Mike, from my own clients and from Hedaya Imports. Money flowed in, more than I could have predicted. I was learning. I was growing. I gained respect. I was exhilarated. Yet all my success did not release me from my worries about my family in Aleppo—my father's deteriorating business, Saleh battling tuberculosis, and Syria's toxic anti-Semitic onslaughts.

* * *

I knew about the November 1947 vote by the United Nations to divide Palestine into two states: Israel and Palestine. I knew Syria joined its neighboring Arab countries, determined to stop the resolution from reaching fruition. Jews living in Muslim lands faced torture, killings, imprisonment and destruction of their homes, properties, businesses, synagogues, sacred books and sefer torahs. I feared for my family's safety.

Reflecting on the prevailing anti-Semitism when I had lived in Syria, I could not imagine it to be any worse, yet it was. I remember my attempts to correspond with my family, but mail was slow and sporadic. Moreover, censorship and mail inspection prevented me from getting much news from them. It was not until years later that I learned from my brothers Ralph and Joe about the ordeal my family endured. I tell their story here because of its timeliness to this period in my life.

A virulent crowd mushroomed. Without exaggeration, their numbers climbed to 100,000. Unrestrained by police, the hysterical mob surged down the main street of Aleppo shouting anti-Jewish slogans, burning and looting Jewish stores, homes, schools, places of worship. They burnt our holy books and desecrated our Sefer Torahs.

Since our family house in Jamalieh sat prominently at a corner on the main street, it became a target of the out-of-control Muslims. Dad thought we would be safe in the basement, so we rushed downstairs and huddled together, hoping to wait out the madness. Then we heard the crowd entering our house and we knew our lives were in imminent danger. Quietly and quickly, we snuck out the side door, hurrying toward the Armenian section of Aleppo. Fortunately, we found refuge in the house of one of Dad's business acquaintances. After three days in hiding, when we thought things had quieted down, someone ventured out to assess the damage to our house. It had been torched and was unfit to live in. Thankful to G-d that we were all still alive, Dad searched for another place for us to stay.

Aunt Eugenie and her family lived in a tiny apartment, yet they opened their arms and their hearts to us. For many weeks, we lived together in these cramped quarters until we were able to restore a few of the rooms in our house so that we could go back and live there.

Meanwhile, anti-Jewish rules became official government policy. We could not leave Syria without authorization, which was next to impossible to get. Jews caught fleeing faced death or imprisonment at hard labor camps. The land which would eventually become the state of Israel was forbidden to us.

No longer could we buy or sell property. Jewish bank accounts were frozen. Jewish schools were closed and handed over to Muslims. Repaying debts to Jews was optional. Jewish businesses were forced to close. And Jews could no longer work for the banks or the government.

Dad, whom we always knew to be proud and self sufficient, found himself helpless, becoming almost a public charge. Having to accept from others shattered his dignity. He had been so fiercely independent, always the one to help others. Now, the tables were turned. He was the one in need, not so much for himself, but for his family. This was his greatest humiliation in life.

Many times, he had to travel outside of Aleppo to collect debts owed to him. Each time, he chanced being caught because freedom of movement to Jews had been restricted. Joe cut classes to go with Dad on these unpleasant and dangerous excursions. In contrast to past times when debtors came to Dad's office and paid him, he now watched Dad beg for what was legitimately his.

Eventually, we experienced a short-lived calmness. Aunt Eugenie and her family permanently left Aleppo and moved to Beirut. Although it was risky, they found a way. Dad finally came to the realization that we could not stay in Syria. We had to leave. Our hope was to make it to Beirut.

At the time, I knew nothing of my family's plight. My limited correspondence with them plus the reports I heard, magnified my concerns. I worried about their security and about Saleh who needed medical care. I did not know my brother had passed away soon after returning to Aleppo.

From left: Moises Shamah, who gave me my first business break, with friends in Shanghai

Left to right: Edmond Esses, Mona Cohen-Esses, David Eskenazi, Lolly Cohen-Choueke, Luba and me

Edmond Esses who hosted me in his apartment, Ted Soskin and me

Saul Reuben, Eileen, John Bialy, Tania, me and Nadia (eventually Saul and Nadia married)

TWELVE

A MAN IS ALWAYS FOREWARNED, WHETHER INADVERTENTLY OR DELIBERATELY, WHETHER AWAKE OR ASLEEP—MISHNAH 2:6

From the time I arrived in Shanghai, I was thrown into a new way of life. Observing the Sabbath was the first thing to go; keeping to my strict dietary laws was the second. Except for rice, a staple in both the Chinese and Syrian cultures, my meals centered around seafood, always in abundance in this port city, as well as dishes of chicken, beef, pork, vegetables, eggs, and soups. In Shanghai, I ate most of my meals in restaurants, in contrast to Aleppo where I ate most of my meals at home. For the most part, my life was free of religion and exempt from my father's rules. I was financially independent and dated girls of differing faiths without making commitments. School and studies were history and medical school would never again be an option. If there were constraints on my life in Shanghai, they were only what I imposed upon myself, such as my unwavering commitment to daily prayer—a seed my father had planted so deeply inside me.

* * *

My business continued to grow and I was earning lots of money. My social life mushroomed and my friends multiplied. I stayed in contact with Johnny Elias who introduced me to his Iraqi-Jewish family. They were as close to a family as I could get in Shanghai. I dated one of Johnny's cousins and enjoyed the time I spent with her.

I also dated Luba, the younger sister of Johnny's non-Jewish Russian girlfriend. Luba worked for Johnny as his office manager and private secretary. Johnny and I were in the same business, but we were not competitors. He exported to Canada while I exported to New York. Because of Luba's position and my business, she and I had much in common. Our conversations were filled with intellectual stimulation and encouraging challenges. Luba captured my heart. She was beautiful, thin, blonde, intelligent, charming, taller than my five feet six inches and she was very popular. Although she was not Jewish, I dated her extensively. Our friends considered us a couple, but to my dismay, Luba had not only a Russian boyfriend but also many other young men vying for her attention. No matter how much I tried, I could not move our relationship past the platonic stage. She liked me, but not in the way I wanted. I was bewitched, she was not. Today I look back and am grateful. Luba could have taken advantage of my vulnerability. She could have held me in her clutches. But she was a decent person who never misled me. She kept our relationship civil and proper no matter how much I wanted it to be otherwise. If she had responded in kind, I am sure I would have married her. Johnny married Luba's sister, Valia. His Iraqi-Jewish family was heartbroken; his mother, especially, grieved.

I continued to expand my circle of lady friends, enjoying the company of young, pretty women. I remember traveling half an hour each way by rickshaw or pedicab to fetch Rachel Abraham. Her family lived in a shack far from the Y. Being British citizens, the family were considered enemies under Japanese occupation during World War II. They were incarcerated and forced to live in a concentration camp. Freed after the War, they had not yet been able to relocate.

Another girl I dated was Chinese. She was quiet, pleasant and subservient, deferring to whatever I wanted. I assumed it was her cultural upbringing that taught her to please the man. She never took me home to meet her family, which perplexed me. When I asked her about it, she was vague. Maybe her parents were protective, maybe she did not want them to know she was dating a non-Chinese, or perhaps she was ashamed of their economic status. I do not know. I liked her but I was not in love with her as I was with Luba.

* * *

From the time of the November 1947 vote by the United Nations to divide Palestine into two states, Muslim countries rigorously built their supply of armaments with the help of governments who were not only sympathetic to their cause but also hungry for a share of Arab oil.

On May 14, 1948, Israel declared itself an independent state. Within 24 hours, Egypt, Syria, Jordan, Lebanon and Iraq sent their armies to invade. Soon after, Morocco, Sudan, Yemen and Saudi Arabia also sent troops. With the British in control, Israelis were not allowed to own weapons of any kind; Palestinians were allowed access to all the weapons they wanted.

To prepare for an invasion, to defend the country and the people, Israelis were forced to operate underground, illegally smuggling in huge arsenals of ammunition. The warfare lasted for one year and the Israelis fought with extraordinary determination, intent on surviving the massive onslaught.

Muslim countries in the region imposed extreme hardships on its own Jewish citizens, making them pay dearly for Israel's existence. Jews living in Muslim lands were subjected to increasing torment as systemic anti-Semitic propaganda spun out of control. Jews were stripped of their homes, their businesses, their belongings and their lives. They were imprisoned and tortured without reason. Fleeing meant they had to leave everything behind; and for many, escape meant risking their lives.

Because of the news seeping into Shanghai, I was aware of what was happening. I thought about my family and imagined the worst, yet I had no way of reaching them, no way of helping them.

Mike and I were were lucky to be out of Syria and far away from Muslim lands. Unfortunately, the rest of my family were not so blessed. My father waited too long. He miscalculated the enormity and speed of anti-Semitism sweeping throughout Syria and all the Muslim lands. I prayed to G-d with all my soul for my family to be safe.

* * *

After living at the Y for 18 months, I decided to upgrade and move to the Park Hotel where my clients stayed. It was directly next to the Y so I did not have to leave my friends or give up my social life. Yet despite these luxurious accommodations and desirable location, I did not remain at the Park Hotel long. My friend Edmond Esses, a compatriot from Aleppo, lived alone in a spacious, two-bedroom, three-bath apartment in a fancy building that his uncle owned. He invited me to move in with him. I quickly acclimated to the change and liked the new posh arrangement, but I did miss the easy access to my friends at the Y, especially the Russian contingent.

Edmond Sassoon, another friend from Aleppo, lived in a ritzy apartment in the French Quarter. The bachelor pad was decorated with impeccable grandeur by a high-end interior designer. Edmond invited me to use his apartment while he was in Japan visiting his older brother, Rahmo. Edmond and Rahmo were partners in a well-established business. Edmond ran the Shanghai office and Rahmo ran the Tokyo office. The brothers decided to close the business in Shanghai because of China's uncertain political situation. They believed it was not wise to hang around and wait for things to get worse. So, for a period, I hosted many splendid gatherings in Edmond's apartment, relaxing and enjoying my parties while Chinese servants did most of the work.

On his return from Tokyo, Edmond took a detour to Hong Kong. He was coaxed by relatives and friends who were bent on playing matchmaker. A Jewish family living in Hong Kong had a lovely daughter of marriageable age. The family had escaped Aleppo by chartering a plane to Beirut. In search of business opportunities, they traveled to Hong Kong and entered into the profitable gold-bullion trade. Edmond married their daughter Yvette in a fancy hotel in Shanghai on August 24, 1948, and I was honored to be one of the ushers. Shortly after the wedding, the newlyweds left China and moved to Tokyo. We are still friends today.

* * *

Almost two years had passed since I left Syria in October 1946. My passport was about to expire and I was foolish enough to assume that I could easily get it renewed. I took a short plane ride north to Nanking, the Chinese capital at the time, and found my way to the Syrian Embassy. Presenting my old passport to an official behind a desk, I looked forward to getting this inconvenient formality behind me. The man glanced at my document, then dourly looked at me and handed the passport back. "This cannot be renewed here," he said. "It can only be renewed in Syria. You will have to return to your country."

"What? How can this be?" I asked.

"There is nothing we can do for you here." He waved me off.

Syria had stripped the Jews of their citizenship and I had no intention of returning to Syria. Feeling the blood drain from my head, the quickening of my pulse, the pounding of my heartbeat, I told myself, *"Relax, Elie, you'll think more clearly if you stay calm."* Intuitively, I knew the reason for this rejection. My Judaism labeled me a pariah, a plague.

Inquiries confirmed my intuition. All Jews living in Muslim lands were non-citizens and did not have rights. Thoughts of my family continued to occupy my brain. Anxiety and worry grabbed tighter on my already unsettled state. I wished I knew they were safe. Most of my telegrams and letters went unanswered. When there was a response, it was cursory due to government censorship. My imagination jumbled my thoughts. I went to a café for coffee and a pastry. I had to clear my head so I could focus on getting my passport renewed.

Continuing to probe, I learned that Shanghai had an office of the United Nations Refugees Administration (UNRA). Its mission was to help resettle displaced persons or refugees who fled the ravages of World War II and/or totalitarian regimes. A light at the other end of the tunnel, I thought. My stateless condition soon would be rectified.

I rushed back to Shanghai and quickly was granted an interview. I took that as a good sign. The interviewer handed me a form to fill out. Carefully, attentively, I completed the document and motioned to the young, pleasant-looking Filipino man. He nodded. I took a seat at the opposite side of his desk and handed him the paper. Slowly, he studied it, then looked at me. I sensed that something was not right. "I must consult with my supervisor. Give me a few moments," he said. I waited. He returned. "I'm sorry, but you do not qualify. Syrian expatriates are not part of our resettlement agenda. I wish I could give you better news. I wish there was a way to certify you, but I have no authority."

I could see that he sympathized with my dilemma. "Please, isn't there something I can do? There has to be another recourse. Please . . ."

The interviewer smiled and handed back my completed form. Keeping his voice to a whisper, he said, "Hold onto this. Forge a signature . . . someone in this office. Perhaps some appropriate government authority will honor it and accept it as an official document. I wish you luck."

This piece of paper, my laissez-passer, was now the only hope to get out of China.

* * *

In time, I developed a strong friendship with John Bialy, a wonderful American from California. He was a professional certified public accountant, a liberal Protestant working for American President Lines, a steamship company headquartered in San Francisco. John Bialy whom I had met at the Y, was the chief accountant, managing a large department in Shanghai. He had been living in the city beyond his normal three-year tour of duty, met a pretty local girl whose parents were of German and Russian origins and married her. The couple were very much in love, but as the situation in China progressively worsened, John grew concerned for his wife. So he arranged for her to emigrate to San Francisco and live with his family until his tour of work ended and he could join her. John became a bachelor again and our friendship blossomed.

American President Lines slowly began pulling out of Shanghai, leaving John Bialy as the only American in the company to remain. He was put in full charge of the entire staff in Shanghai.

American President Lines owned a large, magnificent house in the French Quarter, a residence for corporate executives when they were in Shanghai. John was handed the keys. "This is yours to live in for the rest of your stay here. The amenities are part of the package."

The house came with a Chinese cook, a cleaning lady and a driver. The French Sporting Club was adjacent to the property and its swimming pool was just beyond the garden. "A man should not live alone in such splendor, Elie," John said one day. "I miss my wife and this house is empty. Would you consider moving in? There are plenty of bedrooms."

And so in June of 1949, I took leave from my host Edmond Esses, moved out of his apartment and moved in with John Bialy. I joined the French Sporting Club and John and I fell into a routine. On working days in the spring and summer months, we woke early, played tennis, swam in the pool then showered. Returning to the house, we relaxed on the patio, enjoying breakfast prepared by the cook. Afterward, the chauffeur drove us to work. I wanted to maintain this privileged lifestyle, this opulence fit for royalty.

Moreover, I thoroughly enjoyed John's company, our socializing with our Russian friends and our intellectual and challenging discussions. One of the topics we often spoke of involved the frustrations his company faced as the Communist grip on mainland China tightened and the Nationalists under Chiang Kai-shek retreated to Taiwan. American President Lines began to avoid the port of Shanghai. Instead, their ships were directed to Hong Kong, creating a tremendous problem because some of the cargo was consigned to ministries of the Chinese government. The Chinese Communists and the Chinese Nationalists, embroiled in a civil war, each claimed to be the legitimate consignee for the cargo.

Over dinners, John and I would talk for hours about the quandary, agreeing it would take a King Solomon to solve the problem.

* * *

I continued my membership in the Rose and Leaf Club, socializing with friends, interacting with wealthy business people, widening my contact base and expanding my business. Visitors from the Americas frequented the club. Men came from the United States, Canada, Mexico, Panama and Columbia. Inevitably, I could always find mutually successful transactions, especially among the Syrian Jews from Brooklyn, New York. They wanted Chinese goods and were willing to build their inventory. It was only a matter of time before the Communists would be in full control of China, and importing Chinese goods at far below market value would come to a screeching halt. Until that happened, importers were converging on China, placing large large orders for merchandise while conditions still permitted. Many of the importers were my customers and many others sought me out. My brother Mike had been my protector. From the beginning, I could rely on him not only to send me many big orders but also to send many clients my way.

My business was growing by leaps and bounds. Money poured in, but holding it in Shanghai was getting progressively risky. Mike opened up a bank account for me and deposited some of the payments made to my company in a New York bank. I was barely twenty three years old, had a thriving business with a large office and many employees and I was building a nest egg to await me when I arrived in America.

* * *

I needed a good manager, a person I could trust, someone competent and smart. My responsibilities had become too over-whelming for one person to handle. I was fortunate to have met Sam Raihel, a tall, balding, easy-going white Russian Jew who was born in Shanghai. Although we both had a weakness for a beautiful Russian girl named Nadia, there was no competition or malice between us. We were comfortable in our friendship that we could take it lightly and joke about it. In time, I realized Sam was the right person to be my manager of operations and I asked him to come and work for me. To my delight, he accepted. Not only did this business arrangement work well for both of us, it also cemented our friendship. And Nadia, the Russian girl we were both fond of, she chose Sam over me; she chose a Russian over a Syrian. But that was okay because there were so many other girls to date.

* * *

In spite of the deep concerns about the future of China and the dangers of remaining, no one was panicking, at least from my perception. Restaurants and nightclubs remained busy. Customers shopped in stores. People worked. People socialized. But people carried their cash in bundles because of the escalating inflation. The Chinese currency was losing value by the day, by the hour, under the nationalist government of Chiang Kai-shek. One day as I was returning to my office after lunch, I stopped at a fancy jewelry store to admire an expensive Benrus watch. I bought it for the equivalent of $110 U.S. dollars and paid for it by check. Later that afternoon, I converted some U.S. dollars into the local currency to deposit in the bank to cover the check. By the time the check was cashed, the watch wound up costing me only $75. I kept this watch for many years and took delight in my unexpected bargain.

* * *

John Bialy continued to express his apprehensions. The Communists entered Shanghai in May 1949 and planned to stay. John wished to leave the political upheaval before things got much worse. He also missed his wife in San Francisco. But his company needed him in Shanghai and he was ordered to remain indefinitely.

"Elie," he said, "I'm concerned about your situation. Things here will only intensify. Communism is a completely different form of government, a different system than you and I have ever experienced. One of the things they stress is workers' rights. Workers are urged to report any wrongdoings by their bosses. Even if a boss, the owner of a company, is good, people will always find something negative to report. Be careful."

I lived with John Bialy for more than a year. He was a kind and special man, a devoted and dear friend, my mentor. He continued to urge me to leave Shanghai, but I was not ready to go. I loved my friends and my wonderful social life. I loved my work. I was making more money than I ever dreamed possible. I owned my own business and earned the respect of many people. The respect I once sought by being a good doctor, I now enjoyed as a successful businessman. I wanted to stay a few more years in Shanghai. John advised me otherwise. Still, where could I go? I was stateless. A man with no country. A man with an expired and invalid passport, and a forged document.

* * *

The red-star flags were on the government buildings. The guards wore red army uniforms. All of mainland China was quickly falling to Mao Tse-Tung's Red Army. Soon the entire country would be under communist rule. How much longer could my business survive? This fabulous life I was leading must come to an end. Uncertain times in China were becoming more certain, and that was not good. My friends were leaving while they could still get out.

Where would my future lie? I knew I wanted to go to America. Would destiny take me there? Looking back, I believe G-d paved the way for me. He blessed me with Mike, a kind and caring brother. He sent me John Bialy, a cherished and loyal friend. And he put in my hand, through a Filipino messenger, the forged document from the United Nations Refugees Administration.

Left to right: Nadia, Sam Raihel, Lydia, Ted Soskin, Tania, me, Eileen and John Bialy

John Bialy, Nadia and me —backyard of house in French Quarter

Shanghai 1950, formal evening celebrating French Independence Day (July 14th) at the French Club

Park Hotel

THIRTEEN

I AM SENDING AN ANGEL BEFORE YOU TO GUARD YOU ON THE WAY AND TO BRING YOU TO THE PLACE THAT I HAVE MADE READY. TAKE HEED OF HIM AND LISTEN TO HIS VOICE; BE NOT REBELLIOUS AGAINST HIM—EXODUS 23:20:21

Ironically, Chiang Kai-shek wrote in his diary: *A nation is not destroyed by the enemy from without but rather by the rot from within.* The United States supported this unscrupulous leader who did so little to improve the lives of China's citizens, most of whom lived in impoverishment. To survive a communist takeover, China needed huge economic grants to tackle poverty, unemployment, inflation and social unrest. The United States provided much in the way of materials, military equipment, and financial support, hoping to duplicate the success of the European Recovery Program, also known as the Marshall Plan, which helped Western Europe repel communism and rebuild after World War II. Unfortunately, a similar initiative in China had no chance of success. Chiang Kai-shek and his tight-knit group of dishonest and corrupt colleagues pocketed most of the spoils for themselves, leaving the country ripe for a Communist takeover and the impoverished Chinese people in a perpetual state of hardship.

By late 1948, the Nationalist government of Chiang Kai-shek collapsed and Chiang fled to Taiwan, the tropical island off the southeast coast of mainland China, where he set up his power base. Establishing a dictatorial government in exile, he vowed to take back all of the mainland. He mined and blockaded the port of Shanghai, paralyzing all sea and air traffic in and out of Shanghai harbor. Redevelopment would take months. Steamship lines were forced to circumvent Shanghai and anchor in the far north of China, out of the reach of the Nationalists.

By summer of 1949, Mao Tse-Tung succeeded in occupying much of the Chinese mainland. The people, hoping for a brighter future, threw their support overwhelmingly to the prospective Communist regime. Consolidating his power, Mao Tse-Tung formed a legitimate government, made the city of Beijing the new capital and renamed the country the People's Republic of China. To bring all of China under his regime, Mao continued to push south. Meanwhile, the Nationalist insurgencies under Chiang Kai-shek continued mining and blockading southern ports, similar to what they had done in Shanghai. But in time, the Communists became the victors.

The world now was divided between two camps headed by two superpowers. The United States and its allies represented the side of democracy; Russia and its allies represented the side of communism. Because of the Cold War, the United States extended military protection to Taiwan, recognized the regime of Chiang Kai-shek to be the legitimate government of China and pushed for Taiwan to have China's controlling seat in the United Nations.

The Russian leader, Joseph Stalin, seeking to extend his influence in Far East Asia, supplied Mao and his troops with money and an uninterrupted supply of weapons and training. Chairman Mao, as he was soon to be known, had became Russia's puppet.

* * *

The loss of China to communism changed the entire paradigm of the country. New laws were established to govern business and labor, social culture and customs. Capitalism was out. Socialism and communism were in. A fresh currency was introduced with rules for converting old money, allowing the population to exchange the old money for new, an action that stabilized the Chinese economy and established a realistic money exchange. Announcements were made on which services and enterprises were to become government monopolies. At the top of the list were oil, mining, public transportation and health care. Slowly the list grew to include other sectors such as the fur industry. Some of my friends were affected by this move and promptly emigrated.

For me, I bided my time. I was not too concerned. Matters relating to individual interests like import and export were at a standstill. My business of hand-made linens, tablecloths, pillowcases and accessories was insignificant compared to other industries the government was targeting.

Although we had to cope with new regulations and penalties for even the most inadvertent violations, I did not believe my business or my life were in imminent danger. I hoped to stay on for at least another couple of years. I loved living in Shanghai. The best period of my life was here. I changed from introverted and serious to happy and social. My insecurities faded as I became self reliant and more at ease with myself. I made many good friends. I started a business and steered it to success. I learned to be tolerant and accepting of others who were not of the same persuasion as I. I worked and socialized not only with Syrian Jews, but also with Ashkenazie Jews, Christians, Russians, Portuguese, Chinese—people from different religions, countries and backgrounds. I became versed in Russian, perfected my fluency in English, and even picked up some conversational Chinese. Life in Shanghai allowed me to grow and learn in ways that could never have been available to me in Aleppo with its closed, tight-knit, deeply religious community.

* * *

John Bialy continued to urge me to leave Shanghai. Taking cues from his own dilemma, he was concerned for my safety and about the possibility of my being stuck permanently in the country. Many of our conversations seemed like a repetitive script.

"Elie, why can't you understand the great risks you are taking by staying? You keep insisting that you still have time, but you don't. You are miscalculating, just as your father did. He saw it coming in Syria. You see it coming in China. I don't know your father, but I can bet you are a lot like him."

"Thank you," I would reply with a smile, accepting John's words as a complement. I loved my father. I respected him. To be put in the same category as Selim Menashé Sutton was an honor. "I'm not ready to leave Shanghai. I can't disappoint my customers in the United States. They are counting on me to fill their orders, which are coming in fast and furious. I have to hire more people to keep up with the demand. Who will procure the table linens, the sheets, the pillowcases? I must make sure that agents take them to the homes of the women and the young girls so they can hand embroider them with their beautiful designs. I must make sure the goods are picked up and returned to my office for inspection, for packaging, for boxing. Then they must be crated for shipment to America. My business has been a success because I have kept tight control over my operation. I just can't pick up and walk away from what I have built."

Another time, John would take a different approach. "Elie, even I, who have all my papers in order and a well-established world steamship line behind me, am taking a chance by remaining here. But you, with an invalid and expired passport, with no papers except one forgery . . . how can you not be worried about your stateless position? How much longer can you risk hanging around? How much longer until the gates are locked and your life in China is sealed?" John would look at me and shake his head.

Thank G-d he never gave up. I would have stayed too long for my own comfort.

* * *

In our long distance correspondence, Mike and I would discuss my stateless condition. During one conversation at the end of 1949, my brother told me he was making some inquiries about the possibility of obtaining a permit for me to enter Japan on the pretext of a business trip. By early winter 1950, I got word from Mike that he succeeded in obtaining a permit in my name to enter Japan. *As soon as I receive it from the State Department in Washington, I will send it out to you,* he wrote.

Not long afterward, I was in possession of a three inch by five inch thick folded paper. There was no place for photo identification—only my name and permission to enter Japan. Issued on behalf of the commander of the United States military forces in the Pacific, General Douglas MacArthur, the permit had neither an expiration date nor a window of time for my stay in Japan. I could not believe the absence of time restrictions. To me, Mike had pulled off a miracle. Little did I realize that the permit was issued under the presumption that I was an American businessman, not a stateless foreigner living and doing business in communist China.

It did not take long for anxiety to overtake my euphoria. Questions began to flood my thoughts. Would the permit be honored?

If so, by whom? Would I need to produce more documents verifying my identification? Would conditions be set for me? What if the authorities learn that I am stateless? What if they question my life and my business under communist rule? How could I talk my way out of their interrogations? I was getting cold feet and feared the consequences for things going wrong.

Now that I had the permit from Mike, John hounded me even more about leaving China. Finally, I yielded to his pressure. He convinced me to apply to the authorities in Shanghai for an exit visa to go overseas to promote more business for the Chinese products I exported. In my favor was the fact that I had an office with a full Chinese staff and that Sam Raihel was my manager and would remain to run the business and supervise the staff while I was gone. I was granted the exit visa with an expiration date.

In possession of a permit to enter Japan and an exit visa to leave China made me feel invincible. Nothing could go wrong now, I thought, so I dragged my feet. Why would I give up on the wonderful life I have in Shanghai to venture into the unknown? The tradeoff made me nervous and I was not sure I wanted to make the change.

By mid-June 1950, my exit visa expired and I was still in Shanghai. John's daily hounding grew into daily badgering. "Elie, I can't understand your thinking. The risk of remaining in communist China is far greater than the risk of getting out of here. Personally, I can't wait to leave, to go back to San Francisco, to my wife and my family. I am stressed out waiting for my company to give me the go-ahead.

"You can walk out right now. Start fresh, a new chapter. You're still young. And from Japan, you will make it to the United States. Your brother Mike will make sure of that. So what's holding you back? What are you so afraid of? Just go," he pleaded.

Of course, John was right. So I went back to the authorities in the Shanghai office and requested an extension. At first they were hesitant, then agreed to it with a stern warning: Use it or lose it; there will be no more allowances.

Still, nothing and no one could have propelled me to leave Shanghai, not until a threatening situation emerged to shake me out of my illusions. Korea was the catalyst I could not ignore.

* * *

After World War II, Korea faced two opposing regimes, each fighting for the right to rule. Communist Russia and communist China threw their support to the powers in the north while the United States sanctioned the democratic government in the south. South Korea was in desperate need of defending its people and its territory from daily skirmishes and inhumane attacks, but its military capabilities were weak and inadequate. Without outside help, the country would fall under communist rule.

On June 25, 1950, with Russian-made tanks and Russian-made aircraft, North Korea launched a full-scale military invasion on the South. Swiftly, the United States reacted. President Truman ordered naval and air support, solicited help from the Allies, and moved for the United Nations to quickly condemn the attacks. Still, the onslaughts did not stop. The North Koreans pressed on, at one point reaching as far south as Seoul.

The United Nations Forces under the command of American General MacArthur pushed the invading North Korean forces back. The Chinese government warned MacArthur not to come any closer than 20 miles from the Yalu River, the border between North Korea and China. If MacArthur crossed that boundary, China would consider it to be an act of war. Ignoring the warning and going against the orders of President Truman, MacArthur lined his troops along the Yalu River, provoking China. Seeing this as an act of provocation, China sent 300,000 troops across the River.

Conservatives within the United States advocated an attack on China. However, the Soviet Union had signed a Treaty of Mutual Assistance with China and an offensive action by America could result in direct intervention by the Soviets. General MacArthur pressed President Truman to act aggressively and use the atom bomb. The president hesitated, fearing Soviet retaliation and another world war.

"I'm ready to leave," I said to John.

* * *

Logistically, Shanghai was closed to normal traffic since the Chinese Nationalists under Chiang Kai-shek had mined and blockaded the port. Air and sea traffic were paralyzed and there was no way for me to leave. Rebuilding the harbor would take months.

John Bialy was the sole manager and the only American in Shanghai working for American President Lines. The company's freighters carried massive amounts of cargo. The crews were instructed to bypass Shanghai and travel 600 miles north to the port city of Tientsin, known today as Tianjin. Twelve berths were set aside on each ship and reserved exclusively for American missionaries and their families returning home because conditions in China were too perilous for them to remain. There was almost no hope of anyone but missionaries gaining access to these berths.

John requested special permission from his company's headquarters in San Francisco and was able to secure a berth for me on a ship traveling from Tientsin to Yokohama, Japan. I presume he told whoever was in charge that I was a good customer and did an enormous amount of shipping business with them, which did have some truth to it.

* * *

I hurried to make final arrangements. Sitting in my office, I questioned whether or not to keep the business going, not knowing if I would ever return or if my company would even be there if I did return. I put my trust in Sam Raihel, a good friend and loyal and competent office manager. Together, we decided to keep the office open, providing the government did not close it or nationalize it. Sam and I would stay in touch and once I was settled, wherever that may be, we would decide what to do with the business. I had put so much energy into building my company, it was hard to walk away. But I knew I had to.

I said goodbye to friends still in Shanghai. My connections to them went deep. They had reached out to me, accepted me. Being in their midst brought me so much joy, boosted my moral and self confidence, instilled in me a sense of tolerance that I had not realized was missing in my life. Our farewells were difficult and emotional.

I said goodbye to John Bialy, a Christian who became my most treasured friend and confidante. He watched over me, opened his grand living quarters to me, offered me a way out of a communist world. John and I had shared so much. Never were we at a loss for words. This good man always will hold a special place in my memory.

In Shanghai, I learned that in this world of good and evil, no religion, no race, no ethnic group has a monopoly.

FOURTEEN

On August 2, 1950, I departed Shanghai, leaving my office under the control of Sam Raihel and the Chinese staff. Boarding a passenger train going north, I took my seat in the better section. It was a grueling 36-hour trip. I tried to nap whenever my mind and body allowed, but I was too restless. Struggling with my thoughts, I was preoccupied with having to leave Shanghai and not wanting to go, escaping communist China and apprehensive about my future.

After 600 miles and many stops along the way, I arrived in Tientsin. The monsoon season was just ending and I thought being so far north, the summer weather would be much cooler than Shanghai, but it was not. The ship that would take me to Yokohama was not scheduled to depart until the following day, so I had an overnight stay. Exhausted from the train ride, I checked into a hotel, looking forward to a restful night's sleep, but instead, I went out on a blind date. My Shanghai friends had arranged for me to take out a Russian girl. We went out to dinner and spent a most pleasurable evening. I regretted leaving the next day for I would have liked to see her at least one more time.

* * *

I stood with my luggage at dockside, waiting to be transferred to the ship. The harbor at Tientsin, like the harbor in Shanghai, was too shallow for large ships to approach the shore. Small boats called lighters, stationed at the coastline, escorted passengers or carried commodities back and forth to the ships idling offshore.

Strong rays from the early afternoon sun beat down fiercely, making the intense heat almost unbearable. Seeking shade, some passengers boarded the small boat without asking permission. This infuriated the Chinese security officers who felt their authority had been undermined, so they decided to abort our departure.

I honestly would have liked a long layover in Tientsin to indulge my emotions with my newly-found Russian female friend. Instead, I stood on the dock in sweltering heat for hours, under the dominance of the Chinese security officers toying with us from a distance. Observing the officers confer together on and off for long periods, I can only assume they finally came to their senses and realized that if we missed our connection to the freighter, it would be a lose-lose situation for everyone. Reluctantly, they gestured to us to move quickly onto the boat, lest we miss the freighter which was signaling its impending retreat.

* * *

The ship was comfortable, although not luxurious. The essential crew were American; other crew members were from foreign lands. Everyone was treated well and the food was decent. My berth offered me a quiet place where I could be by myself and quietly think.

I thought about my life in Aleppo, my almost robotic life of daily prayers, holiday rituals, dietary observances and academic studies. I was bound by my father's rules. My father held control and took full responsibility for my welfare. I never questioned G-d's laws and I believed Torah study would make me a righteous, humble human being. I lived among my own people in a tight-knit community. I was accosted by Muslim anti-Semitism and restricted by the edicts of the Syrian government.

I reflected on my life in Shanghai, especially my freedom, my learned appreciation for acceptance of others, and my ability to earn my own way quite successfully. I lived among a conglomerate of people from different religions, nationalities and ethnic backgrounds. I saw no discrimination, no intolerance, no distinctions, no closed circles. People warmly embraced each other without prejudice and judgment. In Shanghai, I was in control and responsible for myself. I experienced both the wonders of becoming a successful businessman at such a young age and the pleasures of an active social life with many good friends.

I grew tremendously over four years. Shanghai was a special place, a place impossible for me to duplicate anywhere else. I had grown both in spirit and in wisdom; my new sense of maturity and self esteem gave me the strength to confront my future. I considered following my young dream, going to medical school, becoming a doctor; I was still young and certainly had the means to do so. But I vividly recalled my father's words just before I left Aleppo: *Elie, once you leave Syria, you will be on your own to make your own decisions and choose what is best for you.* So I chose what I wanted—to be a successful businessman like I was in Shanghai.

* * *

In spite of relaxing my religious obligations in Shanghai, I never stopped reciting my morning prayers, not for one day. My father was adamant: *Missing prayers is never acceptable.*

On the first morning at sea, I carefully removed the tefillin from my suitcase and wrapped the straps attached to the black leather boxes around my arm and around my forehead. I looked out at the rising sun and turned toward Jerusalem. In Hebrew, I recited my prayers without thinking. Tears welled in my eyes. Thoughts of my family absorbed me. The last time I saw my brother Saleh was in Shanghai. I could barely recall his leaving. Our farewell was a blur. I prayed for Saleh's good health, not knowing he had left this world. My parents never liked to impart bad news, especially about family members. It was our way. It was the Aleppian-Jewish culture. In our limited correspondence, they never alluded to Saleh's passing.

I worried greatly about my family's situation, even more now because I was dealing with an unknown and was powerless to do anything. News and information trickled in, alerting me to the difficult situation for Jews in Syria. I was sure my family was affected, but details of their grave circumstances were never disclosed in our sparse correspondence. It was years later that I learned of the ordeal my family had endured.

* * *

Arriving at the Japanese port of Yokohama, American military officers boarded our ship and welcomed us. To my relief, the permit I held was the only paper I needed to enter Japan. My stateless status never came up. Japan, now occupied by the United States under the leadership of General MacArthur, offered free trade and business opportunities, unlike China under Communist dominion and the rules of Chairman Mao.

Based on inquiries I made in Shanghai, I knew to go directly to the Hotel Tokyo where I could connect with acquaintances as well as some Syrian Jews residing there. Immediately after reaching Tokyo, I contacted my brother in New York, informed him of my arrival, and thanked him for my new status. I then checked into the subdued, six-story Hotel Tokyo in a bustling part of downtown. The August weather was hot and humid and dark clouds indicated that rain was on the horizon. I was told that September and October were more comfortable weather months, although no one escaped the frequent rainfalls.

My first contact in Tokyo was with Edmond and Rahmo Sassoon, two brothers who emigrated from Aleppo. It was Edmond who had allowed me to use his lavish apartment in the French Quarter of Shanghai for my parties while he was in Tokyo with his brother Rahmo, planning their exit from China. Edmond and I were friends and I was an usher at his elaborate wedding before he and Yvette moved to Tokyo. Edmond and Rahmo had a thriving business in Japan, bringing in immediate and extended family members to help sustain their rapidly-growing company.

Edmond and Rahmo welcomed me to Japan and encouraged me to continue my pursuit of a new venture. They helped me to establish my base, then encouraged and guided me in applying for a visitor's business visa to the United States. I always will be grateful for the counsel from Edmond and Rahmo.

* * *

While living in Shanghai, I heard so much about the brutal and barbaric ways of the Japanese and the atrocities they committed upon the Chinese people. But my first impressions of the Japanese were nothing like that. I saw them as subdued, polite, respectful and law-abiding. Without making eye contact, they were humble in their own way and eager to help when asked. It was hard for me to perceive their toughness during the War, their savage aggression and inhumane acts, their willingness to die for their country rather than fail in their mission. The trained kamikaze pilots, primed to be suicide bombers, crashed their planes into ships, causing great destruction of life and property. Aircraft with machine guns did not achieve the same success as did the suicide bombers. The Japanese were determined to win their battles at any cost.

When the War ended, the United States helped its enemy rebuild. General MacArthur supervised the American occupation, reconstruction efforts and remolding of Japan into a democracy. By the time I arrived in Tokyo, the city had undergone major renovations. General MacArthur's headquarters were located in a modern, sleek office building in the hub of the city. The official residence of the emperor, the Imperial Palace, was untouched by the War and I easily could see it from one of the main thoroughfares. The Giza, the heartbeat of shopping, restaurants and entertainment, was very much alive, especially in the evenings. Parks with elaborate Shinto temples brimmed with people, particularly young families out for a Sunday stroll.

Unknown to me until then was the culture of the Japanese Geisha girls. These beautiful young women were trained from childhood to entertain men. They served politicians, foreign tourists, and businessmen and their clients. With their white faces and red lips, Geishas entertained with song, dance, musical instruments, story telling, tea ceremonies and skilled conversation. Businessman brought their clients to the tea houses to be charmed by the Geishas. Many successful business deals were sealed in these captivating surroundings. I found the custom magical and wondered why other countries did not adopt it.

* * *

With American dollars always in my pocket, substantial assets in a New York bank account, and a checkbook to procure more cash as

I needed it, I knew my financial situation would see me through for at least some time.

During my stay in Tokyo, I met several people with my background, some of whom stayed at the same Hotel Tokyo where I was residing. All of them were in Tokyo on business. Soon, I found myself spending evenings and Sundays at the Jewish Club of Tokyo. I socialized with new acquaintances, other Middle Eastern Jews, and some friends from Shanghai who had also fled communist China.

I wanted so much to get back into business and believed I could easily contact my Shanghai clients who lived in the United States, offer them the same service from Japan as I had given them in China and get my operation back on track. I soon found out this was not to be. Conducting business in Japan was not the same as conducting business in China. Most of my Shanghai clients had competent agents in Japan and were not prepared to switch to me. I realized I was a novice in Japan. I needed learning and experience before I could generate my first customer. Success here would not come so easily.

Raymond Dweck, a Syrian Jew from New York, was in Japan on a buying trip and staying at the Hotel Tokyo. His father had been my client in Shanghai. Raymond understood my shortcomings and my potential and invited me to sit in on his product selections and negotiating sessions. I learned from Raymond's kindness and thanked him for his recommendations and willingness to teach me.

* * *

With the help of Russia, a strong Chinese Communist Air Force developed rapidly, coming to the aid of the North Koreans. They attacked targets in South Korea, then returned to their home base in China. America faced a dilemma. Should it pursue these fighter planes inside China and destroy them? General MacArthur endorsed retaliatory raids. President Truman saw the situation differently; he was concerned that offensive measures could lead to another world war, bringing into the fight not only China but also Russia.

With this new uncertainty in the region, as well as my business failing to get off the ground, I turned my focus toward the United States, as Edmond and Rahmo Sassoon had been urging me to do. Edmond was so sure I would be granted a visa that he wagered me $100, a lot of money for a bet in 1950.

With much trepidation because of my stateless status, I applied at the U.S. Consulate for a visitor's visa, indicating my desire to explore business opportunities and fulfill social obligations. I was required to produce a doctor's report showing no illnesses or contagious diseases, and I had to prove I had enough money to travel and sustain myself. Once I met these conditions, I was asked how long I would be staying in the United States. I replied 'ninety days.' I wish I had asked for more time. Six months. A year. Forever. But I was apprehensive. Everything had been moving so smoothly and I was so close that I feared a wrong word, a wrong answer might result in a denial. So I responded with what I thought was a safe number. Ninety days.

My visa was approved. I could enter the United States. A miracle! A blessing from G-d! I held the document in my hand, barely able to contain my excitement. I marched over to Edmond Sassoon's office and plopped $100 in cash on his desk. "My greatest pleasure is giving this to you," I said, while euphorically holding up my visa. "If you and Rahmo had not encouraged me, this may never have happened."

Edmond smiled and gave me a warm hug. "I'm elated for you. You're on your way to a new life and I wish you all good things. Use your future wisely."

Over the years, my friendship with Edmond and Rahmo grew evermore significant. Years later, when Rahmo came to me for guidance, I valued the opportunity to give back in some small way for what he did for me.

* * *

My visitor's visa specified my entrance into the United States in September/October 1950. My brother Mike asked me to arrive in time for his marriage to Cynthia Beyda, which would take place in Brooklyn, New York, on November 5, 1950. With no business to keep me in Tokyo and very limited social commitments, I decided to leave Japan in early October 1950.

With my visa in hand, and no home or country in which to put down roots, I placed my trust in G-d. Maybe America will grant me refuge. Maybe America will provide me a place to dwell.

FIFTEEN

I was twenty-four years old. A lot had passed. My life changed drastically. I was not the same person who left Aleppo four years earlier.

On Monday, October 2, 1950, I boarded a Pan American Airways flying clipper. Since there was no such thing as a jet plane in those days, frequent refueling stops were necessary, resulting in no direct flights to anywhere overseas. But passengers were attended to solicitously, seats were comfortable, and food and drink were plentiful.

After being airborne for eight hours, we stopped to refuel at Wake Island, a tropical atoll in the North Pacific with a coastline of 12 miles. We disembarked, grateful for a chance to stretch and move about for an hour before boarding for the next leg of the flight.

After another eight hours in the air, our plane landed in the western Pacific on Guam, another tropical island. We deplaned, went through the same motions as we did at the first refueling stop, then re-boarded.

America was getting closer. From the air, I looked down on the vast ocean below, hoping to spot land, hoping to catch a glimpse of American soil. But all I saw was water. I closed my eyes and slept. We traveled a long time. The stewardess woke me. I heard the local time announced. Looking out the window, Hawaii came into view. This was United States territory. And although Hawaii did not gain statehood for another nine years, at that time it was America to me. I could barely contain my excitement. I looked at my Benrus watch, the one I purchased in Shanghai for the devaluated price of $75. I reset it to the local time and prepared for landing. Twenty-four hours of being in the air, more hours spent on the ground for refueling stops—I was exhausted and ready for a shower, a comfortable bed, a good night's sleep and extended time with my feet on the ground. Friends from Tokyo recommended I break up the trip and spend a few days in Hawaii, relaxing before I embarked on the journey to the mainland.

At the airport, I passed through customs without incident. They asked me the reason for my visit and my length of stay, and inspected the form filled out by the American Consulate in Japan. The immigration officer wrote on it *90 days*. I picked up my luggage. Young, beautiful Hawaiian girls surrounded me, welcoming me with garlands of Polynesian flowers, called leis, which they placed around my neck.

I had reserved a hotel room in Honolulu at a sprawling, ocean-front complex. The grounds were lush, the climate was comfortably tropical, the sand was soft and white. The beautiful blue ocean beckoned me, cabanas lined the beach and everyone spoke English. I could not have chosen a more serene atmosphere. My spirits rose and my body and soul were comforted. I was alone. It was peaceful. I felt G-d's presence. He had been good to me. He watched over me. I prayed for my family.

* * *

I stayed in touch with Mike until my arrival in Brooklyn, New York. Because I had time to spare, he suggested making some stops along the way to sightsee and visit relatives. So with his direction, I left Honolulu on Monday, October 9th, and flew to San Francisco, thrilled to be on the mainland of the United States.

The city overwhelmed me with its many skyscrapers, heavy traffic, abundance of people everywhere I turned. The faces, the hills, the aura of the place were nothing like I had envisioned. San Francisco was physically charming and the weather, with its dry climate, warm days and cool nights, added to its allure. I strolled the streets, experiencing things unheard of in the Middle East or Far East. At Union Square, not far from my hotel, I witnessed a politician campaigning. He asked people to vote for him, telling them why he was the best choice for the job and what he would do to serve the people. I lingered, watching, listening. This was the United States. Democracy at work. A free country. I knew then I would like it here. Somehow, I would find a way to adopt America, to make it my country.

* * *

Mike recommended I call Rachel Gindi, a second cousin who lived in Los Angeles with her husband, Jack Gindi. Rachel was the daughter of Joe and Becky Harary; Becky was our first cousin. Mike had been living with the Harary family almost from the time he arrived in Brooklyn. Not known to me then, I also would live with the Harary family.

I called Rachel. Much to my delight, she sounded genuinely excited to hear from me and invited me to visit. I wasted no time booking a flight to Los Angeles. Upon arriving, I took a taxi downtown, checked into a hotel, dropped off my luggage and took another taxi to the Gindi's house.

The cab made its way through an elegant and tranquil residential neighborhood with lush lawns, magnificent trees and beautiful flowers and bushes. The driver stopped in front of a large house. He turned to me and smiled. I paid him and emerged from the vehicle.

Slowly, I digested the surroundings as I walked to the front door. Rachel greeted me with a hug. She was warm and outgoing. Jack welcomed me with a big, friendly smile. Over a wonderful meal, we chatted incessantly about our family history and relations, the plight of the Jews in Syria, the Syrian-Jewish community in Los Angeles and the Gindi family's successful retail business. Jack and his family had come to Los Angeles and opened many stores throughout the region. Frequently, Jack traveled to New York and visited with family in the Syrian-Jewish community in Brooklyn. It was there he had met Rachel and married her.

* * *

My next stop was Dallas, Texas. There I visited another cousin, Israel Sutton. He was unmarried, not so young and he owned a large children's retail store in downtown Dallas. His overwhelming hospitality enticed me to stay a few days more than I had planned.

Israel had been dating a young woman named Arnette from one of the local Syrian-Jewish families. Eventually, he married her. Years later, I heard that their union had been stormy, although they did manage to have three children. Arnette died at a young age, leaving my cousin Israel a widower.

* * *

On Wednesday, October 18, 1950, I was on my way to New York. There were no direct flights, so I flew through Atlanta. During the short layover, I headed straight for the restrooms in the terminal. What a shock! The signs above the doors read: *White. Negro. Black.* I was in the deep South. No one had alerted me to any segregation laws in America. I was hardly aware of a black population in the United States, no less a race of people forced to live separate from white society. Was this the same America I saw in California? I later learned that, although the Civil War ended in 1865, freeing slaves was one story, joining two races to live equally and harmoniously together was a very different story.

I boarded the last leg of my flight to New York, my final destination, my new home. I put my trust in G-d and prayed for my stay to last longer than 90 days.

At LaGuardia Airport, my brother and his fiancée, Cynthia Beyda, greeted me. I threw my arms around Mike, so happy to see him, so happy to be with someone from my family. Both Mike and Cynthia embraced me warmly, expressing their joy about my arrival.

Mike and Cynthia's wedding was planned for Sunday, November 5th, 1950, a little more than two weeks away. Cynthia's family lived in the Washington, D.C. area. Her parents had a well-established chain of children's retail stores. Cynthia had two brothers. The older was recently married and the younger was still in school.

Cynthia's parents, although residing in Washington with their children, hoped to preserve their roots in the Syrian-Jewish community. They rented an apartment at the Franconia Hotel on West 72nd Street in New York City and traveled from Washington as often as they could. They wanted their children to keep a connection with the community as well as to marry within the group.

* * *

Almost from the time Mike had arrived in Brooklyn, he lived with Joe and Becky Harary, parents of Rachel Gindi whom I had recently visited in Los Angeles. The Hararys had five children, most grown. They lived in an apartment in a two-family house. Mike had been renting a room from them, living like a member of their family.

But now that Mike was to be married, Cynthia's parents invited him to move into their quarters at the Franconia Hotel during those last few weeks before the wedding. Rather than give up the room with the Hararys, Mike arranged for me to replace him as their tenant.

So after leaving LaGuardia Airport, Mike and Cynthia drove me straight to my new home with Joe and Becky Harary. Joe, a quiet man, spent much of his time in New Orleans managing my Uncle Joe Sutton's store. Becky, an outgoing woman, raised the children, ran the house and cooked the meals. They welcomed me and were most gracious.

In my room, I unpacked. The living arrangement was very different for me, so unexpected and disappointing. I wondered if I could get used to it. I longed for Shanghai and wished I could go back.

* * *

The following day, Mike picked me up and we went to his office on Fifth Avenue in Manhattan. In a high-rise building on the fifth floor, Mike rented two small rooms. One room stored his inventory of hand-made tablecloths and other cotton and linen accessories—merchandise that had been shipped from my Shanghai office. The other room, where Mike did his work to keep his business going, contained filing cabinets, a desk and a telephone.

Memories flashed in front of me. I could see my father's office at the khan. Two rooms for his inventory where he stored bolts and bales of fabrics. The third room for his office where he did bookkeeping to maintain the business. My father had left his imprint. Although Mike's office was smaller, the setup was the same.

In the afternoon, Mike and I went for lunch and visited some of my Shanghai customers. During the day together, I learned that Mike had contacted our family in Beirut about his upcoming marriage and invited them to come to America and share in his wedding day. Regretfully, they declined; our father was not well. Concerned, I felt a need to call and speak with my father, but overseas phone service was still in a primitive stage.

* * *

Mike and Cynthia's wedding plans and last-minute details absorbed much of the next two weeks. Honored to be Mike's best man, I accompanied him to a formal-wear rental store where we were fitted with tuxedos, something new and strange to me, but I was assured that this was part of the protocol for getting married in America.

I was invited to Cynthia's bridal shower, an event strictly for females. But an exception was made for me because I was the new guy in town, a foreigner and Mike's only family in Brooklyn. I think it was also because I was an eligible bachelor and perhaps a match for one of the lovely young ladies attending. The bridal shower took place at the Suburban Club, a combination catering hall and restaurant on Ocean Parkway. At first I felt a bit awkward, overwhelmed by being the only male in the company of a large group of chattering females. But with the attention lavished on me, my anxiety dissipated and I found myself enjoying every moment.

Gifts of lingerie and housewares were piled high, waiting to be opened. Guests roasted Cynthia with amusing anecdotes about her life. Then, in a jovial and friendly atmosphere, we gathered for a festive meal. The occasion was my initiation into meeting young, single women of marriageable age and easing my way into dating and socializing within the Syrian-Jewish community.

Mike made every effort to include me in the events leading up to the wedding. His bachelor party was another first for me. In the four years Mike was in New York, he accumulated a wonderful group of friends and relatives who genuinely liked him. To pay tribute to Mike on his final day of bachelorhood, the men took him to a Turkish bath. We relaxed in a steam room, sitting around in towels while sweating, joking, laughing. We cooled off with a swim in the indoor pool, then showered. Afterward, we continued to banter and laugh over dinner at a nearby restaurant. I smiled, happy for my brother. His life was good. He had roots in the Syrian community in Brooklyn. He had a business, found Cynthia, and was surrounded by many people who cared about him.

* * *

The wedding was on Sunday, November 5, 1950, at the East Midwood Jewish Center on Ocean Parkway, a popular place for Syrians to celebrate milestone affairs. Four hundred guests filled the sanctuary. The *chupah* was adorned with garlands of exquisite and colorful flowers. The bridesmaids wore identical pink designer gowns and the ushers sported rented, formal tuxedos.

Mike marched down the aisle accompanied by Uncle Joe, my father's brother who had provided employment to Mike and Saleh in China. Under the chupah, Mike and Cynthia stood facing the respected spiritual leader, Rabbi Halpern. The marriage ceremony began in Hebrew. It was all very emotional for me and I swallowed back my tears. Although I was sincerely happy for my brother, I also was sinking into a depression. My father should have had the joy of marching his first born son to the altar. My mother, my brothers and my sister should have been here to share in Mike's happiness.

Sitting through the ceremony, my father's condition weighed heavily on my mind. *How serious was the brain tumor? Was he in good hands? Was he getting proper treatments? Was he in pain?* So many thoughts and questions ran through my head.

A gala reception with dinner and live Syrian music awaited us as we stepped out of the sanctuary. Guests were already on the dance floor enjoying themselves. Attempting to mask my melancholy, I smiled. Many people approached me and congratulated me on my brother's marriage. They welcomed me to Brooklyn and indicated that they hoped I was here to stay. These formalities failed to lift my spirits. Happiness seemed as far away as China.

* * *

Mike and Cynthia left for their honeymoon. I missed my brother while he was gone. I was just getting to know Mike, to bond with him.

Because of our age difference, Mike and I were not close growing up. Well ahead of me in school, he and his friends were too old to pal around with me. But Mike and I did share family, weekly shabbats, holidays, festive meals and attending synagogue with our father.

While Mike was away, distressing reports filled the newspapers and airwaves. The United States failed to settle the Korean conflict and to stop China from bombing allied forces on the front lines of South Korea. This dire situation prompted America to break off all diplomatic relations with the People's Republic of China. Commerce, travel, communications and transportation came to an abrupt halt. Shipments already in transit, and that included those that already had left my office before the cutoff date, would be allowed to enter the United States. Any shipments thereafter were subjected to an embargo. My business as I knew it to be in China would not survive. My stateless status ensured my isolation. Would it ever be possible for me to return to the wonderful, happy and successful life I knew? Shanghai now seemed like a dream and all dreams come to an end.

I contacted my Shanghai office, corresponding with Sam Raihel, my trusted Russian friend and competent manager. Sam reported that the Chinese staff wanted to keep the office open and take a wait-and-see approach. "I strongly advise against this," he said. "There's no chance for us to continue here. All our export options are closed. We cannot ship to the United States. I suggest we liquidate what we can and quit while we're ahead."

It was difficult for me, but I had to agree with Sam. We arranged to shut down our Shanghai office and approved a severance package for the employees.

* * *

Mike returned from his honeymoon to face a looming crisis. The embargo confronted him just as it had me. What would we do now? Mike needed an answer more urgently than I. He had a wife. His responsibility was greater than mine. As we were debating and exploring the potentials to join forces and pursue a business together, Mike's father-in-law made him an offer that was hard to refuse. He asked Mike to move permanently to Washington and join the Beyda family in their well-established, successful chain of children's retail stores.

Mike was torn, feeling guilty about leaving me. Four years before, when I arrived in Shanghai and needed him, he left for America. Now, with me newly arriving in New York, he would leave me again, this time for Washington, D.C.

I did not want to be the reason for Mike to pass on this opportunity. This time, I was more understanding, not angry, and did not see Mike abandoning me. I urged my brother to go. His place was with his wife and new family. "I will be okay," I said. "You are not to worry about me." Mike deserved to have goodness in his life. Shanghai had matured me.

My oldest brother had lived on his own, cut off from his family for ten years. Five of those years, he lived under harsh conditions, exposed to World War II and Japanese occupation in China. He escaped imprisonment because he was a citizen of Syria and not of America. He struggled to keep going financially, always staying in a small room at the Foreign Y in Shanghai. Then, for four years in New York, he rented a room in the Harary's apartment and managed to put down roots in the Syrian community. Mike opened a small import operation of his own and sent me orders. He also sent me many customers. My company did well because Mike looked after me.

After much soul searching, Mike and Cynthia moved to Washington. Mike worked in the family's flagship store downtown on F Street. Over time, he opened his own stores, became successful and branched out into real estate and other investments.

* * *

After the excitement of the past month, I settled into my place with the Harary family. No longer was I living in the splendid house with John Bialy in the French Quarter of Shanghai. No longer was I living in the lavish, spacious apartment with Edmond Esses. I was not even living in my small room at the Foreign Y. Lodging with the Harary family stifled my independence. Although they were good to me and tried to accommodate me, I was not on my own. My routine was totally out of sequence. My living standards dropped. My outgoing personality, my self-confidence, my smiles—all the positive sides of me that I discovered in Shanghai, faded back to Aleppo. I missed my Russian friends. I missed my international friends. I missed my business, my office, my staff. I missed the income that allowed me to live well.

Yet, thanks to Mike, I did have something—$50,000 in the bank, a substantial amount in 1950. But I could not expect to exist on that forever. I had to be careful not to deplete my savings. I also had to find a way to grow my money. Remaining in Brooklyn in the tight-knit, closed Syrian-Jewish community seemed daunting. How would I ever cope?

I felt like I was sinking in quicksand, unable to free myself. My ninety-day visa was fast running out of time and my foreign status in this land would bring me no privileges. How could I apply for refugee status? I had no passport. I was stateless.

My cousin Israel Sutton
Dallas, Texas

Joe and Becky Harary
I rented a room in their house

Me presenting the ring at my
brother Mike's wedding

Mike and Cynthia Sutton
November 1950

SIXTEEN

WHO IS SHE THAT SHINES THROUGH LIKE THE DAWN, BEAUTIFUL
AS THE MOON, RADIANT AS THE SUN—SONG OF SONGS 6:10

Mike was gone and I was alone. Shanghai was history and
Brooklyn was now.

Dipping into my bank account when I first arrived, I bought
myself a new car, a Buick. This was a bold move because I did not have
a driver's license and I carried only a 90-day visa to accompany my
stateless position. But I was determined. Subconsciously, I made up my
mind to stay in America. Owning a car was my first step toward citizenship.

Remarkably, I did get my driver's license. Then I began to make
friends, socialize and date. I networked and looked to start a business.
My goal was for a long life in the United States. This was the country I
wanted to bring my family, this was the place where I hoped to marry.

* * *

By late November 1950, disappointment in my living quarters
had eased. The Hararys did treat me well and I knew this arrangement
would not last forever.

I approached some people I had known, men who came to
Shanghai on buying trips, men who were my customers. I explored
opportunities for business and friendship. I called some of the girls I
had met at Cynthia's bridal shower and invited them out. Soon, I had
people in my life, Syrian Jews, and I belonged to the community.

I was invited to a meeting about launching a social club for singles. Everyone liked the idea and we quickly moved on it. A search group was formed to find a location. We paid dues and with the money we raised, we rented a one-family house on Avenue R and East 8th Street. We furnished it, not extravagantly, but adequately, and we kept snacks in the refrigerator.

That house was our social hangout where we watched sports on television and played backgammon and card games like bridge and solo. I was an excellent card player, a skill acquired at the coffee houses in Aleppo. In Shanghai, I played such games with my Russian and international friends. My new friends in Brooklyn considered me to be an expert and looked to me to teach them how to play solo, a game similar to bridge but a bit less sophisticated. This elevated my standing in the group and also renewed my self confidence.

Sometime in mid-December, we got a bright idea to throw a New Year's Eve party. Each club member would invite a single girl from the community. The event was a smashing success and our club became an enviable place to be. Our membership grew, we had more parties and invited more girls. The club became a spark for many couples to meet and date; engagements and weddings followed. Our gatherings, whether small or large, were a pastime for enjoyment, socializing and connections.

Everyone grew up adhering to the strict discipline of our parents, never deviating from our ethical and moral upbringings. We remained constant to our close community standards. Heavy drinking, illegal drugs, misbehavior of any kind were taboo. We were a wholesome group and we knew our limits.

* * *

The community in Brooklyn eagerly cleaved to their Syrian ways. Their music, language, foods, values and interactions were engraved into their lives. They upheld their religious beliefs and traditions and safeguarded their Sephardic heritage. I continued to recite my daily prayers as I had done since my Bar Mitzvah, but here in Brooklyn, I did not pray alone as I did in Shanghai. In Brooklyn, I had a community and we prayed together in our synagogue, similar to my days in Aleppo.

On one particular morning, as I left the synagogue after prayers, an old schoolmate and friend from Aleppo caught up with me. He recently emigrated to America and it was good to reconnect with him. As we walked, he spoke about the dire Jewish situation back in Syria. It distressed me to learn about the extent of atrocities inflicted on Jews because of the rampant anti-Semitism throughout Syria. When he said how sorry he was about Saleh's passing, I was taken aback. This was the first I heard of my brother's demise. I knew Saleh was sick with tuberculosis and I feared this news for a long time, yet never in my correspondence with my family was I told of his death.

I thought about Saleh and how he refused to take proper care of himself. In my mind, Saleh's image is vague and I barely remember our goodbye. Still, I am sad for his short life. This must have been very hard on my parents.

* * *

Hoping for an extension to my visa but not fully confident it would happen, I held my breath as I politely requested three more months. Whew! What comfort to see the immigration officer renew my visa. Ninety days more in America. I had to find a way to remain permanently.

My friends suggested I consult the Hebrew Immigrant Aid Society (HIAS). "The organization works with many governments and has helped millions of refugees who cannot return to their homelands. They have a Refugee Resettlement Program and it sounds like you could qualify," they said, urging me to contact HIAS right away, "Don't wait until your visa lapses. Next time you may not get an extension." Thanking my friends, I felt a shred of hope.

I made an appointment to meet with one of the HIAS counselors. "I am optimistic that your stateless status can be changed to refugee status," he said. "You have legitimate grounds and I am going to refer your case to an in-house attorney."

During my second meeting, I met with an attorney who agreed to take my case. "We will submit your application as a displaced person, a refugee. You have been stripped of your citizenship and you are now requesting political asylum."

I nodded, searching the man's eyes, looking for some guarantee that my application would be approved.

He smiled, "While your application is being considered, do not leave the country. If you do, your return cannot be assured. Do you understand?"

"Yes. Thank you."

Anxiously I waited for some news. Finally, a verdict. My heart thumped wildly as I was told that the stay of my visa was confirmed. I would not be forced to leave America for as long as my case was pending. Feeling the stress lifted, I channeled my energies toward the future.

* * *

One of my best customers from Shanghai, Joe Haber of Pan American Textiles Corporation, often traveled to China on business.

Although Joe was quite a bit older than I, we became friends. The main concentration of his business was Chinese imports, but with the trade embargo, Joe's company needed alternative sources to stay alive. In New York, Joe and his partners created a new division, Pan American Handkerchiefs Corporation, to design and manufacture handkerchiefs, scarves, umbrellas and other accessories.

Desperate to find a venture I could latch onto, and not wanting to infringe on Mike who was absorbed in his new life in Washington, I contacted Joe Haber and told him I was looking to get into a business. Shortly after, I was offered a partnership in Pan Am Handkerchiefs. Eagerly, and without thinking even once of what I might be getting into, I jumped at the opportunity. Blindly, I leaped. I did not even stop to ask a question. I withdrew money from my bank account and bought my way into the business.

In Shanghai, I was more sure of myself. There, I would have taken a step back and evaluated the offer, analogous to what I did when Sam Hedaya approached me to manage his office in Shanghai. What happened to that skill I had mastered so well? Was I afraid of not finding a source of income? Did panic cloud my ability to probe or was it the intimidation of being left out?

Pan Am Handkerchiefs did not have strong distribution channels, nor a healthy and loyal customer base, nor a niche in the market. There were too many unproductive, deadwood partners drawing high salaries and splurging on excessive overhead. Our company was being financially drained. Instead of prudently managing our affairs, we made a foolish decision. We hired a high-priced sales and production manager, believing he would save the business and help us grow. Our immaturity, lack of interviewing skills, get-rich-quick mentality and failure to do our homework, led us to choose the wrong guy. We paid dearly for that mistake and incurred huge losses and a massive lawsuit to get rid of him.

* * *

By spring 1951, I still was uneasy about my life in America. I felt the same emptiness I had experienced when I first arrived in Shanghai, when Mike left and I was alone. I was not sure I could ever erase that image from my mind. Adding to this feeling was my unsettled residential status, the nagging insecurity about whether or not I would be allowed to remain in the United States, about where to go if I could not stay. My emotions were in turmoil and I found it difficult to think clearly. "Get hold of yourself, Elie," I said. Once again, the time had come, as it had in Shanghai. I must confront reality, develop a plan and stick to it. I decided to get married and put my legal status to rest. I would not look back. My future was in America and I was not going to live here alone.

I looked to G-d for guidance. Not for Him to do something for me, but to send a sign for me to follow. To this day, I believe He heard me because I received a call from Sam Hedaya.

As I mentioned, I met Sam Hedaya in Shanghai. He and his brothers owned a well established, successful importing business. Sam approached me to manage his Shanghai office. I turned him down, saying the future looked bright for my new company and I wanted to pursue that option. Sam countered with a generous offer. I could move my business into his fancy offices, rent free, and work out of there if I would be his buying agent and add him to my customer list. I accepted. It was a great relationship until the communist takeover.

Now Sam contacted me with another proposal. Would I take out his niece, Tunie Sultan? I was convinced this was the best overture made to me yet. I had been aware of Tunie, we had spoken, awkwardly. Now I could get to know her better. My heart raced with excitement and I could not wait to dial her number. When I heard Tunie's voice, I identified myself and nervously asked her out. My emotions soared when she accepted.

Taking her home after our first date, I knew I wanted more. So I asked her out again, and then again. We had much to talk about, much to share. Our evenings were filled with non-stop chatter and laughter, and the times together passed too quickly.

Tunie was the oldest of five children. She had two sisters and two brothers. Her parents, Abraham and Adele Sultan met when Abe traveled to Aleppo to fetch a bride. They married in 1931. Adele's family tried to follow her to America, but were denied entry because of a quota system, so they had settled in Mexico City.

The Sultan family lived in a big, immaculate, exquisitely decorated house on East 5th Street in Brooklyn. They were one of the first Syrian-Jewish families to settle in the Midwood neighborhood.

To me, Tunie was beautiful inside and out. Extremely bright, she was valedictorian at her high school graduating class. In addition to English, she spoke fluent Spanish, French and Arabic, and attended Brooklyn College. People were drawn to her outgoing personality. She knew how to make others feel comfortable with her warmth and her radiant smile. Tunie and her sister Marilyn seriously studied ballet and piano and had performed at Carnegie Hall. Dating Tunie was exhilarating, challenging, exciting. She was just what I needed to lift my spirits.

During this time, my relationships with extended family members living in Brooklyn were coalescing. One relative, a first cousin, Rachel Haber, had been particularly helpful to and protective of Mike when he was in New York. Now she did the same for me.

Rachel's father and my father were brothers. This remarkable and kind woman became my confidant. I trusted her. When I told Rachel about my relationship with Tunie, she encouraged me to pursue the romance and praised the Sultan family. "They are solid, respected leaders in the community. Good people. Warm, kind, generous. You will love them almost as much as you love Tunie," she laughed.

I decided I would not let Tunie go. I loved her and wanted to spend the rest of my life with her. At less than five feet tall and weighing not much more than a hundred pounds, this petite, feminine, bundle of energy captured my heart.

* * *

My journey back to life in Aleppo began almost immediately, from the first month of my arrival in New York. I found cohesion in the Syrian community, reverence for the rabbis, and addiction to religion and Torah study. Celebrating holidays, observing kosher dietary laws, sharing festive meals, enjoying Syrian food, experiencing Syrian music, living Syrian culture, speaking Arabic, and socializing only with Syrian Jews—did I really want this? Did I want to transplant my life in Aleppo to modern day Brooklyn? Should I allow myself to be drawn in or do I escape? I did not hesitate with the answer. To remain in America, to take Tunie for my wife, I had to absorb the community and allow myself to be swathed into it. I could not return to my Shanghai ways. Shanghai was to become a fantasy, a place forbidden. From now on, my religion, my socializing, my business endeavors, my choice for a lifelong partner would be steered by the community. This was my destiny.

* * *

By April 1951, the community began preparations for Passover. Housewives koshered their homes, cleaning every nook and cranny, checking every inch of their environs to rid it of all the crumbs left from *hametz*, the edibles made from grain and water that are allowed to rise. Foods like bread, cereals, pastas, pastries were either given away or thrown away. Dishes, utensils, pots and pans were either temporarily replaced or made kosher for Passover by washing and boiling them. The Syrian Jews in Brooklyn clung to the directives of Exodus 12:19: *No leaven shall be found in your homes for seven days. For whoever eats what is leavened, that person shall be cut off from the community of Israel . . . .*

Women congregated in each other's kitchens and enjoyed socializing while they masterfully cooked and baked their culinary treasures, preparing enough for everyone to take a portion home. The Brooklyn neighborhood awaited the two seder nights, the chance to once again tell the story of the Jewish Exodus from Egypt before feasting on a banquet of special foods entrusted only to the Syrians.

In Shanghai, there was no Passover seder for me. Nobody included me. Nobody even thought to ask. On this Passover, Tunie and her family invited me. Friends also invited me. It felt good not to be alone. Although I was grateful for the many invites, I chose to spend Passover with the Sultans because in my heart, I wanted to be close to Tunie.

Sitting in the Sultan's dining room with their large extended family, memories gushed forth of my childhood in Aleppo and our yearly seders with aunts, uncles and cousins. I forced back tears as I envisioned my father watching approvingly, satisfied that I made my way back to the fold of the community and the religion that he breathed into me. I thought about my annoyance with him for not counseling me on how to live in Shanghai, but my father was a wise man, wiser than I gave him credit for. When he had said, "*. . . you will be on your own to make your own decisions and choose what is best for you . . .*" he knew, that in time, I would do just that. Selim Menashé Sutton implanted in me an indestructible foundation, believing that after I tasted the outside, I would come back to my roots and never leave. He could not force me. He could not steer me. I would arrive on my own. My father was certain of it.

The large dining room table was set with all the ritual accoutrements needed for our seder. A special platter displayed the roasted egg, roasted shank bone, bitter herbs, parsley and haroset. Salted water filled a small bowl. Ornate boxes held sheets of matzoh. At every place setting was a goblet brimming with Manischewitz grape wine and a Haggadah to read, to tell of the Hebrew's Exodus from Egypt.

Tunie's father, Abe, was dressed to look like a very old man. He was hunched over and struggled to walk as he entered the room. Wearing a large unkempt hat, baggy pants, and carrying a small sack over his shoulder, he portrayed an ancient Israelite with a heavy load to carry as he relived the Exodus. This amused everyone at the table. The sack held three slices of matzoh, one of which was the afikomen to be hidden for the search later in the evening. The sack had another purpose as well. We all took turns carrying it on one shoulder, then crossing it over to the other shoulder, mimicking the harsh journey from Egypt to Jerusalem.

* * *

I recalled my summers in the mountains of Lebanon when many of the Syrian Jews would escape the hot Aleppo summers. In the small mountain towns, they rented rooms, apartments, houses. We Syrian Jews were a cohesive group, keeping to ourselves, interacting and socializing within our own community, carrying out our religious practices as one people.

Ironically, the Syrian Jews of Brooklyn were exactly the same, but instead of heading for the mountains in the summers, they headed for the beach—Bradley Beach, New Jersey. By June 1951, wives and mothers, with the help of their live-in maids, packed the family belongings while the husbands worked. Rooms, apartments, houses by the Atlantic were occupied all summer, every summer by the Syrian Jews. I found it humorous to witness how these Aleppian descendants did not deviate from the blueprint of their past. They may have left Aleppo, but Aleppo did not leave them.

Tunie's family rented a house in Bradley Beach. Abe, like so many other husbands, worked in New York during the week and spent long three or four-day weekends at the shore, enjoying time with family and the community. I did not want to be left out and I did not want to be away from Tunie, so I rented a room in a boarding house, not far from where Tunie and her family resided.

Bradley Beach is a compact town by the ocean, with nothing more than a few blocks in any direction from Main Street. The beach is within walking distance of everything. I found Bradley Beach similar to belonging to a private club because everyone knew each other and our days were filled with socializing, sunning, swimming, eating and a host of other fun-filled activities.

On any given day, one could find families trekking to the beach, lugging their food, chairs, towels and blankets. Young and old, singles and families congregated on the beach or walked the boardwalk, stopping at the Sand Bar to get sandwiches, drinks and ice cream. In this hubbub of action, dates were made, engagements announced and weddings planned.

Romance was in full bloom and dates meant either going to the movies and a snack at a glorified luncheonette, or a special night of dinner and entertainment at one of the various nightclubs, most notably the Green Grove which featured Arabic music and belly dancers.

Our synagogue and social club, the Magen David Congregation, had a sanctuary for prayers and a social hall for playing cards and backgammon and for special events such as parties and celebrations.

The men in our community who commuted back and forth from the shore to Manhattan to go to work, often traveled on the Jersey Coast Train. The regions's permanent residents who used this same means of transportation on their daily commutes to work did not like this infringement on their space. Often, they attacked our men with strong anti-Semitic slurs, despite the fact that they benefitted financially from our being there.

* * *

Tunie and I were wildly in love. Every time I knew I would see her, my senses heightened. We were happy when we were together and I missed her when we were apart. By late July, I proposed marriage. Eagerly, she accepted. Her family was elated. "We must have an engagement party. It is our tradition," they pronounced joyously.

More than 200 people filled the Magen David social hall. Family and friends celebrated with us. A caterer supplied the kosher food. A band played Arabic music. And everyone was on the dance floor enjoying themselves.

Right after this occasion, Tunie's parents began planning a fancy wedding for their first child. The tumult of activities began in August and lasted until our wedding day. It was hard to imagine that everything would get done in time. Tunie's parents took care of everything. They reserved the place, the caterers, the band. They confirmed the rabbi, worked on ceremony preparations and guided the *ketubbah,* the writing and design of our Jewish marriage contract. They selected flowers and chose gowns and tuxedos for everyone in the wedding party.

* * *

Sunday, November 4, 1951—our wedding day arrived. We were married at the Forest Hills Jewish Center in Queens. Newly built and newly decorated, it was an hour's drive from Brooklyn. I arrived ready to change into my wedding apparel. Ooooops! I forgot my tuxedo. Amidst all the excitement, I left it behind. A two-hour round trip—I had to go back to Brooklyn to retrieve it.

"You can't leave," said my in-laws. "You're the groom."

"But my tuxedo . . ."

Tunie's cousin Morris Hedaya volunteered to go back and get it. To this day, I am grateful for his kindness.

Waiting for my clothes to arrive caused a delay in starting the wedding, but no one seemed to mind. During the cocktail hour, 400 guests happily socialized around the massive buffet table. In addition to family and friends, there were Abe Sultan's business contacts, presidents of major companies and merchandise heads of J.C. Penney and Sears.

I missed my family and wanted so much for them to share this day with me. Although I was happy, an empty feeling gripped deep in my stomach. Within me, I prayed for them, especially for my father to be well. My mother was in Beirut with Ralph, Morris, and Edgar, living in an apartment. Joe and Margo were in Israel, staying close to my father where he was getting medical treatment.

Tunie and I signed our ketubbah. Tunie's uncle and a rabbi served as our witnesses. The ceremony began. Mike marched me to the altar. Tunie looked so very beautiful as she came down the aisle with her parents. Jacob Kassin, Chief Rabbi of our Syrian community, officiated. To me, it all seemed like a dream. I could not believe it was happening.

After the ceremony, everybody entered the banquet hall. The lights were low, the band was playing, the tables were exquisitely set and strikingly colorful flowers filled every empty space. The room was magnificent.

Tunie and I were prompted to dance. Guests watched us glide across the floor, allowing us our first undertaking as husband and wife before converging on the dance floor with us. The band played American music, Israeli music and Syrian music. Guests feasted on rich, savory cuisine. As the evening wound down, it was time to cut the cake. Everyone watched as a magnificent, multi-layered, five-foot high wedding cake was wheeled in. Today, I think about it and laugh. The cake was taller than Tunie.

* * *

My application for permanent residency at the immigration department still was pending. I was told my marriage to an American would speed it along and hoped that was true.

Since I could not leave the country, Tunie and I settled for a two-week honeymoon to Florida, New Orleans, and Washington, D.C. In Miami, Tunie's father booked us a room at the Saxony Hotel, the most exclusive and desirable accommodations in the city. From there, we traveled to New Orleans where my Uncle Jack Sutton had a fancy linen store off the lobby of the Roosevelt Hotel. Uncle Jack treated us royally, providing a tour around the city and introducing us to New Orleans' famous night life. Our last few days were spent visiting Mike, Cynthia, and the Beyda family as well as sightseeing around Washington.

With Tunie now in my life, it seemed like nothing could go wrong. But then we returned from our honeymoon and I had to face my failing partnership in Pan Am Handkerchiefs and suffer the consequences of my foolish move.

Rabbi Jacob Kassin handing Tunie booklet on family purity

Mike marching with me down the aisle

Tunie's family at our wedding; from left clockwise: Adele, Tunie, Abe, Marilyn, Diane, Morris and Joey

Marriage ceremony - Elie and Tunie Sutton, November 4, 1951

Cutting the very tall wedding cake

SEVENTEEN

AND THE DUST RETURNS TO THE GROUND AS IT WAS, AND THE
LIFEBREATH RETURNS TO G-D WHO BESTOWED IT
—ECCLESIASTES 12:7

It was decided that when Tunie and I returned from our honeymoon, we would look for an apartment. My in-laws graciously invited us to move in with them until we found a place of our own; little did we know of the surprise awaiting u s. Abe and Adele took it upon themselves to rent an apartment while we were away. They said they had been looking for a while and found us the ideal apartment. It was in an excellent location and if they waited until we got back, it would be lost to another renter, something they could not let happen.

The rent on this two-bedroom apartment was $140 a month, a lot of money in 1951. Because it needed updating, Abe and Adele took charge of hiring and paying for a high-end interior designer to do extensive decorating and furnishing. Tunie and I did not comprehend the enormity of the project and had no grasp of how long we would be residing with my in-laws until the project was done. Still, I could not complain. The Sultan's large, luxurious house with extravagant furnishings and live-in maids was an indulgence compared to my room in the cramped quarters at the Hararys where I had been living.

After honeymooning for two glorious and hectic weeks, we had expected to return to Brooklyn and find some degree of calmness, but we did not. Settling in with Tunie's family, we allowed ourselves to be swooped into their daily lives. Another round of wedding plans was underway. The marriage of Tunie's sister Marilyn and her fiancé, Joe Chira, was planned for March 28, 1952, four months away. I could not imagine more preparations and more expenses on the heels of our nuptials, but Abe and Adele seemed to thrive on their children's joy. In addition to the hustle and bustle of plans and activities leading up to the wedding, Tunie and I found ourselves working with the decorator almost daily. We were anxious to get the job finished so we could move into our apartment.

* * *

Pan American Handkerchiefs could not keep its head above water and the company carried a heavy load of inventory that neither my partners nor I could unload. To avoid going deeper in debt and to salvage whatever we could, we shut down the company. Each of us agreed to take on a share of the damages. Using whatever money I had left, I bought the entire inventory.

My father in-law, in partnership with his two brothers, Judah and Raymond, ran a successful manufacturing business. The three worked harmoniously, complementing their divisions of responsibilities. The company was named Joseph Sultan & Sons out of respect for their father, Joseph Sultan, although he was never involved in the business with his sons. Their office, four floors of rented space in a high rise building, was located between Fifth and Sixth Avenues on West 40th Street in Manhattan. The first floor was devoted to executive offices and to several showrooms that displayed samples of their products. In the basement, were stored small quantities of selected items, mostly for on-the-spot sales to peddlers who stopped by to purchase goods to take with them.

Generously, Abe offered me not only office space on the first floor so I could conduct my business but also a portion of the basement to stock my inventory. He did this without ever asking for anything in return. Tunie's father was as much of a blessing in my life as Tunie was. This benevolent and kind man touched me in so many profound ways. I think I will forever be indebted to him.

Grateful to have a place to do business without carrying much overhead, I attempted to run Pan American Handkerchiefs on my own. Aware of the need to unload my existing merchandise, I hired a young, local salesman who I hoped would bring in orders and free me to focus on reviving the company. The man brought in a few sales, barely enough to be worth maintaining him, but I was patient. When he asked me to teach him the inventory so that he could help fill orders and hand deliver the goods to the customers, I was elated, believing he wanted to prove himself. I was overly anxious for an employee I could trust, for someone dependable, smart and competent like Sam Raihel, my wonderful friend who managed my office in Shanghai. Foolishly, I once again allowed my vulnerabilities and eagerness to triumph over my common sense.

In time, a customer was kind enough to caution me. The salesman had my merchandise in his possession and was offering to sell at discounted prices if cash were paid to him up front. Literally, he was helping himself to my goods.

Angrily, I confronted him. The salesman denied it. I persisted. He held to his denial. I demanded the truth. More denial. This was getting me nowhere, so I changed the dynamics of the game and threatened to report the theft to the police. As I reached for the phone and began dialing, he stopped me and confessed to his exploits, offering to pay for all that he took. Unable to quantify my losses and not wanting to press charges, I guessed at a sum, fired him, and added the incident to my growing list of learning experiences. What else could I do?

It was times like these that I found myself wishing I had never left Shanghai. There, I trusted the people who worked for me and I dealt with a more honest and ethical fringe of humanity. But that was then and this is now. Shanghai was no longer the city I knew. China was a communist country. Trying to run my business in New York as I had done in Shanghai would be like trying to mix oil with water, an impossibility.

* * *

I wanted to stop accepting from my father-in-law and I longed to earn my own money again. I hungered for success and wished to gain my rightful place in the Syrian-Jewish community. I sought to keep the friends I had and also to make new ones. My social life was just as important as my business life. As in Shanghai, I needed both.

* * *

Trying to sort out my life, I knew that marrying Tunie was the best thing I had done for myself since coming to Brooklyn. She was warm, kind, caring, and giving. The more I knew her, the more I loved her. Within Tunie's tiny frame lay an immense heart and a towering soul. I could not imagine what my life might be without her.

Because of Tunie, my American wife, I was afforded priority status in my application for permanent residency to the United States. By nature, these procedures take a very long time, but thanks to HIAS working on my behalf, and to Tunie supporting me, my petition did not sit at the bottom of the pile.

* * *

By late August 1952, we moved into our apartment. Our new home was on the first level of a two-family house on Ocean Parkway, close to Tunie's family and within the confines of our community's neighborhood. It was good to finally be in our own place. The wait had been long but our home was elegant. Every piece of furniture, every adornment, every detail was chosen with impeccable taste. We were thrilled with our new surroundings and hurried to settle in before the birth of our daughter Adele in early September.

With a home to run and the arrival of our first child on September 4, our roles changed and our responsibilities increased. While I worked, Tunie needed support, so we hired a live-in maid to help with the cleaning, cooking, laundry and caring for the baby. This was not an unusual undertaking because, for Syrian Jews, having servants was a normal way of life, a tradition brought to America from the old country. Not having a servant was the exception; even my own family in Aleppo had two live-in maids to help my mother.

So now, in addition to the $140 a month rent and the expenses that go along with having a home and a family, I had to come up with $40 a week for the maid. I needed to earn enough money to pay for all that we had so we could keep up with the customs in our community. Maintaining a living standard comparable to our friends and relatives who were close to us stressed me at times and I wondered how much longer I could, or even if I should, continue to accept from Abe. But parents in the community, whether in Aleppo or in Brooklyn, always helped their children. It is our way; it is embedded in our culture. So although my situation was not an unusual one, I nevertheless yearned for a breakthrough in my business so I could take full responsibility for my family.

* * *

When our daughter was born, we named her after my mother, Adele Sutton. The custom among Sephardic Jews is to name after the grandparents, whether they are living or not. When Tunie was pregnant, I hoped for a girl, but prayed for a healthy, perfectly-formed child. Adele was beautiful, a good infant. As she began to grow, her display of affection charmed everyone and her delightful mischief brought us joy and laughter. I could not wait to return home each day to spend time with my daughter, to feed her, to change her, to play with her, to spend hours ooohing and aaahing over her. I found solace in this little miracle that I held in my arms.

With a new baby, a wonderful wife, a stylish apartment, a big-hearted extended family, many friends, and an active social life, my place here in Brooklyn had taken root and my life in the community was forged. The culture and the customs that I grew up with in Aleppo, came alive in Brooklyn. My religion, given to me at birth from my parents' seeds, from my brit milah, from my covenant with G-d, had once again returned, latching on ever so tightly. This time there was no escape, no taking flight to Shanghai, no looking back on those sensational four years. This was my life now, but with a twist of Western modernity. The community and the rabbis owned me and I owned them. Divine intervention set my fate in motion.

* * *

My company was struggling to stay alive and I did not know what to do next. Someone suggested that I hire a secretary and recommended an ultra-orthodox Ashkenazie Jew. I found her to be efficient when she worked, but she spent way too much time on the phone with her private conversations. Yet I kept her on. Next, since I still could not travel out of the country because my application for refugee status was still pending, I linked up with some Japanese trading companies with branch offices in New York City. I also kept myself informed of anyone in the community who would be going overseas on business or for vacation, asking them to sample shop for me, such as looking for scarves in Paris.

I focused on my work as best I could. In the office, I did not allow my mind to wander or accede to outside distractions. I maintained a strong work discipline, intent on becoming financially successful as I once had been in Shanghai. But one particular day, my concentration went haywire. I felt exceptionally downhearted as if a black cloud was hanging over me. My family, whom I had not seen in years, consumed my thoughts. The receptionist noticed my melancholy as she was distributing the mail. Approaching me, she put an envelope on my desk and smiled, "Cheer up! You have a letter from your brother."

* * *

I knew my father to be proud and independent, a take-charge man, a family man with a big heart beneath his stoic exterior. Long after I left for Shanghai, after Muslim extremists entered our house and torched it, making it unlivable, I learned about my father. He became a beaten man. Much money was owed to him by Muslims who, under new government laws, were released from any obligations to Jews. Anti-Semitism reached unbearable levels and my father's business slumped. Devastated, his mental and physical being deteriorated. Painful, debilitating headaches soon followed. Then my father was diagnosed with a brain tumor and told he needed radiation treatments, something not available in Syria. He would have to go to Beirut.

Making my father's care their top priority, my family wanted to be with him as he went through therapy, but that was impossible. In

Syria, a Jew could not leave the country except for medical emergencies, and only after paying a hefty sum to the government. Entire families were forbidden from departing together; under prevailing law, it simply was not tolerated under any circumstance.

By mid-1950, my father received special dispensation, a temporary exit permit to seek medical care in Lebanon. My brother Joe, then 16, and my sister Margo, then 21, were allowed to go with him. Margo hoped to find a cure for her elephantiasis, a condition that plagued her almost from birth. The huge, unsightly swelling in her foot which caused her to walk with a pronounced limp, inflicted a heavy toll on her self esteem and emotional strength.

* * *

During the time in Beirut, my father's health grew worse and the radiation treatments exacerbated his declining condition. Margo could not find a doctor to help with her affliction. It was suggested they go to Israel where medical care was held to higher standards. Hurriedly, Joe made risky travel arrangements for Margo and my father to be smuggled into Israel while he remained in a rented apartment in Beirut, waiting, hoping for the rest of the family to be safely smuggled out of Syria.

* * *

Arriving in Tel Aviv, Margo and my father were helped by my mother's sisters, my Aunts Milo and Ramiza, who compassionately stepped in and accompanied my father to Hadassah Hospital for observation and treatment. A neurologist named Doctor Feldman took on the case. In spite of excellent care, my father continued to decline and suffered from headaches so excruciating that even the pain medication could not alleviate his intense agony. His eyesight was failing, his motor skills diminished and control over his faculties waned. Doctor Feldman said the brain tumor had progressed too far and nothing more could be done. My father had to be discharged from Hadassah Hospital, but where could he go? Joe was notified to come quickly. He was needed at a conference with Doctor Feldman and the Hadassah Hospital staff. Hastily, Joe found a way to smuggle himself out of Beirut and into Israel.

At the conference, a temporary solution was reached. Doctor Feldman owned an interest in a private nursing home. My father could move there temporarily until his application to a state-run nursing home was accepted. To pay for the cost of my father's stay at Doctor Feldman's nursing home and to cover their living expenses, Joe and Margo worked for Doctor Feldman in his medical practice.

* * *

Meanwhile, at great peril to their lives, Morris, Edgar and my mother courageously traveled with their paid smuggler and crossed the border into Lebanon. From there, on their own, they found their way to Beirut and settled in the small apartment that Joe had rented.

Remaining behind in Aleppo, my 18-year-old brother, Ralph, worked to salvage whatever family assets were left. Soliciting help from some of our cousins, and with the assistance of their Muslim partners, Ralph sold what was left of our father's inventory. He then rented our house to a Muslim sheikh and collected three-years rent in advance, knowing none of us would ever return to live there. Finally, Ralph memorized and practiced some basic Muslim jargon, camouflaged himself in Muslim attire and concealed his money under his clothing. Then, in perpetual fear of being caught, he fled Syria, just as other members of his family had done. With his heart pounding so fiercely that he thought it would burst from his chest, Ralph followed the lead of his professional smuggler. Reaching the Lebanese border, he breathed a sigh of relief and joined the remainder of his family in Beirut.

* * *

Although none of us could ever go back to live in our family home, the house does have a continuing story. At the termination of the three-year lease, the Muslim sheikh and his family were forced to move out and the Syrian government took full possession of the property, boarding it up, not allowing it to be transferred or sold, and keeping it empty all these years. The official policy of the Syrian government, hiding behind a pretext, stated: *We admit your ownership. You are free to come back to live in your house.* They carried out this same course of action on every house that a Jewish family had owned—confiscating the premises, boarding it up, leaving it vacant.

To justify its actions, the Syrian government declared: *We are not taking over your properties as the Israelis took over the properties of the Palestinians in 1948. We are allowing you to return, contrary to the Israelis who will not allow the Palestinians the right of return to their homes. Palestinians are refugees; Jews are not.*

In reality, this declaration is a farce, cloaking the real intentions of this Arab state, because even today, Jews are denied entrance into Syria and barred from homes once rightfully theirs.

Ten years ago, in 2,000, my brother Joe and his wife, Eileen, risked their security to travel to Syria for a visit. A friend who was doing business in the country, prodded Joe and Eileen to join him and his wife, and assured their safe passage.

In Aleppo, my brother stood in front of our old house, visited the khan where our father had his office and showroom, and explored the places of his youth. Although Joe was able to revisit his past, we were all grateful when he and Eileen returned unharmed to America.

* * *

By spring 1953, my father's application to the state-run nursing home was accepted and he was transferred. Joe, seeing there was nothing more he could do for my father, wanted to leave Israel. He feared being drafted into the Israeli Defense Forces if he remained in the country. Resorting to smuggling once again, Joe joined a group looking to leave the country; he was unaware of the smuggler's inexperience. Everyone got caught at the border and Joe was sent to an Israeli jail. After a month of incarceration, he was released. Settling in Tel Aviv, he tried to establish a routine by living with our aunt, getting a job and visiting our father in the nursing home. Biding his time, Joe waited for another chance to slip out of Israel.

Meanwhile, Margo met a Sephardic Jew from Morocco while she was working for Doctor Feldman. She and Nessim Mizrahi married and settled in Israel. Unfortunately, my sister's elephantiasis remained with her all her life, leaving a permanent scar on her psyche.

On Joe's last visit to the nursing home in August 1953, he was informed of my father's passing. In a cemetery in Petach Tikvah, then a suburb of Tel Aviv, Selim Menashé Sutton was buried. There was no funeral, no one to be with his body those first few hours after death, no one to sit shiva for him. My father passed away, a man all alone.

Joe made another attempt to flee Israel. This time he succeeded. Returning to our family in Beirut, he was convinced they all must find a way to alter their stateless condition and journey to America. Until that was possible, Joe and Ralph found jobs and took responsibility for the family, just as our father would have done if he were with them.

* * *

In Manhattan, sitting by myself in one of the showrooms at Joseph Sultan & Sons, I reached inside the envelope and withdrew the letter from my brother Joe. He was sorry to inform me that Dad was gone, passed away several weeks ago.

Memories of my father instantly flooded my brain and I relived those last difficult moments with him at the airport in Beirut when we said goodbye, knowing we would never see each other again. Tears gushed, running down my cheeks. I began to sob. I wanted my father with me. I wanted him back. This was not fair. He did not deserve that kind of ending. From deep within my soul, I begged G-d not to let this be true, I begged to see my father just one more time.

Without my mother and my siblings to mourn with me, I felt terribly alone, abandoned. Sitting at the desk, I cried uncontrollably. My wails intensified, reverberating throughout the workplace. The Sultan brothers and their staff rushed to my side, each trying harder than the other to console me. My sobs magnified and I lost all my self restraint.

Aware that this could not go on in their busy office, my father-in-law asked one of his salesman to take me home.

* * *

For one year, I mourned for my father, clinging to the ritual of our Judaic law. I refrained from listening to music, refrained from attending celebrations and happy occasions. I commiserated with my brother Mike who lived in Washington, and with my father's two brothers who had businesses in New Orleans. During the week of shiva, friends and relatives stopped by our home bringing food and offering condolences. Still, nothing could soften my father's strong presence that is still with me today.

I am grateful for all he did for me, for all he did for our family. I praise him for the sacrifices he made to give us a better life and for reaching out to help those less fortunate. I looked up to my father, respected him, loved him from as far back as I can remember; yet there was never an opportunity to express my feelings. Our parents' stoic ways did not foster outward displays of emotion.

Although twelve months of grieving never quite justified his passing or my loss, my life has gone on, but with a different meaning. My memory recaptured the time we lived in Mersin, Turkey when I was four years old, walking down the sidewalk, holding the hand of our maid. Vividly, the scene flashed in front of me: the horse-drawn open carriage, the Christian funeral procession, the maid lifting me up to view the perfectly adorned dead man in the uncovered coffin. " Everyone dies eventually," she said. "Even Jews."

Margo on her wedding day

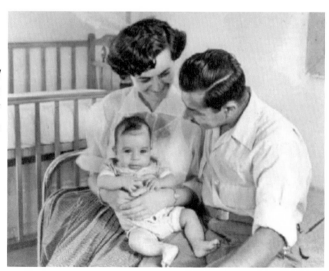

*Margo and
Nessim Mizrahi
in Israel
with first son*

EIGHTEEN

BE CONTENT WITH WHAT YOU HAVE; REJOICE IN THE WAY
THINGS ARE. WHEN YOU REALIZE THERE IS NOTHING LACKING,
THE WHOLE WORLD BELONGS TO YOU—LAO TZU

Pressures mounted as I continued to go to the office each day and work every business angle available. Keeping up with our living standards in the community and having all the things we wanted required money. I longed to see light at the end of the tunnel, but when I looked down the shaft, the only thing visible was a muted shadow. Still, I tried to maintain a positive attitude and be grateful for my blessings: a wonderful wife, a remarkable daughter, extraordinary in-laws and many good friends. If my business life pulsated as vigorously, as solidly as my personal life, all would have been ideal.

* * *

By early 1954, I detected a light flickering in the distance. Toward the end of the tunnel, I saw a glow. My sixth sense told me that change was on the way.

I hired a veteran traveling salesman named Harold Fried who commanded a strong following in a lucrative and wide-ranging territory. His customer base stretched up and down the east coast, into the deep south and westward into Texas. He serviced an abundance of independent and family businesses in every small town and city in his territory; the concept of major discount retailers was still a futuristic concept.

This time, I did my homework. I had learned from two hard lessons: blindly getting involved with Pan American Handkerchiefs and anxiously hiring a salesman who attempted to exploit me. I could not afford another desperate, impulsive move.

Harold Fried was recommended to me by Judah Sultan, my father-in-law's brother. Judah had a brother-in-law whose main product line was handkerchiefs, merchandise closely akin to my own. Judah came from the same mold as my father-in-law. Both men were of a rare quality—credible, ethical, responsible, charitable. I trusted Judah's endorsement of Harold Fried.

My new salesman was a confirmed bachelor with no family ties. He loved living on the road and made it his home. Harold Fried said he had the perfect job. Hiring him was my smartest business move thus far because orders began to trickle in. As my company approached survivability, my spirits began to lift.

* * *

Shortly thereafter, I received word from HIAS that the Justice Department granted me permanent residency. Soon, I would have my green card, privileges to travel freely in and out of the country and a guarantee I could apply for full citizenship. Euphoria enveloped me; I was beside myself with joy. No longer would I be a man without papers, a man without a country. I belonged to America and America belonged to me.

The immigration office instructed me to leave the country and go to the United States Consulate in Toronto, Canada, where I would be granted my official residency document, my green card. To my surprise, a classmate from Aleppo, another Syrian Jew living in Brooklyn, who also was waiting for his green card, received the same directive and the same appointment date as I. David Shamah and his wife Julie joined Tunie and me as we drove to Canada. Sharing this significant milestone is a time I will always remember, for it ensured my life in America. After leaving Toronto, we decided to extend our trip a couple of days to visit Niagara Falls. We had never before experienced the roar of waterfalls plummeting with such force.

Ironically, David and Julie Shamah eventually moved to Brazil and permanently settled there to live near their family. In the big city of São Paulo, a thriving Syrian-Jewish community exists, a near image of our community in Brooklyn, but on a smaller scale.

I always will be grateful to my brother Mike who got me a permit to enter Japan, a prelude to my obtaining a visitor's visa to come to America; to my wife, Tunie, for if I were not married to an American citizen, this good fortune would not have come my way so easily; and to the people at HIAS because without their benevolent efforts on my behalf, I would be somewhere in limbo, a stateless being.

* * *

While continuing in this upbeat mode, a masterful proposal was placed in my lap. My father-in-law, Abe, wanted so much to see me succeed, especially because I was married to his daughter, Tunie. Moreover, Abe's brother Judah had a son-in-law named Ellis Safdeye and he wanted to see him succeed, especially because Ellis was married to Judah's daughter, also named Tunie. Both Tunie Sutton and Tunie Safdeye were cousins, named after their paternal grandmother. Ellis was born in Bogotá, Colombia, where his father owned a textile mill. After a time, the family moved to Manchester, England, settled there and became legal residents. Now, living in the United States, Ellis had just closed down a failing textile-fabrics business.

The two fathers-in-law cleverly put their heads together and brokered a business partnership between Ellis and me, carving a path for Elie Sutton and Ellis Safdeye to form an alliance and establish E.S. Novelty Corporation. Interpreting our identical initials as a good omen, we eagerly prepared a business plan to design, manufacture and import women's apparel, scarves and accessories. Our imports would come largely from Japan, but also from other countries in the Far East. We needed customers to buy our goods and storeowners to stock and sell our merchandise. This would take a strong sales force strategically positioned throughout the country, a sales force good enough to generate a continuous flow of orders to E.S. Novelty Corporation. We wanted to make money, lots of money, and we set our sights high.

Although our new company required travel to the Far East, we initially tried to avoid that route. Until we could afford our own travel expenses, we sourced through two large Japanese trading companies with offices in New York, C. Itoh and Mitsubishi.

As we established the groundwork for our partnership, we were advised to call Joseph R. Beyda & Company, a respected accounting firm. Joe Beyda, a Syrian Jew from our community, introduced Ellis and me to Manufacturers Hanover Bank. They gave us a line of credit, enabling us to supplement our limited capital and finance our foreign imports. Feeling more secure, we hired additional salesmen to service other regions across the country—Florida, the Midwest, the West Coast.

Then Abe and Judah recommended us to some of their important clients who, in turn, gave us business. We were thrilled to have these customers and catered to them with flawless attention, meticulously filling each of their requests. Building a solid reputation was a priority, a key to our success.

With new orders rolling in from our salesmen, plus repeat business from customers that Abe and Judah sent our way, E.S. Novelty was outgrowing the space our fathers-in-law so generously apportioned to us in the office building on West 40th Street. It was time for Ellis and me to venture out on our own.

After carefully searching for a new location, we found adequate space in a building on West 37th Street, a property known for its concentration of companies that specialized in ladies' accessories. Although we were excited to open our own office and showroom in New York City, and believed that in the long run it was the right move, I worried about meeting our new expenses and about Ellis and me reconciling our headstrong personalities.

Ellis and I made conscious efforts to get along and not allow our differences to obscure our objectives. We worked out a system of sharing responsibilities in everything, with the goal of molding E.S. Novelty into a company of unlimited heights. Over time, we took turns traveling to the Far East on sourcing missions, searching for companies, manufacturers, factories and mills that could work with us to produce original, creative samples of our designs. When we identified well-matched establishments, we negotiated for quality, pricing and completion dates. Once satisfied that our requirements were fully met, we placed our orders and committed to a payment schedule.

Each trip lasted four to six weeks. Being away was not only strenuous on us but also difficult on our growing families. There were no jet planes, no cell phones, no computers, no e-mails, no Internet, no video-conferencing and, as far as I knew, Blackberry was a kind of fruit. These innovative, modern technologies, unknown to us and taken for granted today, would have deemed our physical presence in the Far East unnecessary or greatly shortened the durations of our journeys.

* * *

The forward momentum of 1954 spilled over into 1955. E.S. Novelty was on slow but steady growth. Tunie was pregnant with our second child. Our social life mushroomed, our friendships grew stronger, and the tight-knit Syrian community encompassed us with its solidarity, vibrancy, religion, culture and philanthropy.

Ellis and I now had the confidence to seize on carefully planned risks for the expansion of our company. Each month, revenues exceeded those of the month before and we always managed to fill enough orders to get us through and propel us to the next level. Cautious not to put ourselves into financial overload, we maintained a core group of salesmen and hired just enough office staff for what we needed. As long as we could cover our expenses, pay our bills, make our payroll, give ourselves each a decent salary and increase our capital, we were in business.

Money in my personal life was no longer the great concern it had been. I was not rich, at least not by the standards of the wealthy in our community, but I earned enough to take care of the needs and wants of my family and maintain a lifestyle prevalent among the Syrian Jews in Brooklyn. No longer did I have to rely on my generous father-in-law for help. Standing on my own felt good.

* * *

Tunie and I were elated about the prospect of another baby, another bundle of joy to fill our home. At the end of the year, Adele would have a sister or brother. My in-laws were overjoyed. Tunie was devoted to Adele and me, and anticipated another addition to our lives.

Throughout all of our married years, Tunie remained the one person in my life that I could always trust, always depend upon. We shared so much together. We loved playing bridge, socializing and traveling. Tunie was as knowledgeable in foreign languages as I and always ready to explore new places and new experiences with me.

Our circle of friends kept widening and we joined with several other young married couples to form a Mister and Misses Club which we christened the Esquire Club. Some of those in the group included my partner Ellis Safdeye and his wife Tunie, Renee and Izzy Shamah, Eva and Mosey Rahmey and Tunie's sister Marilyn and her husband, Joe Chira. In all, there were about eighteen couples, a snobbish clique that hand picked our members. Eventually, the Shamahs, the Rahmeys and the Chiras became our closest friends and Tunie and I shared many wonderful times and memorable vacations with them.

The Sephardic Community Center on Avenue P and Bay Parkway, established in the early 1950s, sought to increase its membership. Graciously, they set aside a room for our Esquire Club, providing us a place to gather not only on Saturday nights but also on some weekday evenings. This venue allowed us to comfortably mingle, celebrate events, play cards and plan special mystery nights. We and the Center were an ideal match, so we enrolled in the struggling establishment and volunteered to help promote its membership. But in the end, the Center failed and we were forced out. A powerful, wealthy, respected leader among the Syrian Jews, Isaac Shalom A"H, wanted the Center converted to a Jewish day school for our children. Many people were angry and resented the arbitrary decision, but we could only watch this man's determination as he filled one room after another, transforming the floundering Sephardic Community Center into a Jewish day school called the Magen David Yeshivah.

For four years, we tried to hold onto our group, then we disbanded. Ten couples eventually reunited, including Tunie and me.

We formed our own, intimate Mystery Night Club. Meeting once a month, each couple took turns planning a mystery evening. We enjoyed magicians, hypnotists, off-Broadway shows, nightclubs, fancy restaurants and so much more. In between, we continued to socialize on a smaller scale, getting together on Saturday nights at each other's houses for card games and light meals of bagels, lox and eggs.

Meanwhile, the Magen David Yeshivah continues to flourish to this day. In two locations, it caters to elementary and high school students. More than 1,500 children from our community are educated in the religion of our ancestors, anchoring them to our strict Sephardic heritage and keeping them from assimilation. To ensure the school's forward strides, parents assume active roles in the school's growth and success.

Isaac Shalom A"H also committed himself to saving Jewish children from assimilation wherever they exist in the world. Through Ozar HaTorah (treasure of Torah), his non-profit society, Isaac Shalom's intentions have been felt. First-class religious, cultural and secular education continues today, especially in Asia, Africa and Europe. Moreover, this well-connected, successful businessman helped dozens of young men from our community by taking them into his company, teaching them, then giving them wings to fly so they could be successful in their own right. He asked only two things in return: that the men become charitable in causes he holds most dear and that they help others who are less fortunate.

To me, this man was a visionary who possessed strength in purpose and passion for what he believed in. I speak of Isaac Shalom A"H only because I am in awe of him and what he accomplished in his life. He is my role model and I have strived to follow in his footsteps.

I think, above all else, Isaac Shalom A"H was obsessed with preserving the Syrian-Jewish community and keeping our people from assimilation. Understanding the need for a spiritual leader, a chief rabbi to guide us, he collaborated with other community leaders and then contacted the prestigious Porat Yosef Yeshiva of Jerusalem, a school specializing in grooming rabbis to lead congregations.

By 1933, Rabbi Jacob Kassin was hired as our chief rabbi. Within two years of his arrival in Brooklyn, he convened a meeting with the other community rabbis and addressed the problem of intermarriage and the critical need to issue a proclamation rejecting assimilation. Unanimously, they agreed to counteract this situation and signed their names to an edict stating that no one in the community is to marry someone from outside the religion. Further, converts to Judaism shall not be recognized as Jews and always will be identified as those outside our religion. No rules are to be bent, no exceptions are to be made. This is our law. Anyone going against the edict, anyone marrying outside the religion, shall be expelled from the community, forbidden to ever return. To this day, this proclamation is held in the highest esteem and our people cleave to its mandate well after Rabbi Jacob Kassin's passing in 1995. Our community remains intact and our survival is secured. We Syrian Jews are one people committed to our G-d, dedicated to our heritage and linked to the souls of our ancestors.

Framed copies of the edict hang in all of our synagogues, prominently displayed for all to see, for all to know and obey. Rarely is this edict challenged; those attempting to do so, do not win.

Isaac Shalom A"H, who strongly championed this proclamation, revered Rabbi Kassin for his masterful achievement. He took pride in his own foresight to bring Rabbi Jacob Kassin into our community and for guiding him in the ways of our people.

As for the Sephardic Community Center, it took two decades and a second generation to pave the way for ground to be broken on property on Ocean Parkway in the middle of our Syrian-Jewish confines. How we functioned without this structure for so long is an enigma to me because the Center is the heartbeat of our community. Flurrying with activities 18 hours a day, serving our members from the very young to the very old, its growth has been phenomenal. A recently completed expansion to the building now provides its burgeoning membership with 50,000 square feet of space that houses a gym with the latest equipment, a basketball court, an indoor swimming pool and breakout areas for plays, classes, lectures, health fairs, book clubs, bridge groups, Alzheimer's support, fundraisers and so much more.

Ongoing life at the Center is supported by dues, private donations, Jewish philanthropies, UJA, Jewish Federation and grants from our city and state. A staff of dedicated workers and volunteers ensures the vitality and spirit of our Center's active life.

* * *

Over the years, I have reflected on my life in Shanghai, on the non-Jewish girls I dated and the ones I was tempted to marry. How grateful I am to have escaped the allurement. How grateful I am to be with my own people, to be living in the community of my roots.

* * *

In early May of 1955, we heard from my brother Ralph in Beirut. He was coming to Brooklyn. The news was exhilarating. Ralph was stateless, like I had been. After fleeing Syria, he was in Lebanon, stuck with no way out, no papers, no documents. That did not stop him from hoping, searching for an escape, a route to come to the United States. Through the local Jewish community in Beirut, he discovered that the Iranian ambassador to Lebanon may be the answer to his prayers.

The ambassador lusted for the excitement of the casinos of Beirut, the gambling, the nightlife. He played with the high rollers, the rich oil barons whose pockets ran deep. Needing money to support his habit, the ambassador, through a confidant, offered passports on the black market to anyone who could claim ancestral roots to Persia and who could pay the hefty sum required. Ralph not only invented a believable story about his Persian background but also managed to come up with enough money to satisfy the ambassador and his confidant. Once Ralph procured an Iranian passport, he applied for a student visa from the American Consulate and made arrangements to travel to the United States.

I discussed with Tunie where we could find a place for my brother to stay. "He will stay with us, of course," she said.

Living in a two-bedroom apartment, having one child and a second one on the way, and the maid sleeping in a bed in the basement, I wondered where we could possibly put my brother. I must admit that Tunie's kindness and compassion superseded mine. Inheriting these traits from her warmhearted parents, Tunie put the needs of others before her own. She insisted that Ralph move in with us, at least until he could manage on his own. "We will welcome him and help him all we can," she maintained. Tunie was right, as most times she was, and I spoke with my partner, Ellis, who agreed to give Ralph a job in our company.

After having lost both my father and Saleh, I wanted my remaining family members to be together in America. Unfortunately, tragedy struck once again. Ralph arrived bringing the sad news. Our youngest brother, Edgar, died suddenly at the age of 14 from kidney failure, triggered by a careless and erroneous medical diagnosis. Mom was devastated. It had been difficult to console her.

Ralph lived with us for ten months. To ease his initiation into New York life, Tunie went to great lengths to ensure his comfort and I welcomed him into our office. Although we could not pay Ralph much at the beginning, he managed his earnings well and was able to save money, especially since he took a second job working evenings in a retail store. Surprisingly resourceful, my brother adjusted well to his new environment. I hoped this would pave the way for my remaining family to buy Iranian passports and come to Brooklyn.

* * *

On December 8, 1955, our son Sammy was born at Brooklyn Jewish Hospital where Tunie and the baby remained for eight days until the brit milah—Sammy's ritual circumcision establishing his covenant with G-d. We named our son after my father, Selim. I felt Sammy was my father's blessing to me.

The hospital provided a small room for the circumcision. Joined by the mohel and our rabbi, I held my son and entered the sterile chamber in a surgical gown. Family members and friends assembled in the adjacent room, observing the circumcision ceremony through a large window. Our big concern was ensuring the presence of a minyan—a quorum of ten Jewish men to recite prayers—kaddish, blessing over the wine, Shehecheyanu thanking G-d for a long life and reaching this milestone. Guests partook in wine, challah, coffee and pastries.

* * *

Once we brought Sammy home, I cherished every moment with him. He was an easy baby, a joy from the moment of his birth. Tunie was thrilled to have a son. Adele, now three years old, was taken with her baby brother, although we needed to watch her when she was with him. In her determined display of affection and love for Sammy, Adele sometimes got carried away, not understanding that she could not play with him like one of her toys. We learned not only that raising two children was definitely more challenging than raising one but also that a new baby heightened the hectic pace of our lives and added to the overcrowding in our apartment.

* * *

By the end of the year, my brother Morris managed to acquire an Iranian passport through the same channels Ralph did. I was happy to have another brother coming to Brooklyn and pleased that my father's dream was slowly being realized, but I wondered where Morris would reside. We found him a room in a house, similar to my accommodations when I first arrived and lived with the Hararys.

Morris was in the rented room for barely two weeks when Mike invited him to Washington to live with his family. There, Mike registered Morris in a school that teaches English to foreigners.

* * *

Respecting the need for our space, in March 1956 Ralph rented a small apartment on East Third Street within the domain of the Syrian community. He hoped the move would tide him over temporarily until our mother and Joe arrived. They were working on obtaining Iranian passports from the black-market ambassador.

Morris soon returned from Washington to live in the Syrian community in Brooklyn, and moved in with Ralph.

Our sister Margo seemed to be doing well with her husband in Israel, or so we thought. They had started a family and we believed it was best not to disturb her life there.

*My certificate
of naturalization*

*1956 after traveling with
David and Julie Shamah to
Toronto to receive American
residency status, we visited
Niagara Falls*

*Isaac Shalom A"H
innovator and respected leader
of the Syrian community*

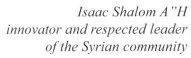

1935/5695

A
RABBINICAL PROCLAMATION
Adar 5695 (February 1935)

FREE TRANSLATION OF THE ORIGINAL HEBREW DECREE

HAVING OBSERVED the conditions prevailing in the general Jewish community, where some youth have left the haven of their faith and have assimilated with non-Jews; in certain cases they have made efforts to marry Gentiles, sometimes without any effort to convert them, and other times an effort is made for conversion to our faith, an action which is absolutely invalid and worthless in the eyes of the law of our Torah. ~

WE HAVE therefore bestirred ourselves to build and establish an Iron Wall to protect our identity and religious integrity and to bolster the strong foundations of our faith and religious purity which we have maintained for many centuries going back to our country of origin, Syria.

WE, the UNDERSIGNED RABBIS, constituting the Religious Court, together with the Executive Committee of the Magen David Congregation and the outstanding laymen of the community, do hereby DECREE, with the authority of our Holy Torah, that no male or female member of our community has the right to intermarry with non-Jews; this law covers conversions, which we consider to be fictitious and valueless. We further DECREE, that no future Rabbinic Court of the Community should have the right or authority to convert male or female non-Jews who seek to marry into our community. We have followed the example of the community in Argentina, which maintains a Rabbinic Ban on any of the marital arrangements enumerated above, an edict which has received the wholehearted and unqualified endorsement of the Chief Rabbinate in Israel. This Responsa is discussed in detail in Duar Shaul, Yoreh Deah, Part II to Part VI. In the event that any member of our community should ignore our ruling and marry, their issue will have to suffer the consequences. ANNOUNCEMENTS to this effect will be made advising the community not to allow any marriage with children of such converts. We are confident that the Jewish People are a HOLY PEOPLE and they will adhere to the DECISION OF THEIR RABBIS and will not conceive of doing otherwise.

SIGNED: CHIEF RABBI HAIM TAWIL

Rabbi JACOB KASSIN, Rabbi MURAD MASALTON, Rabbi MOSHE GINDI, Rabbi MOSHE DWECK KASSAB

1935 Rabbinical Proclamation

2006/5766

WE, THE LEADERS

of the Congregations, Yeshivot, Centers, and all our organizations of the

SYRIAN AND NEAR EASTERN SEPHARDIC COMMUNITIES

of Greater New York, New Jersey, and other U.S. cities, in conference assembled, do now and hereby solemnly declare, proclaim, and

REAFFIRM

our commitment to uphold, enforce, and promulgate the ban on conversions as declared in the original decree of 1935 and as reaffirmed in the subsequent declarations and proclamations in 1946, in 1972 and in 1984. In witness whereof we have caused this document to be prepared and affixed our signatures hereto, on this fifteenth day of Sivan 5766 corresponding to the eleventh day of June, 2006, in Brooklyn, New York.

RABBI SAUL J. KASSIN, CHIEF RABBI

2006 reaffirmation of the Rabbinical Proclamation

NINETEEN

WE DO NOT SEE THINGS AS THEY ARE, WE SEE THINGS AS WE ARE
—ANAIS NIN

After moving into the apartment with Ralph, my brother Morris needed a job, so Ellis and I assigned him the task of selling our products to local stores. Now both of my brothers were employed by E.S. Novelty. I was glad I could offer them support and if I could have paid them more at the time, I would have. Ralph, working two jobs, favored the one in retail. Morris, instead of a second job, chose to study Torah with the rabbis and raise money on behalf of Jewish institutions. Over the years, after Joe had arrived, Ralph, Joe, and I became Morris's main source of support until his two sons, Sammy and Gaby, were old enough to be productive and helpful to their father.

* * *

In 1956, I took my first business trip to the Far East. On my return to the United States, I planned to stop in Beirut and visit Joe and Mom. It had been so long. I was anxious to see them; however, I could not obtain a visa to enter Lebanon. Although I easily received visas to travel to Japan and other Far Eastern lands, the Lebanese Consulate in America denied me entry into the country because I did not have citizenship and my American residency status would not be honored. In reality, the reason was my Jewishness.

When I told this to Joe, he suggested I take a flight from the Far East with a destination somewhere in Europe, but with a fuel stop in Beirut. He would make arrangements for someone to meet me at the Beirut airport who held a permit for me to enter Lebanon for a few days. I could not have been more delighted.

Joe approached a member of the Beirut Jewish community who was well connected with many government ministries, including security and intelligence. Relating his dilemma, Joe asked the man to please use his influence to get a permit for me.

Meanwhile, I booked a flight from Hong Kong to Istanbul with a scheduled two-hour refueling stop at Beirut International Airport. Upon landing in the city, I was whisked to the transit lounge with the other passengers to await takeoff. A gentleman named Mister Elia, accompanied by immigration officers, approached me. Mister Elia welcomed me to Lebanon, handed me a two-day visitor's pass, asked the airline staff to unload my luggage and instructed me to visit the Pan American Airlines' office in town to rebook my continuing flights. I graciously thanked him for his efforts.

My mother and Joe were waiting at the airport. As I caught sight of them, I felt a burst of adrenaline race through my veins. I had left them in Aleppo ten years before, never knowing if I would see them again. For such a stoic family, our emotions were now in full view. We embraced, not wanting to let go. Tears welled and the words we had not spoken for so long poured forth in a constant stream of chatter. I stayed with Mom and Joe in their apartment. Together, we visited extended family members who also fled Syria by smuggling out and defying the travel ban imposed on all of Syria's Jews.

During this visit, my mother and I spent time together catching up on lost years. Mom recounted the story of Edgar's stomach pains, his misdiagnosis and tragic passing. She needed to talk, she needed to cry, and I cried with her. My brother was so young, only 14 years old. I was surprised that she did not mention Saleh's passing, but felt it was not wise to bring up the subject if she was silent about it. While her tears continued to flow, my mother spoke of my father and how much she missed him, how he was left alone to die without any family by his side.

I reflected on the perils inflicted on my family and on all Arab Jews. Virulent anti-Semitism has been raging like an inferno across the Muslim world for too long. Is it possible to believe that it will ever cease? I don't think for a moment I could find it in my heart to forgive these people and the atrocities they committed against humanity, against my family, against my people. Like those who survived the horrors of World War II and Hitler's maniacal genocide, how could the European Jews forgive? I prayed for the day when Mom and Joe would join the rest of our family in Brooklyn.

My time in Beirut passed quickly. I wished to extend my visit, but that was not possible. I found my way to the local Pan American Airways' office. The staff was cold and resistant, unwilling to accommodate me. They did not appreciate my presence in Beirut and were determined to make my departure as unpleasant as possible.

Several months later, on another business trip to the Far East, I replicated the flight path. Mister Elia greeted me at the airport, the immigration officers and the Pan American Airlines' staff treated me amicably and my visit with Mom and Joe was more easygoing.

In late fall, I again traveled abroad to shop for designs and explore the best sourcing establishments. My first stops were Paris and Italy. From there, I boarded an Alitalia flight with a destination to Beirut. Arriving at midnight, I found no trace of Mister Elia. As passengers lined up to pass through immigration formalities, I stalled, hoping my delay would allow more time for Mister Elia to come. Immigration officers recognized me, asked if I would like to join them for coffee, and informed me that I would not be allowed into the country without a permit from Mister Elia.

"Alitalia should never have allowed you on the flight without an entry visa. Now they are responsible for taking you back to Rome. We would like to be of help but our hands are tied. We could lose our jobs," one of the officers said, expecting me to understand. Escorting me to the transit lounge, I was allowed a short time with my mother and brother who were waiting for me. After a twenty-minute visit, they were asked to leave. I was stranded, confined to the transit lounge.

At 3:00 AM, all employees had completed their shifts. The airport was securely shut down, every door locked. With no way out, I was imprisoned in the terminal, distressed about having so little time with Mom and Joe, puzzled about being abandoned by Mister Elia and anxious to get the next flight out.

By 8:00 AM, the hustle and bustle of airport life resumed. I pleaded with the new immigration shift for permission to visit the terminal's airline offices that were already opened for business. Accompanied by the watchful eyes of an officer, I reserved a seat on a flight to Hong Kong which was, by chance, the place I had planned to travel next. As I gathered my things, preparing for the departure gate, someone stopped me. I felt my blood curdle and attempted to resist the fear rushing into my brain, the panic ready to overtake me. "Yes?" I asked, thinking I would be taken into custody, afraid I would be barred from leaving.

"Mister Elia is on his way," the intruder announced. "He asks that you wait in the transit lounge for him. He has a two-day pass for you to enter the country."

I hesitated, not sure whether or not to believe him. Quickly, I made a decision to stay. Time with Mom and Joe was too important to give up. I cancelled my flight and waited, restricted to the transit lounge. One hour. Two hours. Three hours. Four hours. I grew more irritable, more desperate to escape the confined space. Fourteen hours had passed and I regretted my choice to stay. Stress was taking its toll, even as I tried to convince myself that I would soon see Mom and Joe.

By mid-afternoon, in came Mister Elia, profusely apologizing for the mixup and the delay, handing me a two-day permit to visit with my family, and wishing me the best. Whew!

In November I became a naturalized citizen of the United States. Four months later, Mom and Joe arrived in America. Thank goodness I never again had to make that trip or be held captive in a transit lounge.

Mom and Joe used the same channel to the Iranian ambassador that Ralph and Morris had used. They procured Iranian passports and visitor's visas to America under the pretext that Mom wanted to see her family and Joe, a student, wanted to expand his studies.

* * *

Arriving in New York, Joe encountered complications. The immigration officer insisted Joe must put up a bond to get his student visa approved. Not having enough money to post his own collateral, a kindhearted Egyptian Jew traveling on the same boat with Mom and Joe agreed to help. But before he could act, HIAS stepped in, providing the money to guarantee Joe's visa. HIAS, the same organization that helped me, is still in existence today, intervening on behalf of Jewish refugees seeking safety and security from violence, repression and poverty throughout the world.

The American State Department expected Mom and Joe to honor their time-limited visitation visas, never intending for my family to remain permanently in the United States, similar to my story when I first arrived on American soil and had a 90-day visitor's visa. As HIAS had helped me, I prayed for HIAS to also help my family— and they did. Always, I will be grateful to HIAS for what they did for us. I often remember the organization in my charitable giving.

* * *

Mom and Joe arrived in Brooklyn in March 1957. Ralph rented a larger apartment in anticipation of their coming. My three brothers, along with my mother, moved in together. Right away, Joe found a job. He even found a second job. Soon, Ralph and Joe each held two jobs, paying for the apartment, paying the expenses, supporting our mother and helping Morris who spent even more time on his Torah studies and soliciting donations for various Jewish causes.

Both Ralph and Joe worked in various stores, learning the trade, understanding the operations and proving to themselves their own value, astuteness and insightfulness. With money put aside for their future, they rented space on 14th Street in Manhattan and opened their own retail store, naming it R & J Discounts.

* * *

On Monday, April 15, Tunie, I and our children, Adele and Sammy, celebrated the first night of Passover in my family's apartment. Tunie and my mother cooked the meal, we brought our maid to help with the cleanup, and together for the first time in eleven years, we told the story of the Jewish Exodus from Egypt.

* * *

Tunie and I wanted more children, more brothers and sisters for Adele and Sammy, but our two-bedroom apartment already was congested, even with Ralph moving out. With our family of four plus a live-in maid, we were running out of room, so we decided to search for a larger place. We found what we thought was the ideal apartment. It filled our needs and was in a desirable location close to our family, community and synagogue. However, entering into price negotiations was senseless because the owner, a Syrian-Jewish woman, added more and more items to a long to-do list and insisted we pay for everything. When her demands became so great, Tunie and I backed off, having no desire to prolong such a pointless arrangement.

Searching for something more affordable, we found a good-size house on East 19th Street, just outside the boundaries of our Syrian community. It was in move-in condition, was large enough to accommodate a growing family and would tide us over until the time we could afford something more to our liking in a location within the Syrian-Jewish confines. We bought our first house for $22,000, made a down payment of $3,000 and took out a mortgage for the balance. The year was 1957. Little did I understand back then the value of location and of escalating equity, nor could I imagine a great future in real estate. All I knew was that I was struggling in my business with Ellis.

* * *

By September, with Sammy not quite two years old, Tunie enrolled Adele in kindergarten at the nearby public school. Most girls from the community did not attend a yeshiva; in those years, that prerogative was mostly reserved for boys. It was not until Adele reached age 12 that she began her Hebrew and religious studies in an after-school class that Tunie started at the synagogue near our house.

* * *

My vision had been for a large family, at least six children, but Tunie had several miscarriages after Sammy. Thank G-d our prayers were finally answered. Our third child, a beautiful daughter, was born on Passover Eve, April 22, 1959. With our first daughter named Adele, in honor of my mother, we were in a quandary as to what to call our second daughter. According to Sephardic tradition, she should have been named for Tunie's mother, also Adele. In the end, we decided on April for the month of her birth and for the letter "A" which begins the name Adele. April held a special place inside my heart, especially since I believed she would be our last child.

* * *

In time, E.S. Novelty Corporation began to prosper. Ellis and I could hardly contain ourselves as we watched the fruits of our labor pay off, our business exponentially multiplying. Although our personalities periodically clashed, we tried not to let that interfere with our responsible work ethics, our zealous energy, and our commitment to succeed. We worked hard, motivated by the desire to make lots of money so we could reach the levels of upscale lifestyles and charitable gift giving prevalent in our community.

As the market for our women's apparel and accessories grew, so did the demand for us to come up with more designs and expanded inventory. Business trips for Ellis and me became more frequent. We traveled to American and European cities seeking new designers, new creations, new styles. We journeyed to the Far East on sourcing missions to find the right factories, the right mills, the right manufacturers.

During these long trips, I found myself lonely for Tunie. Often, I persuaded her to join me when we could use my in-laws as babysitters, taking advantage of their kindness and love for their grandchildren.

* * *

Over time, those business trips expanded into the realm of personal travel. We were very close with Tunie's sister Marilyn and her husband, Joe Chira, and had formed solid friendships with Renee and Izzy Shamah and Eva and Mosey Rahmey. We were four couples who clicked in our personalities, values and lifestyles. Our unbreakable bonds of friendship still continue and our travels together as a group of eight spanned a thirty-year period.

Over the years, I was fortunate to have business opportunities come my way, opportunities that would have passed me by if I were not so enterprising and intuitive, so willing to take risks. I made money, lots of it for Tunie and me and our children. We lived very well, well enough to afford the luxuries of our extensive vacations, especially those with our group of four couples. Tunie and I together journeyed the world. We had a passion for knowledge, for exploration, for connection with different peoples, different cultures, different lands. I think, at times, Tunie's fascination surpassed mine, but on occasion she did get homesick and missed the children.

Marilyn's husband, Joe, although he did not have a formal education, was diligently coached when he was young. His father taught him to be street smart, have good business sense and to work hard. With this mindset, Joe fostered financially rewarding undertakings. He and Marilyn shared an immeasurable level of love and trust. Comfortably, they joined us on our many global excursions.

Renee's husband, Izzy, came from a large family and grew up poor. He had to quit grade school, go to work and contribute his modest earnings toward the family's sustenance. Not a stranger to heavy labor, Izzy's workdays began at six in the morning. In time, his efforts grew into a blossoming business. He and Renee have had an incredibly wonderful marriage, always putting each other's welfare above all else. They have been able to savor the excitement of their worldly journeys with us.

Eva's husband, Mosey, was a class unto himself. He enjoyed the best things in life, the latest model cars and the most up-to-date technical gadgets. Mosey was an adventurer with an incredible sense of direction who flew his own plane and steered his own boat. His lust for travel equalled his love for good food. Following a dream, he joined with two partners to build a highly successful, well known national travel agency. All of us in the group benefitted from his expertise as he guided us to the best vacation spots in the world. We were happy to let him take charge and make all of our travel arrangements. Together, Mosey and Eva radiated harmony, mutual respect and an uplifting union filled with love and joy.

For the eight of us, the earth has been a captivating planet. We discovered the congested cities of Hong Kong and Singapore, the two busiest ports in the world. We traveled through China, Japan, Thailand, and Cambodia. We visited Poland, Russia, Bulgaria, Italy, England, and France. We basked on the French Riviera. We ventured south into the earth's lower hemisphere, exploring Brazil, Argentina, Mexico, and Uruguay. We indulged ourselves in the Mediterranean regions of Greece, Turkey, Lebanon, Morocco, Egypt, and Israel. We flew over the Grand Canyon in a helicopter and rode mules to the bottom of the ravine. We went on safari in Nairobi, Kenya, and hiked the Canadian

Rockies. We cruised the waterways of the world. In the Caribbean, we rented a fully-staffed villa on the beach and we even chartered a yacht with a crew of seven.

Sadly, those globe-trotting days with our friends ended when Tunie died. Today, I can only hold those happy times in my memory.

March 1956 - *A letter from Tunie to Elie*

March 26, 1956

Dear Sweatheart love, & honey

I just received your letter of 3/21. I hope that you will keep up the good work of writing. As far as I'm concerned this whole trip is a nightmare. Now with the holidays here, & all the new home for so many days it's not so easy either. And it's not very pleasant to hear Adele nag for you. But I guess I have to live though it. I told you this is not the proper way to live. I'm sorry that you are having it hard. really. Anyway, hurry up so it can all be over with.

Do you remember those 5 big pearls that Choneke showed us that night at the Waldorf? Well, Saturday, Marilyn & I got the shock of our lives. My mother presented us each with a PEARL ring set with diamond hearts at each side. How do you like that? Mine is because I had the baby Marilyn for her anniversary, Big Tunie for her anniversary & then Mommy made one for herself. Almost like a fire sale, but they are absolutely gorgeous. I got my wish finally.

You want a quote from Adele? OK. Marilyn & Adele were talking about Daddys. Adele asked Marilyn, "what is her Daddy?" so Marilyn said "My daddy is a man. what is your daddy?" Adele promptly replied "My daddy is a gentleman." Then Marilyn asked her "Who told you?" Adele thought & thought. Then she said: "I found out." As far as Sammy is concerned, words can't describe him. I can never stop kissing him. He loves when Adele plays with him. He blinks his eyes when she gets near because he knows she's rough. Bunna doesn't stop blessing him. He's nice & big. There is something to him. You will never recognize him. I didn't get around to making pictures.

Page 1

The plans for Mexico are tentative. My mother feels like going by herself around April 15. Then my father & Joe will follow the first week in May for 10 days. Marilyn & Joe are undecided. She'll probably convince him.

Today I'm going to cash my bonds so that I can invest them in G.M. Right now I'm in Marilyn's house putting my things in her dishwasher to kosher them. Ralph bought us cake from synagogue. So I guess we're all set.

Marilyn, Joe, & my mother are the only ones who try to see that I'm not alone. So I guess that it's true when they say that your family are the only true ones.

Page 2

2.

Last night my parents, Marilyn & Joe & I went to the Town & Country Club. (The Old Roadside) It is fabulous. We saw Harry Belafonte. But believe me going to a night-club like that depressed me terribly.

Terrie & Ellis haven't said boo! Paulette spent some time with me yesterday. She is the best of my friends. ----------

Tonight's seder is at Aunty Margie's. Tomorrow's by my mother.

Marilyn says that Ellis is nervous & that Terry is getting nervous from Ellis. Ralph hustles off early every morning. Maybe the change is finally coming. I hope!

Page 3

3.

I'm not going to tell anybody to write because I'm hoping you'll be home soon. I'm praying anyway. You don't mention at all if your trip is proving to be successful. All I know is that you are not buying anything. That's what the office says.

Today is the first one with decent weather.

That's all,
We all send love & kisses to you
Love
Tunie.

P.S. Now I know for sure that you are my other half.

HURRY UP!!!!!!

Page 4

TWENTY

FOR THE MOUNTAINS MAY MOVE AND THE HILLS BE SHAKEN,
BUT MY LOYALTY SHALL NEVER MOVE FROM YOU,
NOR MY COVENANT WITH YOU BE SHAKEN
—ISAIAH 54:10

By 1962, Ellis and I ended our business relationship, and not too amicably. All that we worked so hard to build, the huge successes that we reached, could not outweigh the ill-match of our personalities. In 1954, we had been so full of hope, grateful to our fathers-in-law for handing us a wonderful opportunity. Together, we had resolved to make our dreams a reality. We took risks, became self supporting, opened our own offices on West 37th Street and shared our responsibilities. We really tried. But I perceived Ellis to be stuck on his Manchester blue blood, putting himself in a higher realm than those of us who came from Aleppo. I am sure he had perceptions of me that also were not wonderful.

Our split was hostile, and although we divided the inventory in a somewhat equal manner, we became competitors, stoking the flames of the fiery battle we were waging. With duplicate merchandise to sell to duplicate customers, and using the same salesmen, we locked ourselves into a quandary. We were in a mess, each of us wanting to keep the business we had, each of us wanting to unload the huge inventories we just inherited and each of us refusing to consider other options. Neither Ellis nor I wanted to be forced out into the unknown to face starting over, switching to a new product line, developing a new market of customers, finding a new partner and raising capital for a new venture.

Once again, our fathers-in-law, Abe and Judah, stepped in, facilitating the breakup, limiting the bickering, softening the lingering contention, overseeing an agreeable division of E.S. Novelty. But their noble efforts could never mitigate the unsettling turbulence between Ellis and me. Our strained relationship has lasted to this day.

* * *

It took a long time for Ellis to move on, switching his product line to footwear, taking in another partner and renaming his privately-held company. Ellis succeeded in building a huge following, becoming a leader in the shoe industry.

In the meantime, my brothers Ralph and Joe poured their energies into their newly opened store. They were able to make a decent living and continued to wisely manage their money.

Early in 1963, soon after the breakup with Ellis, I moved to a ground floor location on 5th Avenue in New York, continuing my business in ladies' wearing apparel and accessories such as scarves, umbrellas and slippers. By spring, I asked Joe to join me in the business. Both of us wanted Ralph to be our third partner and for the three of us to work together, but this was not possible at that time. Ralph had to remain with the store, manage a going-out-of-business sale and find a buyer to assume the balance of the lease. In addition, my new company was barely generating enough earnings for Joe and me.

In our new venture, E.S. Sutton, Inc., Joe and I applied for a line of credit from a bank to keep us solvent. We had to provide information to show our qualifications, how our company was solidly sound and a secure risk, and how we could repay the money. Fortunately, we got the loan.

Left to our own wits to make a success of this new enterprise, Joe and I struggled in our 5th Avenue Office with the fancy showroom on the first floor and the dingy warehouse in the basement. There were times when huge cartons filled with merchandise we had ordered were dropped off outside on the sidewalk or, if we were lucky, left inside our front door. Sometimes, the cartons remained in those drop-off places for hours until Joe and I and our staff could get around to hauling the big delivery onto the freight elevator and down to the warehouse.

* * *

During this time, Tunie and I sold our house on East 19th Street for $25,000—$3,000 more than we paid for it. We wanted to live within the community's walls and for our children to experience their friends and family within the tight radius of our people, the Syrian Jews.

On East 8th Street in the Avenue J corridor, we bought a house for $60,000, made a $15,000 down payment, took on a $45,000 mortgage and spent several thousand dollars in renovations and interior decorating. Despite the fact that our newly-purchased upscale home was commensurate with the high-society social status we hoped to achieve, I had not yet reached the level of financial wealth widespread in our community. However, my family did enjoy the indulgences of a live-in maid and a materialistic lifestyle, although at times the pressures on me to pay for the unending, high standard of living was demanding.

Searching for guidance to balance the stress of my financial obligations, I looked to my religion for solace. Soon after moving into our new house, I wrote a letter to Congregation Beth Torah, a synagogue located just around the corner on Ocean Parkway. Introducing myself as a new resident in the neighborhood, I indicated my desire to become a member and to play an active and helpful role in the synagogue's growth. Promptly, I received a reply inviting me to join a committee. This newly formed orthodox congregation struggled to bring in a minyan each day and held services at Club 100 while its own building was under construction.

Rabbi Zevulun Lieberman, who guided the shul's development back then, is still at the helm today, soundly leading an ever-growing congregation. My strong connections with the members of Beth Torah congregation have been sustained. My solid bond with Rabbi Lieberman is ongoing; he continues to nurture my spiritual growth and crystallizes my sacred awareness with his presentations on esoteric meanings to our prayers, rituals, Torah and Talmud.

* * *

While settling into our new home, Tunie registered Adele in the local public school while Sammy attended Yeshivah Flatbush. Because the Yeshivah was near our new house, Sammy walked to and from school. However, as each day passed, Sammy grew progressively reluctant to leave the house. Suspecting the problem stemmed from school, we made an appointment with the teacher who assured us that Sammy was an outstanding student, well behaved and very smart. Sometime later, we learned from our neighbors who saw Sammy standing at the curb, teary-eyed and hesitant, afraid to cross the street alone. After that, Tunie or I drove him. Reflecting on this incident now brings a smile. If only all of life's problems could be solved so easily.

* * *

By October 1963, Joe had married and moved out of the apartment. Tunie and I held a wedding reception for the newlyweds in our house. Joe took his bride, Eileen, to the Far East, combining a business trip with his honeymoon.

In January 1964, Ralph moved out of the apartment and married Sondra. Although Mom and Morris were left alone to live together, Ralph, Joe and I always looked after their welfare and made sure Mom had an active and good life in Brooklyn. She kept busy with her children, grandchildren, card games, cooking and community affairs.

In the fall, when April began school, Tunie and I faced a challenge from both our mothers. They began to hassle us about having another child. We were content with our son and two daughters and did not want Tunie to risk the possibility of further miscarriages, especially after her struggle to conceive April. But our mothers were determined. Succeeding in their efforts, they imprinted upon us the joys and blessings of having a large family, following a concept imbedded in our Syrian culture and our orthodox way of life.

* * *

On January 29, 1966, after more than seven years, we had a second son. Etched in my heart forever, this bundle of joy was so perfectly formed, so perfectly healthy, so very beautiful. Knowing that Abraham would surely be my last child, I planned to dote on him and hold him dear every moment of his infancy and childhood. I was already experiencing how quickly my other children were growing up and how the early years of their childhood were fast turning into memories. Adele was 13, developing into a lovely young lady. Sammy was ten, already showing signs of maturing into a fine young man. April, at six, kept us hopping with all her youthful exploits and displays of independence. Abraham was our baby, and our joys overflowed.

Abraham's brit milah was very different than the one we had for our first son. Ten years brings many changes. With Sammy, Tunie was in the hospital for eight days and the brit milah was held at the hospital in a special room behind a glass window. Our biggest worry was that there may not be ten men for a minyan, but there were. Wine, challah and pastries were served to those in attendance.

Abraham's brit milah was held in our home. More than 100 hundred friends and family members attended and there were more than enough men for a minyan. The mohel performed the ritual circumcision and our rabbi conducted the service. We hired an exceptional caterer who, with her staff, served a wonderful lunch to our guests.

* * *

The success of our business came gradually, but it nevertheless did grow. Joe and I had been in business together almost two years; it was time to ask Ralph to join us as a full partner.

With the three of us working together, dividing our areas of responsibility, the growth of E.S. Sutton, Inc. continued unabated. My brothers and I shared a common goal, an unbending commitment to succeed. We were family and our allegiance to each other was secure. I thought our partnership would last our lifetimes. We worked by the sweat of our brows and surrounded ourselves with trusted, competent, loyal staff. Nothing happened overnight, as we once hoped it would. Becoming rich took years to accomplish.

Eventually, we moved to bigger offices, opening more spacious showrooms, building our own warehouse and developing new sourcing initiatives that reached into South Korea, Taiwan, Japan, China, Hong Kong, Philippines, Thailand, Singapore, Italy and Poland. As our company grew, so did our banking connections. At any given time, we worked with a half dozen banks. We three brothers turned our business into six profitable divisions.

* * *

While I was enjoying the comforts of my life in Brooklyn, the story was different half way across the world. Always, our Syrian community has felt deeply connected to the land of Israel, going back to our patriarch Abraham and to our survival as a people. Many of us, including me, have children and grandchildren studying in Israel. Family members live there. We do business in Israel. Often, we visit the holy sites of our heritage and celebrate the bar mitzvahs of our sons and grandsons at the Western Wall, the site of our ancient Temple. We rally for Israel's survival and make substantial donations to help ensure her existence. For these reasons, I have a need to share with you some of Israel's history and how, as I moved through my life during the decades of the 1960s and 1970s, watching Israel fight to stay alive.

* * *

Yassir Arafat, a guerilla fighter who led the Palestinian crusade against Israel, was born in Cairo in 1929. He claimed Palestinian origins and, as a young man, fought on the side of the Grand Mufti of Jerusalem, a Muslim leader who was determined to finish what Hitler had started. As head of the Fatah movement, Arafat conducted numerous attacks against Israel, killing and maiming many innocent civilians, attempting to blow up Israeli water-pump stations and rallying Muslims in the Arab world to join a war against Israel.

By the spring of 1967, the Soviet Union, hoping to incite an Arab attack on Israel, deliberately lied to President Nasser of Egypt, informing him that the Israelis had mobilized their troops on the northern border and were ready to invade Syria. In response, Nasser's first action was to close the Straits of Tiran, blocking Israel's oil imports. Thus, a massive buildup for a major assault on Israel was planned by Egypt and backed by the Soviet Union. Strengthened by its neighbors Syria and Jordan and reinforced by six other Arab nations, Egypt's invasion would doom Israel's future and send the young state, not yet twenty years old, into extinction.

Learning of the imminent onslaught, the Israelis, on June 5, launched a preemptive strike before the Egyptian military could complete its buildup and reach Israel's borders. The Israeli army succeeded in pushing the Egyptians back across the Sinai, away from Israel, and wiping out much of the Egyptian and Syrian air forces. Within six days, the Israelis gained control of the Sinai Peninsula, Gaza Strip, West Bank, East Jerusalem and Golan Heights. This victorious assault to save Israel from annihilation was accomplished in six days and viewed by many around the world as a miracle that could only have been realized through Divine intervention.

At this point, Israel found herself in a position of superiority and could have continued striking, advancing into Amman, Damascus, Cairo, but she did not. Israel did not seek a bloodbath, only to defend herself against annihilation, to secure the survival of her people. Sadly, Israel's struggle for survival continues as this book is being written.

Most Arab countries have adopted a position toward Israel of "no negotiation, no recognition and no peace." They continue to denounce Israel and her right to exist, and actively work toward hastening Israel's destruction by fueling the flames of hatred and by funding terrorist operations.

Israel, although a strong military power, is at risk. Her size and hostile neighbors expose her, the intifada rages on with no sign of easing, and the potential for another regional escalation is a possibility that never ends. Israel could find herself wishing for that Divine intervention she experienced in June 1967.

* * *

By 1968, Fatah, residing in Jordan under the leadership of Yassir Arafat, became an uncontrollable force, intent on murdering the Jews and gaining control over Israel. It also planned to assassinate Jordan's King Hussein and take Jordan for itself. On March 21, Arafat led Fatah to victory in a skirmish with Israeli Defense Forces in the Jordanian village of al Karameh. After 150 Palestinians and 29 Israelis were killed, Israel withdrew rather than expend any more lives. On December 13, 1968, Time Magazine featured Arafat on its cover with an inside story depicting him as a hero who dared to confront the Israelis. Followers of Arafat were motivated and scores joined the ranks of Fatah. Shortly thereafter, Arafat was appointed leader of the Palestinian Liberation Organization (PLO).

Meanwhile, tension between Palestinians and Jordanians mounted as heavily-armed Palestinians created a state within a state, controlling many strategic points in the country, including Jordan's large oil refinery. By September 1970, known in history as Black September, several attempts to assassinate King Hussein failed. The Palestinians resorted to hijacking three international airline flights. To bring world attention to their cause, they invited television crews to film them as they removed passengers and dramatically blew up the planes. These acts had the full support of the Syrian government.

On September 15, King Hussein declared martial law and on September 16 Jordanian tanks attacked the Palestinian headquarters in Amman as well as Palestinian camps around the country. On September 18, Damascus intervened on behalf of the Palestinians, sending Syrian tanks into Jordan.

King Hussein now was faced with threats not only from Palestinian refugees in his country but also from Syrian military forces crossing Jordan's borders. The King asked Britain and the United States for help, and also requested Israeli intervention against Syria. Israel found this appeal a mockery, but could not deny America's request for support, so she performed simulated air strikes against the Syrian column. Alarmed at the potential for an armed conflict with Israel, Syria retreated, causing a severe blow to Palestinian hopes. On September 27, the Palestinians agreed to a cease-fire. On September 28, Egypt's President Nasser died of a sudden heart attack which resulted in the Palestinians losing Egypt's protection.

In time, Arafat and the PLO were expelled from Jordan, but they quickly found a new home in Lebanon, setting up operations as an independent state, pressing on with their aggressive terrorist strikes against Israel.

* * *

Shortly after the 1967 Six-Day War, I had to make another business trip to the Far East. To my delight, Tunie made arrangements for her parents to watch the children so she could join me. It was summertime and we made a stop in Israel. For some unexplained reason, I felt compelled to visit my father's grave. What I saw saddened me beyond words.

In a cemetery, tucked away in the city of Petach Tikvah, I found my father's burial site, isolated in the far back. I touched the tiny tombstone inscribed with my father's name and date of death; nothing more was written on it. No date of birth. No epitaph. Unsettled, I stared. One would never know if buried underneath this stone was a baby or an old man, a homeless person or a father and husband, a righteous man or a beggar. But I knew. This was my father, a good man who devoted his life to his family. "There is no man that I love more than you," I whispered, hoping my words would somehow reach him. For several moments, I can't remember exactly how long, I stood there frozen. None of us had the chance to fulfill our duties to him, to eulogize him, to give him a proper funeral and a proper burial. None of us sat shivah for him. Filled with distraught, tears trickled down my cheeks. My father did so much for us, yet we could not do right by him in death. He suffered and died with his mortal spirit stripped of all dignity. Heart wrenching memories will plague me all my life.

* * *

By the end of 1967, my brother Morris, then 30, decided it was time to take a wife. Encouraged by aunts and cousins in Israel, he was lured to the holy land to search for a bride. A match was already in the works as Morris journeyed across the ocean. In Tel Aviv, he was introduced to Frieda Gindi. Their meetings went well and they decided to marry in Israel and settle in the United States, in our community in Brooklyn.

My mother traveled with Ralph and his wife, Sondra, to be with Morris on his wedding day. My sister Margo and her family, then living in Israel, attended the nuptials, as did our extended family of aunts, uncles, and cousins. Although Tunie and I could not personally be there, I was with Morris in spirit, happy for my younger brother.

After his marriage, Morris returned to New York and continued working sporadically for Ralph, Joe and me, collecting a stipend. We left him undisturbed to pursue his spiritual life. Fortunately for Morris, he saved enough money to buy a house before the big real estate boom. He purchased a two-family house and set in motion an ideal situation for Mom to live in the downstairs apartment and Morris and Frieda to live upstairs. Mom and Frieda got along well, sharing their common Arabic language while attempting to perfect their splintered English. They helped each other, shared sabbaths and holidays together and summered together at the shore in New Jersey, first in Bradley Beach and then in Deal. When Frieda and Morris' sons were born, Mom was there to help with Sammy and Gaby. The extent of her bonding and displays of affection toward her grandsons was something I had never before seen from my mother. And though her bias toward Sammy was obvious, I was happy to see her stoicism soften and joy permeate her life.

* * *

On a beautiful Saturday morning in May, 1968, with the sun shining brightly in the sky and a gentle breeze tempering the air, I walked with Tunie and our children to the synagogue, dressed in our finest new clothes. On that day, our son Sammy would become a man according to the laws of Moses, to the laws handed down by G-d on Mount Sinai. On that day of his Bar Mitzvah, I was incredibly proud of my son as I watched him go up to the bimah, accept his first aliyah and recite his first reading in the Torah. I beamed as he chanted his haftarah and explained the weekly portion of the parashah. That day ushered in a new level of accountability for Sammy. As a Jew, he was now responsible for performing the mitzvot, participating in minyans, reading from the Torah, wearing tallit, laying tefillin, reciting the daily prayers and fasting on Yom Kippur. In our synagogue, the service with all of its orthodox ritual protocols advanced smoothly. For a moment, I thought about my own Bar Mitzvah in Aleppo, wondering if my father was as proud of me as I now was of Sammy.

In the evening, we celebrated at our house with a big party, catered by the most sought-after caterer in our community. Two hundred guests enjoyed an array of the finest, succulent, mouth-watering Syrian foods while being entertained by the well-known Israeli singer, Avram.

* * *

By 1970, more serious approaches to our religion began to take hold. Learned elders spearheaded Torah study classes. Kollels sprang up for core groups of scholars engaged in full-time, advanced Torah study. The Sephardic Heritage Foundation emerged, undertaking the role of modifying and updating our prayer books. Cantors composed songs appropriate for specific milestones. And patiently, our Chief Rabbi, Jacob Kassin, waited for the right time to strictly enforce G-d's fourth commandment: Remember the sabbath day to keep it holy. He wanted the entire community, men, women and children, to unite in observing this holy day of the week.

Although many always honored the sabbath day, there were many who did not. With Rabbi Kassin's new dictate in place, more and more men adjusted their work practices, closing their businesses on Saturday. However, insisting on shutting down a retail store on Saturday, the busiest day of the week, and foregoing a major chunk of income, would have exacted a great sacrifice, a major cut in one's livelihood. So Rabbi Kassin consulted with other rabbis in the community to develop a solution in which everyone could live. As a result, store owners could arrange to sell their stores to trusted non-Jews for the sabbath day and then buy back their stores after the sabbath. In this way, businesses could stay open and earnings would not be lost. This arrangement met most everyone's approval. Today, observing the sabbath is characteristic of our community, it is part of what makes us religious Jews. There is no hesitation, just as there is no hesitation in adhering strictly to our kosher dietary laws. We just do it. It is part of who we are.

After this accomplishment, attention turned toward the children in our community. With American society evolving so rapidly into an open, progressive culture, the young were vulnerable. We could not risk losing our children to unscrupulous temptations, so an unstoppable movement began to remove our children from the public school system and enroll them in our community yeshivot. These schools follow not only the state-approved curriculum, but also instruction in Hebrew, religion and the moral and ethical paths by which to live by. In addition, we established schools that cater to the physically and mentally challenged children among us, schools with small, structured classes and compassionate teachers that provide less demanding state-approved programs which blend with instruction in our customs and religion.

Keeping our community together, holding onto our heritage, always has been a major concern, from the time Syrian Jews arrived on America's shores in the early part of the 20th century.

Our people first tried to settle on the Lower East Side of Manhattan and merge with the European Jews, but the Ashkenazie Jews would have nothing to do with the Sephardic Jews. They looked down on our people, labeling us as uneducated and dirty, asking, "What kind of Jews don't speak Yiddish?" They sneered and taunted the Syrian Jews, refusing to accept them into their midst, saying, "Jewish Arabs. Unheard of!"

In addition to facing humiliation, the small community of Syrian Jews witnessed many Ashkenazie Jews following the path of assimilation. My people could not continue in this environment, so they found another area to live, a place to call their own where they could freely practice their religion and preserve their culture. With a mass exodus to Brooklyn, they first took up residence in Bensonhurst, then chose the lower end of Ocean Parkway and its surrounding neighborhoods, a place where 75,000 Syrian Jews live today.

Marrying within the group, socializing with our own populace, adhering to our religious beliefs and rituals, and protecting our Syrian heritage—these things are paramount to our survival as a cohesive people. These practices reach far and wide. Today, we have united with Lebanese and Egyptian Jews living among us. We are strongly bonded with the Syrian Jews who reside all year in New Jersey, and to those who make their homes in Manhattan, Great Neck, Myrtle Beach and Beverly Hills. We, in Brooklyn, are the largest of the Syrian-Jewish communities, the mother community that sets the example for all others. In Panama, Mexico, Argentina, Brazil, Chile, Israel, France and Great Britain, our people live much the same as we do, following the laws according to Moses, following the culture of our Arabic heritage.

Our women adhere strongly to our traditions, maintaining orthodox homes, caring for their families, raising their children within the doctrines of our community. They open their palatial homes to raise money to support humanitarian needs and serve the community at many levels.

Moreover, a number of organizations serve our community: Bikur Holim cares for the needy and delivers food to the home bound, the elderly, the handicapped, the poor. It provides medical referrals, social work and employment guidance. Bikur Holim is run by a staff of professionals and volunteers with a budget in the multi-millions. It is funded by private donations from our community as well as some government assistance.

Our own rabbinical college educates young men to serve in our community as rabbis and rabbinical teachers. They receive full remuneration while studying so they can focus exclusively on learning. Similar studies are open to women to help secure teachers for our children.

SAFE, Sephardic Addiction Family Education, helps people with addictions. Link provides matchmaking services for single adults. Sephardic Federation is our lobby, serving as a liaison to local, state and federal governments. The Sephardic Voters League guides the community in electing the best candidates to safeguard our people and preserve our country. The Sephardic Food Fund helps those struggling economically, discreetly providing them with credit cards to purchase food at designated supermarkets. The Angel Fund counsels those grappling with failed businesses or job losses.

* * *

More than 100 years ago, Syrian Jews began arriving in New York. They were penniless, spoke no English and had no professions. They were not a burden to society and they asked for no help from the government or anyone. Today, we are a cohesive community, succeeding on our own, helping our own, looking toward G-d's light to continue guiding us.

My family clockwise: Adele, Sammy, Tunie, Abie, April

Sammy's Bar Mitzvah

Sammy's Bar Mitzvah - my family, 1968

Morris and Frieda's wedding reception in Israel, 1967

Brother Ralph and his wife Sondra at Morris and Frieda's wedding

Brothers Ralph, Joe and me

TWENTY-ONE

BUT WHENCE DOES WISDOM COME? WHERE IS THE SOURCE OF
UNDERSTANDING? IT IS HIDDEN FROM THE EYES OF ALL LIVING
—JOB 28:20

When I visited my father's grave shortly after the Six-Day War, I also went to see my sister. At the time, Margo expressed a desire to live in the United States and be near her family. She said she wanted her children to grow up knowing us. As I listened to her speak, a queasy feeling gripped me and I grew apprehensive. Margo was different. It was not just her physical deformity, but more so, it was her narrow mindset and strong Israeli morés. She was locked into a disposition out of which she could not reason. Margo rambled on in her restricted logic, nagging, complaining. Her words, her attitude alarmed me, so I made no commitment except that I would think about her request. Personally, I did not believe Margo could assimilate into American society and I did not trust her to blend into our Syrian community.

Nonetheless, by 1972, with our business flourishing, our financial situation strong, our marriages warm and sound and our children blossoming, my brothers and I thought the time might be right to bring our sister and her family to America, to bring us all together. We could not argue with my mother when she said, "This is what your father would have wanted."

So Joe, Ralph and I made the arrangements. We paid for the journey, settled the family in an apartment, gave Margo's husband a job in E.S. Sutton, Inc., and ensured the family an adequate and steady income.

* * *

Margo and Nessim had arrived in New York with their two sons and one daughter. They moved into an outmoded apartment in a seven-story building in Brooklyn, on East 3rd Street and Avenue X, about 20 blocks from where Tunie and I lived. The elevator in the complex was rickety, but it worked, and the family's simply-furnished apartment matched their simply-coping lifestyle.

Margo came to America full of hope for a new life, a life of acceptance. But this was not to be. From the beginning, Margo was stigmatized and people in the community avoided her. She was a foreigner who spoke little English, one foot was permanently disfigured and she limped. Plagued by elephantiasis, Margo's handicap brought her long bouts of depression. Her husband, Nessim, short, unassuming and shy, tried to please Margo and protect her from the unkindness around her.

Tunie, with her enormous compassion, reached out to my sister, but it seemed Margo's emotional needs were too great to fill. The more we gave, the more Margo wanted. Over time, and with greater desperation, Margo turned to our mother. But because of Mom's stoic nature and Margo's endless need for attention, my mother quickly ran out of patience.

Moreover, we all were busy and involved with our own lives. Tunie and I had four children to raise, charity work, community involvements, friends, social life, trips, and I had a business to run and financial responsibilities. Yet we did look after Margo and her family to the extent we could.

* * *

In 2002, on the roof of the seven-story building where the family lived for 30 years, Nessim lay dead. The police never learned what happened nor did they seem to care. Follow-up was almost non-existent.

Nessim's passing took a heavy toll on my sister. With no one to care for her the way Nessim did, Margo was unable to carry on. She spent her remaining years confined to a nursing home. Her children and I visited her often, until the spring of 2010 when she passed away.

* * *

Margo and Nessim's middle child, a pretty young woman, struggled with the indifference exhibited toward her and her family by our community. Today, she lives in Florida with her husband and two daughters.

Margo and Nessim's eldest son is married to an Israeli, a teacher. They live in New Jersey with their two children. He works in our warehouse, where he has competently held a stable and responsible position for many years.

Margo and Nessim's youngest son, a modest and humble man, leads a pious life of Torah study and fundraises for the underprivileged and the needy. He is married to a teacher, an Israeli of Moroccan descent; they have eight children and reside in Brooklyn.

TWENTY-TWO

MANKIND MUST REMEMBER THAT PEACE
IS NOT G-D'S GIFT TO HIS CREATURES,
PEACE IS OUR GIFT TO EACH OTHER—ELIE WIESEL

All day on Saturday, October 6, 1973, I sat in the packed synagogue with my fellow congregants. Rabbi Zevulun Lieberman led us in fervent prayer. I fasted; I atoned; I repented. This day was not only our sabbath, but also Yom Kippur. No day of the year could be more holy for Jews.

Our ten days of introspection and meditation that began on Rosh Hashanah had reached its crescendo. Our Talmud explains it in the following way: *The Book of Life is open for the righteous on Rosh Hashanah so that G-d can inscribe their names; the fate of all others for the coming year is on hold until Yom Kippur.*

After the late-morning Torah reading, I joined the worshippers in reciting special memorial prayers for deceased members of our immediate families. I prayed for my father and for my brothers Saleh and Edgar. Soon after, we learned of the Yom Kippur War in the Middle East.

Jews all over Israel had been in their synagogues, praying, fasting. It was two o'clock in the afternoon Cairo time when Egypt and Syria launched coordinated surprise attacks in the Sinai and the Golan Heights. Israel was stunned and an international crisis developed.

* * *

Egypt's President, Anwar Sadat, had tried unsuccessfully to obtain American mediation for a peaceful solution in the Middle East. President Nixon assigned Secretary of State William Rogers to negotiate, but Henry Kissinger, then Nixon's national security advisor, sabotaged the effort, fearing that Rogers and not himself would get the credit. This was a tragic blunder.

Disgusted with White House in-fighting, Sadat turned to the Soviets for military support. Hundreds of Soviet espionage agents poured into Israel, infiltrating the country's secret intelligence, but reneged on their promise of military aid to Egypt, so Sadat threw the Soviets out. He would redeem Egyptian honor by a force of arms.

After the 1967 Six-Day War, King Faisal of Saudi Arabia was even more emphatic than Egypt's President Sadat about destroying Israel. Unfortunately, Israelis grew overconfident after the six-day miraculous victory, believing they were invincible.

As October began, the Israelis, still absorbed in their 1967 haughtiness, were blissfully ignorant of the tsunami looming before them. The best-kept secret in the Arab world was about to be unleashed—an attack on Yom Kippur day when all of Israel comes to a complete standstill. The only outsider to be informed of the plan was America's National Security Agency (NSA) which, on October fourth, had a good grasp of the situation. However, the Nixon White House ordered NSA to sit on the information and let the attack happen. Nixon knew that American Jews did not vote for him and that the Israelis had enough information about his past to cause him major political damage.

If Israeli generals had learned of the imminent onslaught before it was upon them, they could have devised a defense or even a preemptive strike, but with no time to prepare, Israel was in trouble. An Israeli mobilization plan required 16 hours to call up its reserves and to give their soldiers time to grab their weapons and hitchhike to the fronts.

* * *

In shul, as we discussed the situation during a break in our prayers, we were not concerned, having full confidence that G-d was on our side and the Israelis would quickly triumph, just as they did in 1967. Still, we prayed, beseeching Hashem to protect Israel. By late afternoon, following Mincha prayers and the reading of the Book of Jonah, we received information about Israel's heavy losses.

As the sun set and dusk came upon us, our holiest day of the year was about to end. Our congregation joined together for Neilah, the final prayer before the blowing of the shofar, the time when G-d makes His final decision about who is forgiven and who is not. As we stood in supplication, distressing news spread quickly throughout our sanctuary. In the Sinai Peninsula, Egypt's Third Army took Israeli defenses by surprise. Syria attacked the Golan Heights. Israel stood alone to defend herself.

* * *

Brigades, weapons and money came from Iraq, Saudi Arabia, Libya, Sudan, Morocco, Kuwait, Algeria and Tunisia. King Hussein of Jordan did not want to get involved in the fight, but knew the consequences if he refused the other Arab leaders. The Lebanese encouraged Palestinian terrorists to inflict their own brand of insurgency, to shell Israeli civilian settlements from Lebanon's terrain. The Soviets, who earlier reneged on providing military support, sent anti-tank guided missiles in addition to an array of other advanced weaponry. Even the United Nations did not voice objection to the onslaught.

On October 6, Yom Kippur Day, two hours after noon time, the shelling began. On the Golan Heights, 180 Israeli tanks faced an onslaught of 1,400 Syrian tanks. Along the Suez Canal, 80,000 Egyptians attacked over 400 Israeli defense soldiers stationed there. An Iraqi division of 1,800 men moved hundred of tanks into the central Golan. Libya supplied Mirage fighters to Egypt along with $1B in aid. The Saudis sent 3,000 of their best fighters to help Syria. Algeria deployed three aircraft squadrons of fighters and bombers, plus an armored brigade of 150 tanks. Two-thousand Tunisian soldiers were positioned in the Nile Delta, and 3,500 Sudanese troops arrived to help Egypt. Morocco discharged three brigades plus an additional 2,500 men to Syria. Syrian air defense forces made use of Lebanon radar units. King Hussein of Jordan sent his two best brigades to Syria as well as three artillery batteries and 100 tanks.

In desperation, Golda Meir ordered Simcha Dinitz, her ambassador to the United States, to tell President Nixon that Israel needed help fast. Nixon arranged to be unavailable. Dinitz tried to reach Secretary of State Henry Kissinger, who by then had replaced William Rogers, but Kissinger was conveniently incommunicado at the Waldorf Astoria Hotel in New York.

Israeli front-line units were crushed as the Egyptian army used high-powered water cannons to blast down Israeli sand forts, then cross the Suez into Israel. In the north, Syrian tank brigades obliterated significant sections of the Israeli battle line. Israel suffered its most significant losses during those first few days. Close to 2,000 soldiers were killed and 5,000 were wounded.

Prime Minister Golda Meir was desperate. With Nixon and Kissinger unreachable, and American help reduced to a fantasy, she made the most excruciating decision of her life. Dimona! If Israel was going down, she would not let her country go down alone.

For years, Israelis worked in secret to develop nuclear weapons. Just months earlier, with the help of France, Israel had completed its nuclear weapons site in Dimona. Golda Meir gave the orders to aim the nuclear missiles at Cairo, Damascus and Moscow. Then she called Simcha Dinitz, telling him that the nuclear weapons were in place, ready to be deployed. She begged Dinitz to find a way to get word to Kissinger— if Israel does not receive American help within 24 hours, the missiles would be unleashed.

To the world, Israel was an expendable commodity. It did not matter that Jews brought life to a barren desert. It did not matter that Israel was the only democracy in a region surrounded by countries ruled by theocratic, oligarchic, political despots. It did not matter that Israel was producing some of the best doctors on the planet who accepted anyone who came for help. It did not matter that Israel pioneered some of the greatest medical breakthroughs and shared the findings with the world. And it did not matter that technical innovations produced through Israeli ingenuity improved the lives of people all around the globe. None of this mattered. What mattered was oil, black gold. The Arabs had it and the Jews did not. Except for the Dutch, even the Europeans sided against tiny Israel, not wanting to upset their oil supplies, not wanting to trigger price hikes.

* * *

Oil was the reason Kissinger was eager for Israel to comply with U.N. Resolution 242, reversing all territorial gains that Israel had made in 1967. Yet doing this would put Israel in a position of maximum vulnerability. The Nixon administration adopted a policy of stalling, not rushing to Israel's side, keeping a low profile to avoid an Arab reaction in the oil markets. The Arabs had given an ultimatum: Any nation that helped Israel would see their supply of oil cut off.

* * *

Simcha Dinitz succeeded in reaching Kissinger. Hearing that Israel's nuclear arsenal was in place and that Israel was not going down alone, Kissinger went into a tailspin. Kissinger reached Nixon and on October 12 a decision was made. Israel would immediately receive all the supplies and military support it needed, as long as it was done in secret. However, the secret quickly surfaced when bad weather and botched-up maneuverings forced American military deployment to be carried out in broad daylight instead of being concealed in the dark of night.

Still, the American airlift of arms rushed to the the battlefronts gave Israel the advantage it needed to change the tide of the war. An Israeli counteroffensive pushed the Egyptians back just as they were on the verge of destroying the tiny state. Israeli soldiers attacked key points on the Canal's west bank and trapped Egypt's Third Army. Once across the Suez Canal, Israel began its drive toward Cairo.

Only diplomatic intervention from America could save the Egyptian forces from being wiped out. Syria fared far worse, with Israeli forces winning back control of the Golan Heights and moving troops within striking range of Damascus.

On October 16, the Soviet prime minister flew to Cairo and advised Sadat to call for a cease-fire. A meeting of Arab members of OPEC unilaterally announced a huge price hike in petroleum and a planned oil embargo on America. On October 19, Nixon announced more than $2B in military aid to Israel, hoping to force negotiations and preserve the military balance between the Jews and the Arabs.

By October 25, the United States and Russia squared off in a nuclear confrontation. To contain the alarming situation, Kissinger pressured the Israelis to allow the Arab armies to retreat unmolested. A cease-fire was ratified on October 26, 20 days after the onset of the Yom Kippur War. Israel would survive; Nixon would not. The Watergate scandal and the energy crisis eventually brought him down.

* * *

I thanked G-d for Israel's survival. To me, G-d had heard our prayers. The Yom Kippur War ended, to be recorded in the history books.

The price of a gallon of gas jumped from 36 cents to 55 cents cents. The Arab oil embargo reduced America's supply of crude by 25 percent. Long lines formed at the pumps. Twenty percent of gasoline stations across America had no fuel. Rationing was imposed, where those with license plates ending in an odd number could only fill their tanks on odd-number days and those with license plates ending in an even number could only fill their tanks on even-number days. The 31st day of a month was open, meaning the restrictions did not apply. This system lasted until 1976.

Oil had become more precious than gold. Gasoline rationing led to violence at the pumps, siphoning from others' gas tanks, brutalizing the striking truck drivers, establishing a maximum 55-miles-per-hour speed limit, producing smaller and more energy-efficient cars, initiating year-round daylight savings time and creating a Department of Energy in Washington.

* * *

Like most Americans, I moved on with my daily life. Our daughter Adele was getting married and Tunie and I began plans for an extravagant wedding, an affair to set the standard for unrivaled elegance. We booked the upscale Pierre Hotel across from Central Park, on Fifth Avenue in Manhattan.

Preparations had to be made for the music, flowers, decorations, photographers, food and drink, hotel rooms for the overnight guests, valet parking, the cocktail buffet, the ceremony and the main ballroom for the banquet and for dancing. Adding to this long list was shopping for the bride's wedding dress, gowns for Tunie and April, tuxedoes for Sammy, Abraham, and me. Everything had to be perfect.

On January 12, 1974, Adele Sutton and Ed Hamway married under a magnificent chupah, with our chief rabbi, Rabbi Jacob Kassin, officiating. From the moment our 400 guests entered the Hotel Pierre's magnificent hotel lobby with its hand-painted murals and plush furnishings to the cutting of the wedding cake and the last dance in the floral-adorned ballroom, everything moved with meticulous precision. The emotional high from this lavish extravaganza lingered with Tunie and me for a long time.

* * *

We thought nothing could interfere with our prolonged joy of Adele's wedding, but it did. Tunie's mother, Adele Sultan, was in her mid fifties when she was diagnosed with dementia, which took over her life. As her mental instability progressed and jeopardized her physical welfare, she had to be placed in a nursing home. This was especially hard on Tunie because she was very close to her mother. Tunie took courses to learn about dementia and Alzheimers and started a support group at our community center for family care givers of the disease.

Adele was in the nursing home for 20 years, until her passing. Tunie's father, Abe, took full responsibility, making sure she had the best care, even though he divorced Adele and remarried. The family accepted Abe's subsequent marriage with compassion and understanding, realizing that he needed not to be alone. The rabbis sanctioned the marriage as being within halacha (Jewish law), even while my mother-in-law was bedridden. Abe's second wife, Gladys, proved to be a wonderful and kind woman and we grew to love her.

* * *

By 1976, Tunie, I and the children journeyed again to Israel to attend the Bar Mitzvah of Tunie's nephew. Israel was experiencing relative calm after the war, although occasional terrorist attacks carried out by Palestinians did disrupt the country's tranquility. However, we were not concerned. Israeli military troops were everywhere, visibly armed with guns and rifles. With their keenly trained eyes scanning every inch of the land, we felt safe, protected.

At the Kotel, the Wailing Wall in Jerusalem, we celebrated our nephew's Bar Mitzvah and enjoyed a festive reception afterward. Our group consisted of the Bar Mitzvah boy and his family as well as Tunie's father, Abe, his new wife, Gladys, and members of our extended family. In total, 30 of us, men, women and children, enhanced our stay in Israel by touring extensively around the country. We climbed to the top of Masada, savoring the breathtaking views overlooking the Dead Sea. From high up in the Golan Heights, we could see Syria. In Haifa, we toured the magnificent Baha'i Shrine and Gardens on the slope of Mount Carmel. We spent time in Safed, a seat for kabbalistic learning, comfortably mingled with Israeli Palestinians and rode a camel. Ending our trip in Eilat, we swam in the Gulf of Aqaba and then cruised in a glass-bottom boat, mesmerized by the array of underwater sea life, fish, coral and vegetation.

* * *

The land of Israel pulls me in. Perhaps it is because of G-d's promise, leading my people to a land of milk and honey. Perhaps it is because G-d watches over the soil, never allowing Israel to meet her final destruction, always miraculously bringing her back to life. And perhaps it is because of my own emotional and religious relationship to this piece of earth, the place where my ancestors, Abraham, Isaac, and Jacob lived.

Tunie and me

Adele and Ed Hamway at their wedding, January 1974

Adele and Ed Hamway and their children

My brothers and I - Giving of a new Torah, 1994;
left to right: Morris, Joe, Ralph, me, Mike

Brothers and our wives at Torah dedication

TWENTY-THREE

LOVE BEGINS WITH A SMILE, GROWS WITH A KISS, AND ENDS WITH A TEARDROP

The idea of moving permanently to Deal, New Jersey, became more tempting despite the fact that two years earlier, Tunie and I spent a small fortune for an accomplished and pricey interior designer to redecorate our home in Brooklyn.

Decorating and redecorating had almost become a way of life for us. Tunie loved the excitement, the newness, the change, as well as keeping up with many of our friends and relatives who were doing the same thing. For me, I was happy as long as Tunie was happy.

By late spring of 1977, workmen and decorators completed the remodeling of our summer house in Deal, just in time for us to move in. Every year, during this warm season that brings a long school break for students, Brooklyn loses its Syrian Jews to the shores of central New Jersey.

As we began to enjoy the summer, the beach, our friends, our very active social life, we received word from the police that our house in Brooklyn had been robbed. The robbery sealed our decision. We would live in Deal all year round. Selling and getting top dollar for our house in Brooklyn would not be difficult. Residences within walking distance to one of our community synagogues were always in demand. Our newly-decorated Brooklyn house, close to almost everything in the community, was highly desirable.

* * *

Living all year in Deal brought many advantages. No heavy traffic. No horns honking. No trying to get around double-parked cars blocking the streets. More space between houses. More living privacy. Friendlier people. Better county services. Safer environment. Tunie and I liked our new surroundings. There was a synagogue for our community and a yeshivah for our children.

When the summer ended and much of the community returned to Brooklyn, we thought our lives would quiet down, but that was not to be. We joined the Deal Synagogue that served the burgeoning year-round Syrian community and I was elected to the synagogue board. We registered April in Asbury Park High School, a public school with a 50% black-student population. Tunie and I held our breath, mildly concerned about her welfare and the level of education she would receive. Our apprehensions were needless because everything worked out fine. We enrolled Abie in the Hillel Yeshivah and I was invited to be a member of its board. I then held two board positions—the shul and the yeshivah. Eventually, Abie completed his yeshivah studies and moved on to Asbury Park High School, following his sister's path.

My daily commute to work involved going into our office in Manhattan and also to our warehouse in Jersey City. I hired a local man, a Deal resident named Jessie, to be my personal driver.

Meanwhile, Ralph, Joe and I had grown our company into a huge, thriving enterprise. We were sharp-witted in our business dealings, worked hard and put in many hours. Conscious about maintaining a loyal, competent, trustworthy staff, we treated our employees well. We were fair to our customers and insisted that our merchandise pass strict quality control measures. Our company benefitted from a sound reputation and steadily rising profits. The growth of E.S. Sutton, Inc. went far beyond our wildest dreams.

Tunie and I maintained an active social calendar, staying connected to our friends and family in Brooklyn, attending performances at the Lincoln Center and having season tickets to the ballet. We could always count on our chauffeur, Jessie, to drive us into Manhattan and wait for us.

* * *

In the summer of 1978, we celebrated Abie's bar mitzvah. On a Saturday morning, Tunie, I and our children were joined by 300 guests who filled the sanctuary of the Deal Synagogue. Rabbi Isaac Dweck guided Abie in his bar mitzvah ceremony, conducting the service with the ritual and protocol of our orthodox tradition. Our youngest child, our second son, was to become a man. Brimming with pride, I watched this majestic young man in his new suit ascend to the bimah, accept his first aliyah and recite his first Torah reading. I reflected on my oldest son, Sammy, who, ten years before, had brought me just as much joy, just as much pride. I wanted to take Tunie's hand and hold it, but our orthodox ways require men and women to sit separately in different sections. Still, I felt her euphoria as much as I felt my own.

That evening, our guests streamed into our backyard and into a huge, elaborate tent set up especially for the affair. A band played through the night, entertaining us with Israeli, Syrian and American music. A large buffet spread across several tables consisted of succulent appetizers, heavenly cuisine and lavish desserts. As always, Tunie was magnificent, attending to every detail. In her warm and outgoing nature, she reached out to everyone.

* * *

Soon after our simcha, Rabbi Dweck of the Deal Synagogue approached me, prodding me to host a fundraiser for Bill Bradley, an American Hall of Fame basketball player who had played for the New York Knicks. Bradley was challenging moderate Republican Clifford Case for his seat in the United States Senate. I agreed to sponsor two fundraising events in support of Bradley's campaign.

In November 1978, Bradley was elected junior Senator from New Jersey. It felt good to be part of the winning campaign. With a group of selected supporters, I was invited to his Washington office and, for many years afterward, Bradley and I continued our contact with one another.

After three 6-year terms in the Senate, Bradley became disillusioned with Congress and decided to run for president, hoping to be a catalyst for change, hoping to serve the American people with new leadership. He challenged then vice president Al Gore for the Democratic presidential nomination. I supported his candidacy and was sorry he failed in this endeavor. I think Bradley would have been a great leader. He deeply cared about our country and the American people.

* * *

Tunie and I enjoyed year-round living in Deal, but we missed our grandchildren who lived an hour away in Brooklyn. We wanted them closer to us. So we spoke with our daughter, Adele, and our son-in-law, Ed, presenting them with a list of advantages for moving to Deal permanently. When they agreed, Tunie and I were ecstatic.

Sammy was attending New York University and living in Manhattan. On weekdays, after classes and homework, he was more inclined to spend his free time in our company's showroom rather than hang around campus with his friends. He liked the environment and the exposure to the working world and was quick to learn our business. I saw that Sammy had a good head on his shoulders and I looked forward to one day bringing him on board. He wanted to quit school and start working in the company right away, but Tunie and I would not let him. We insisted that he graduate first.

In 1979, April met her future husband, Mickey Shabot, who lived with his family in Deal. By October, we celebrated another milestone—April's marriage. With 350 guests and Rabbi Dweck officiating, we held the wedding at the Beth El synagogue, which could accommodate all our guests in the sanctuary and a sit-down catered reception in the large social hall. The wedding was elegant, not as lavish as Adele's wedding at The Pierre, but it was what April and Mickey wanted—a graceful wedding to share with family and friends, a wedding that held charm and memories.

After returning from their honeymoon, April and Mickey settled in Deal. Tunie and I were thrilled to have both of our daughters nearby.

* * *

About this time, religious fervor within our community gained a deepening momentum. More and more Syrian Jews took on greater adherence to the laws of our Torah, to the precepts of Leviticus, to G-d's 613 commandments of which 365 are negative and 248 are positive. Our rabbis set the standards, spinning interpretations, keeping us together as one people. My family life, social life, business life, all centered around attending synagogue and reciting our daily prayers, observing the weekly sabbath and celebrating our holidays, adhering to our dietary laws and clinging to the community, living among ourselves and abiding by Rabbi Kassin's edict.

The number of hours each week dedicated to Torah and Talmud study soared. Men in our community exchanged a life of work for a life of learning, with greater mastery of G-d's laws. Kollels sprang up for those wanting to follow a rabbinical life, to serve on a pulpit or to become an educator or tutor. Schools of study also opened for women. These learning centers, called seminars, began to train women in the wisdom of our Torah, the ways of purity, how to be teachers, how to serve our community and carry G-d's message.

* * *

In 1981, we received an invitation by mail to join a group of benefactors at Mt. Sinai Hospital in New York, called "The Committee of a Thousand." One thousand members pledge a prescribed amount of money each year to fund research and development at the hospital's school of medicine. As a reward, those donors are recognized on rosters and invited to prominent events hosted by faculty, practicing doctors and hospital executives. The 1,000 members are guaranteed VIP status with privileged access to a roster of doctors practicing at the hospital, and to receive top priority in attention, care and treatment if and when it should ever be needed. Tunie and I did not hesitate. We made the first of our large donations and were inducted into this prestigious group.

* * *

Meanwhile, Tunie and I never lost our enthusiasm for the excitement of city life. Our close friends, Renee and Izzy Shamah, had been living in Manhattan for some years and we often met them in the city for dinner at upscale restaurants, to attend theater performances or to visit the museums.

Over time, Renee and Izzy persuaded us to move to Manhattan. So, in 1983, we decided to try city life, renting a plush apartment for a year. Our married daughters were busy with their lives and families in Deal. Sammy was living alone in Manhattan and Abie was attending Cardozo School of Law. We were free to go wherever we wanted. Tunie and I loved the excitement, the intensity of city life with its culture and many activities at our fingertips. The following year, we bought a duplex in a new building, although we did keep our home in Deal.

Through my hectic business and social life, I continued my daily prayers and observance of the sabbath and holidays. I attended both the Fifth Avenue Synagogue, an orthodox Ashkenazie shul that accommodated the Sephardim, and the Ashkenazim Sutton Place Conservative Synagogue where I enjoyed the Saturday afternoon bible classes with Rabbi David Kahane.

* * *

On the second of June 1985, we had another wedding. Our son Sammy married Jane Massry at the East Midwood Jewish Center in Brooklyn. Four hundred people attended. A catered reception with sit-down dinner and lively music followed the ceremony.

On June 11, 1988, the last of our children married. The wedding of Abie Sutton and Mary Arazi was held at Shaare Zion synagogue on Ocean Parkway in Brooklyn. Six hundred guests enjoyed a lavish catered buffet dinner and dancing on a crowded floor. Abie and Mary's honeymoon to Europe and the French Riviera was cut short to return home and pay respects to our family when my mother, Adele Sutton, died on June 24th. With my brothers Mike, Ralph, Joe and Morris, and my sister, Margo, I sat shiva. For one week, we observed a mourning period, received visitors paying their condolences, recited prayers and shared meals.

For 30 years, my mother had enjoyed life in America with her family, attending weddings, bar mitzvahs, brit milahs, sharing shabbats and holidays and sometimes vacationing with us.

In the fall of 1988, Tunie and I moved back to Brooklyn and rented a house for a year and a half. Then we purchased a lot with an older house on it. After contracting to have that house demolished, we hired an architect, a builder and an interior decorator. We then built a large, magnificent home. We stayed in our rental until construction of our new residence was completed. After moving in, we rejoined Beth Torah synagogue and eased ourselves back into the Brooklyn community.

* * *

The extraordinary growth of E.S. Sutton, Inc. continued unabated. Ralph, Joe and I were all living well, thanks to the business. Over time, friends approached us to invest as silent partners in real estate deals. This began our business expansion into real estate that garnered huge returns on our investments.

* * *

In the fall of 1993, my world began to cave in as three heartbreaking events unfolded, one right after the other, shocking my reality and shattering my spirit.

It began on Saturday, September 25, 1993, Yom Kippur Day. Our highly esteemed Rabbi, Zevulun Lieberman, led our congregation in prayer. After the late morning Torah reading, I prayed for the souls of my father and my brothers, Saleh and Edgar, during the memorial service. Shortly thereafter, news began to trickle in, quickly spreading among us. Rabbi Lieberman's son, Hillel, a rabbi in Israel, was captured by Palestinians.

The first Intifada that began in 1987 had escalated to a savage crescendo. For six years, the intifada festered, feeding on virulent anti-Semitism and violent opposition to the Israeli occupied territories—lands that were seized during the 1967 Six-Day War when Israel was defending herself from annihilation.

In shul, we discussed the situation during a break in our prayers. By early evening, as we joined together for Neilah, our concluding prayer before the shofar blowing, news of Hillel Lieberman's murder reached us. The bullet-ridden body of our rabbi's only son was found in a cave outside Nablus.

Rabbi Hillel Lieberman was married and the father of seven. He lived in Elon Moreh, a settlement in the Samarian Hills just northeast of Nablus, and was one of the founders of *Od Yosef Chai Yeshiva*, located on the compound of Joseph's Tomb, a shrine he dearly cherished.

Palestinians went on a wild rampage with intense fighting at the compound of Joseph's Tomb, scorching the monument and desecrating the Sifrei Torah and holy books. When Hillel Lieberman heard the news, he rushed out on foot to save all that he could. Rabbi Lieberman was last seen walking toward the compound to save the synagogue's Torah scrolls and the Jewish religious books at the yeshivah where he taught. He was unarmed and wearing a tallit. The IDF reported that he was murdered in cold blood by Palestinian terrorists as he made his way to Joseph's Tomb.

Absorbed in this misfortune, our congregation offered consolation to our rabbi and his wife. The couple suffered greatly from their tragic loss. We pulled together to raise money, creating an endowment fund for the children who must grow up without their father. We offered our rabbi a generous severance package so he and his wife could retire to Israel and live near their grandchildren and daughter-in-law. Although Rabbi Lieberman owned an apartment in Israel, he declined our overture. He and his family had strong roots in New York. It would be hard to pick up and leave.

Rabbi Zevulun Lieberman and his wife have remained in Brooklyn all these years, and although he continues to lead Congregation Beth Torah, he is a changed man. The hardship of his loss, knowing that his beloved son, his only son, met a violent death at the hands of a gruesome mob of Palestinian terrorists, has been an agony from which he and his wife shall never be free.

* * *

Two weeks after the death of our rabbi's son, my beloved Tunie was diagnosed with ovarian cancer. Four months later, my grandson Robbie was diagnosed with autism spectrum disorder. Then Tunie's mother died. At age 75, after 20 years in a nursing home, Adele Sultan's dementia and failing health took a final toll.

Tunie's devotion to her mother continued until the very end. When Adele Sultan was first diagnosed, Tunie joined an Alzheimer's association, attended classes and learned more about the disease. She wanted not only to help care for her mother but also to share what she had learned with others. Tunie started an Alzheimer's support group that is still in existence today. She wanted to reach out and offer guidance to those in the community who were struggling to cope with family members affected by Alzheimer's.

* * *

Initially, our grandson Robbie's situation was a great concern to us. But as we watched with amazement at the remarkable way Sammy and Jane handled Robbie and at how Robbie's siblings reached out to their brother with kindness, compassion, and love, we knew our son's family would become a shining example for others to follow. Over the years, Sammy and Jane have expended a great amount of time and energy seeking medical and therapeutic help for Robbie. They learned that no schools or community organizations existed in New York to deal with the wide range of manifestations within autism. Recognizing that if Robbie were to get the specialized care he needed, they would have to find it themselves.

They equipped their home with therapy rooms, gadgets, appliances and security to accommodate Robbie's needs. Sammy and Jane's persistent research and probing to find answers led them to join forces with four other families in our community, all with similar challenges. Together, they started the Imagine Academy for Autism where well-trained professionals provide unparalleled care, working one-on-one with each student. The academy has an ambitious agenda. Construction of a new building to accommodate the growing number of applicants is near completion and there are plans to someday open a resource center and a residence to house individuals who cannot remain at home.

* * *

Hints of Tunie's cancer first surfaced in September 1993 during the Sukkot holiday. Tunie and I went to dinner at my brother Ralph's house. When we returned home that evening, Tunie complained of pain in her abdomen. As the pain intensified, we grew concerned. We found a family doctor who would see her right away. He did not believe it was anything serious, but suggested, as a precautionary measure, to see our regular doctor at our convenience. The next day, Tunie called and made an appointment.

After a thorough checkup, blood work and a CT scan, the doctor did not like what he saw. He recommended Tunie see a gastroenterologist. We decided to use our privileged status as members of "The Committee of One Thousand" at Mt. Sinai Hospital and were able to make an appointment with the dean of the faculty for the following week. A scrupulous review of the scans, blood work and examination report revealed tumors encasing Tunie's ovaries. The dean called a friend, a respected surgeon, and scheduled a consultation for Tunie for the following week. By then, it was mid-October and each day of waiting compounded our distress.

That evening, after our meeting with the dean, we mentioned the situation to a family member who encouraged us to contact ECHO (Ezrat Cholim/National Jewish Institute for Health), an organization specializing in medical referrals. We called. The next day, we had an appointment with a surgeon at Sloan Kettering Hospital. Impressed at how quickly ECHO responded to our urgency, we decided to cancel the appointment made for the following week.

All of our children accompanied us to Sloan Kettering. We waited for the surgeon's opinion, hoping it would not be as bleak as we were suspecting. "Immediate surgery is needed to determine if the tumors are malignant or not," said the surgeon.

* * *

I checked Tunie into the hospital on Sunday, October 24, for pre-op tests. Her early morning surgery on Monday, October 25, coincided with a commitment I made to speak to a group at the Sephardic Community Center about launching and operating a successful enterprise. Of course, I cancelled the class. My place was with Tunie. I vowed to see her through this illness and would not accept the possibility of losing her. Tunie was the love of my life.

Close friends and family sat for hours with me in the waiting room. Some read psalms, others busied themselves with phone conversations. By mid-afternoon, after a long and agonizing wait, the surgeon emerged. Anxiously, I searched his face, looking for good news, praying that all was okay. It wasn't. The tumors covering Tunie's ovaries were malignant. My beloved wife would have to undergo six months of chemotherapy. "If Tunie responds well to treatment, then she has a favorable chance of recovering, or at least keeping the cancer in remission for many years. If the cancer is difficult to control . . . let's wait and see how she responds to the round of chemo," he said.

* * *

The surgeon put Tunie in the hands of his team of oncologists who explained the procedures for administering the chemotherapy, the potency of the drugs and the side effects. They said sometimes the chemotherapy would be taken at home and sometimes it would require overnight hospital stays. Tunie would suffer side effects, some of which might be fatigue, hair loss, nausea, vomiting, bruising, bleeding, joint and muscle pain.

At this point, my life lost all sense of normalcy and my daily routine shifted 360 degrees. Instead of going into the office, channeling my zeal toward continued growth of E.S. Sutton, instead of an active social life with friends and family, instead of trips with my cherished wife, my life and my energies turned toward sustaining Tunie. A life without her was not an option for me. Our existence centered around the next chemotherapy treatment, the next hospital stay, weekly doctor visits to monitor the drugs' effectiveness and caring for Tunie, who was bravely enduring the dreadful side effects. Coping with this lifestyle change was not an experience I could ever have imagined.

For support and guidance through this difficult period, I turned to ECHO, especially to Rabbi Aaron Weitz, Founder and Executive Director, who endorsed the course of treatment.

* * *

In May of 1994, Tunie's chemotherapy treatments ended. Exploratory surgery followed to determine if the malignant cells were eradicated. My family and I anxiously awaited the diagnosis, praying to G-d for a positive outcome. The same doctor who performed the first surgery also performed the second surgery. We waited at the hospital, expecting the surgeon to appear and speak with us. He did not. He sent the head operating-room nurse in his place. She told us the surgery had been completed, but offered no further information. I was concerned and pursued an answer, needing to know if the months of chemotherapy had been successful. She smiled and took me to the recovery room to see Tunie.

My apprehensions, my questions went ignored. The surgeon made no attempt to speak with me. I detected something very wrong, so I left Tunie's side and ventured into his office. I found him sitting calmly, reading. He disregarded my presence. I became angry at his indifference and pressed for answers. In a cold, insensitive tone, he announced his evaluation. "The operation went well but lesions are still present. Call my office and make an appointment to discuss future options."

What callousness, I thought. Is this proper behavior for a doctor?

* * *

With the chemotherapy discontinued, Tunie's spirits lifted marginally. Her hair grew back, she discarded her wig and she regained some of her weight. To recoup a degree of normalcy to our lives, and with the approval of the surgeon, we planned a trip, although this did not diminish Tunie's fear of the future.

In October, with our close friends Renee and Izzy joining us, we set out for a ten-day vacation to Atlanta, Charleston and Hilton Head. Tunie appeared eager for a change, but in hindsight, this was a bad idea. No sooner did we arrive in Hilton Head, we had to rush back home.

* * *

Tests showed a widespread recurrence of the cancer. The surgeon refused to operate again. He gave up hope, but I did not.

I called Rabbi Weitz, desperate to find help for Tunie. Rabbi Weitz sent copies of Tunie's medical records to doctors at major hospitals in Boston, Houston and Los Angeles. A surgical oncologist at Mt. Sinai Cedar Hospital in Los Angeles responded. "Contingent on a physical examination, surgery might benefit the patient."

I prayed this doctor would be our answer. Rabbi Weitz, a one-time resident of Los Angeles, offered to make all the logistical arrangements for Tunie and me. He set up an appointment with the surgeon and his team of oncologists, and he reserved a room for us in a hotel in a Jewish neighborhood. The hotel had a kosher dining room and was situated across the street from a Sephardic synagogue.

* * *

We landed in Los Angeles quite late on a Thursday night. Tunie was exhausted from the trip. She needed a good night's sleep, especially since her medical appointment was scheduled for the following day. We took a cab to the hotel. The lobby was dull and colorless, and added to my somber frame of mind. I thought about leaving, going somewhere else, but Tunie was tired and needed to rest, so I checked in. Our room was drab and dismal, even more so than the lobby. I felt my depression deepen. These were not the kind of accommodations I was accustomed to and I did not want to be there. I did not like the dilemma I was in. Tunie was exhausted and I had to help her get ready for bed; I could not start looking for another hotel room. Moreover, to move to better accommodations in the center of the city, away from the synagogue and the kosher kitchen at the hotel would be an insult to Rabbi Weitz who made the arrangements for us. So, at least for the night, we stayed put, but I had every intention of moving after Tunie's oncology appointment.

I rose early on Friday. Tunie was still asleep. I showered, dressed and went across the street to the synagogue to recite my morning prayers. When I returned to the room, I found Tunie too tired to go down to the kosher kitchen for breakfast. Inquiring at the reception desk, I was told of a kosher bagel store nearby.

I did not mind walking a few blocks, especially since the weather was so pleasant. Inside the shop was a line of people, each holding a number, each waiting to buy bagels. I took a number and stepped in line to wait my turn.

Within seconds, something unusual happened. I struck up a conversation with a delightful woman and found myself deep in dialogue with a stranger, divulging private information to her. This is quite unusual for me, not my normal demeanor. Perhaps our meeting was meant to be because, all of a sudden, she invited Tunie and I to spend Shabbat with her and her family. I hesitated, but she would not take 'no' for an answer.

* * *

We arrived at Mt. Sinai Cedar Hospital on time for the appointment. The doctor greeted us warmly, making us feel at ease. He carefully examined Tunie and then spent a long time speaking with us about his medical views and our options. We agreed to surgery on Tuesday. When I asked him about a good hotel in which to stay, he recommended the upscale Sofitel, conveniently located across the street from the hospital.

I called our prospective host and accepted her invitation, then booked a room at the Sofitel Hotel for check-in Saturday night.

On Friday afternoon, we arrived at a large house where the entire family welcomed us. We settled into the big, cheerful guest room with a private bath. We attended synagogue services with the family on Friday evening and on Saturday morning. We had wonderful sabbath meals and warm conversations. Constant chatter from the teenage children filled the house. Tunie and I felt our spirits lift. I will forever be grateful to that special lady who reached out to me in the bagel store.

After sunset on Saturday night, we moved into the Sofitel Hotel. On Tuesday, Tunie was in the hospital for surgery. Tunie's sister Marilyn flew in from New York to be with us.

* * *

Marilyn and I waited at the hospital for Tunie's surgery to be done and for the doctor to come out and speak with us. Our son Sammy was returning from a trip to the Far East and stopped in Los Angeles to be with his mother and to provide moral support.

"The surgery went well," the oncologist said, "except for a minor flaw. Extensive cutting to remove the tumors perforated Tunie's intestine causing a fistula, a sometime unavoidable consequence. The opening has to be closed or it will pose a greater risk to Tunie's already fragile condition."

More surgery was performed to repair the fistula, but tests afterward showed the hole had reopened. To avoid infection by a leak, the doctor recommended a colostomy, an alternative channel for intestinal waste to leave the body. He was willing to do the procedure immediately, but we wanted to return home for a second opinion. We called Rabbi Weitz, seeking his guidance. He made an appointment for Tunie with a New York surgeon.

Our trip home was gruesome as we sat on the plane in a constant state of attending to Tunie and the incessant intestinal leak from the fistula. Poor Tunie. I hurt so much for her and wished I could remove her suffering and make her well.

* * *

A quick consultation with the New York surgeon confirmed the need for a colostomy. The procedure was done within days. Tunie also had to repeat another round of chemotherapy treatments. The severe side effects were immediate. Tunie, who was not a complainer, endured the invasion to her body in silence. I think she was too weak to fight anymore, too resigned to hope for a positive outcome.

I resolved to devote all of my moments caring for Tunie, attending to her needs, making her comfortable. I neglected my business, a choice that brought me anguish and near ruination in the coming years.

Rabbi Weitz had a friend, a doctor with whom he engaged in weekly bible study classes. The doctor's practice was in Westchester, New York, an hour's drive each way from Brooklyn. Rabbi Weitz recommended we use this man for Tunie's next round of chemotherapy.

At our first meeting, we found the doctor full of compassion. It appeared we had his undivided attention as he assured us of a positive prognosis. Little did we know his wonderful bedside manner would last only so long. Tunie became another number on his assembly line.

Tunie's colostomy was meant to last six months, to give the fistula time to heal. She was on a liquid diet, initially prepared by a visiting nurse before I was taught how to take over. Liquid entered Tunie's body through a port that was surgically inserted into her chest.

As Tunie's resilience strengthened, her spirits lifted. She began to joke, invited friends to visit and play bridge and proudly displayed her many get well cards. She expressed her gratitude to Rabbi Weitz, his assistant, Judith Rackovsky, and to the ECHO staff. "ECHO saved my life," she said, and wished for me and the children to introduce ECHO to our community so that more people could reap the benefits of this organization.

By December 1995, Tunie was admitted to the hospital to repair the fistula. One last string to tie and we would return to normalcy. Our hopes were high. I put on a business suit, expecting to go into the office, expecting to resume my obligations to our company—right after the surgeon delivered the good news. At the hospital, my family and I waited . . . and waited . . . and waited. Time dragged on. Strangers wandered in and out of the visitor's lounge, their faces were a blur. Fear and anxiety took over, darkening our initial optimism. Where was the doctor? Why didn't he come out? We paced the floor for what seemed like an eternity. Then, out of the corner of my eye, I spotted the surgeon walking toward us; a cloud of sadness hung over him. He had grown fond of Tunie and now he had to bring us the news.

"I'm in shock. I truly didn't expect this," he said. "Tunie's abdomen is full of cancerous tumors. There was nothing more I could do except close her up. It's a matter of time for . . . " his voice quivered and his words trailed. He placed his hand on my shoulder, "I'm sorry, Elie."

Devastation overcame me. My world, my love would soon be gone. I broke down and cried. Family and close friends surrounded me and cried with me. Teary-eyed, I faced the doctor, "Where do we go from here?"

"The cancer will continue unabated. Its ferocity will multiply, gradually attacking every organ in her body," he replied. "Tunie will suffer from extreme pain, but we will medicate her to ease the agony. We could try other options, but most are experimental. Tunie has about a year and I can't see inflicting her with more treatments. In her final months, I suggest you make her comfortable, and love her. Don't try to fight a losing battle."

* * *

In the months that followed, unbearable pain wreaked Tunie's body, depleting all her energy, leaving her with no strength to fight the disease. Trying to alleviate the pain with medications and frequent trips to hospital emergency rooms became my main function. Then, in late spring, Tunie's kidneys failed, requiring dialysis three times a week, initially in the hospital and then at home. Her weight tumbled to 80 pounds. Her body was black and blue from needles, ports, and patches. Seizures became a daily occurrence. My heart, my insides, ached for Tunie. Wishing to ease her torment, I asked G-d to have mercy and take her. Then quickly, I regretted my thoughts and prayed for forgiveness.

Tunie's sisters were a tremendous help supporting us through this nightmare. They cooked meals and arranged for our daily nourishment. Friends and family visited constantly, always ready to pitch in and help with whatever was needed. My children were as devastated as I was. They loved their mother and did whatever they could to keep her comfortable. Rabbi Weitz of ECHO became Tunie's spiritual caregiver, preparing her to accept the inevitable, instilling in her an afterlife, her soul basking in G-d's splendor. Rabbi Farhi from our community came to the house on Rosh Hashanah to blow the shofar for Tunie, which seemed to awaken a mystical spark.

I am grateful to Gladys Sultan, Tunie's stepmother, and her daughter, Ellen, who spent hours with Tunie, playing the guitar and singing Israeli melodies. Tunie looked forward to their visits, which never failed to lift her spirits.

Toward the end, Tunie became delirious, then silent. On December 10, 1996, at 10:30 PM, with her son Sammy and her brother Joe at her side, Tunie closed her eyes. She was 64 years old.

Tunie left me with many blessings—four children, 17 grandchildren, seven great grandchildren. Through my family, I keep Tunie alive. No matter where I am, no matter what my frame of mind, Tunie is with me.

* * *

Rabbi Weitz devoted untold hours nurturing Tunie's spirit. He directed us to reputable doctors and the finest hospitals. He offered comfort, understanding and religious wisdom at times when we needed it most. His staff, especially his assistant, Judith Rackovsky, treated us with kindness and compassion and provided us constant attention and feedback to every detail of Tunie's care.

To show our never-ending gratitude and to honor Tunie's memory and her wishes, my sons, Abraham and Sammy, and I brought ECHO to Brooklyn, to serve and benefit the Syrian community.

It did not take long for us to raise money, including our own sizable donation, to establish an office and hire Rabbi Mordechai Kenigsberg to manage ECHO's latest branch. We dedicated the new ECHO office in memory of Tunie Sutton.

Today, I continue my commitment to ECHO, raising funds to maintain the budget, ensuring that when someone in our community is in need of finding good, specialized medical care, our well-trained office staff is ready to serve.

Celebrating my 60th birthday with family,
Concord Hotel, Upstate New York

Sailing trip in the Caribbean, 1984

Outside Athens on way to cruise through Turkey and Russia

IN MEMORIAM

TUNIE SUTTON

The Sephardic Community suffered a tremendous loss recently when Tunie Sutton passed away at the age of 64 after a long illness. Tunie was a devoted wife, loving mother and grandmother. Her energy and enthusiasm coupled with her kindness and compassion brightened the lives of all those who were fortunate to know her. Tunie stood for family values, modesty, education, and was always concerned with the health and well being of our community. The establishment of Congregation Beth Torah in Brooklyn and the Hillel Yeshivah High School in New Jersey were both fuelled by her dynamic efforts.

Tunie's mother, Adele Sultan, suffered from Alzheimers disease for over 20 years before succumbing to the illness. In 1981 recognizing how this disease affected an entire family, Tunie dedicated herself to raising the community's awareness of Alzheimers. She organized and led support groups for the families and care givers of Alzheimers patients at our Sephardic Community Center. Despite her absence, these support groups still meet helping many families during difficult times. Tunie was also involved with the Alzheimers Association, the National Organization committed to finding a cure for this dreadful disease.

During her illness, Tunie and her family became acquainted with the ECHO Organization. ECHO is a medical referral service based in Spring Valley, New York, created to help families suffering through medical crisis. Realizing the tremendous support ECHO offered, and organizing the need for such a service in the community, Tunie and her husband Elie with the help of several other community leaders, worked diligently to open a Sephardic division of ECHO. This office opened several months ago in the Ocean Parkway area of Brooklyn and is currently serving our community at large. In recognition of her endless desire to help others, the Sephardic division will soon be renamed in her memory.

Tunie was an inspiration to her colleagues, family and friends. Tunie Sutton truly made a difference and is sorely missed. Tunie is survived by her husband of 45 years Elie, 4 children, 15 grandchildren as well as her father, Abraham Sultan, 2 sisters and 2 brothers.

*   *   *   *   *

Tunie Sutton has touched the lives of our family for four generations. She has brought sunshine, warmth, sincerity, and joy to all of our lives.

Tunie was very dedicated to her family. She loved life and approached every day with enthusiasm and joy. She used her intelligence and compassion to always try to help others. Tunie was active in a variety of community projects.

The memory of her smiling face will have a special place in all of our hearts forever. ❑

Isadore & Renee Shamah & Family

Tunie Sutton - In Memoriam

My son Sammy and his family

My son Abie and his family

My daughter April and her family

Family picture taken at my grandson Lee and Sally Hamway wedding

TWENTY-FOUR

THE PERSON WHO TRIES TO LIVE ALONE WILL NOT SUCCEED AS
A HUMAN BEING. HIS HEART WITHERS IF IT DOES NOT ANSWER
ANOTHER HEART. HIS MIND SHRINKS AWAY IF HE HEARS ONLY
THE ECHOES OF HIS OWN THOUGHTS AND FINDS NO OTHER
INSPIRATION—PEARL S. BUCK

While devoting so much time to Tunie, I completely neglected my business responsibilities. My commitment to Tunie and my obsession for her to get well, consumed me. To their credit, Ralph and Joe not only picked up the slack and covered for me, they also continued to provide me with my substantial income.

After Tunie's passing, I was completely distraught. All hope was gone. My efforts to care for her, to save her from the inevitable were now history. I missed Tunie. I wanted her back. For weeks, I cried inconsolably. I mourned. I sobbed. I wailed.

After three-and-a-half years, my brothers recognized that they could run the business without me, that I was no longer indispensable. Yet, out of kindness and compassion, they did not force me out. They remained patient, waiting for me to return to work full time.

* * *

Noting my severe depression, our close friends of more than 40 years, Renee and Izzy, insisted I spend time with them in their Florida apartment. They said a break from the harsh winter would do me good, exposure to the sunshine and warm weather would lift my spirits. But I knew that going anywhere without Tunie would only exacerbate my depression. Still, I went. At night, I cried myself to sleep and wanted only to be near my family, so I returned to Brooklyn.

The winter was grim and I was lonely. Time dragged. Each day seemed to be heavier than the one before. I forced myself to go back to work, but found it too difficult. My children and grandchildren showered me with attention and love, yet I could not pull myself out of my sorrow. I sought out a bereavement therapist and consulted with my family doctor. "Time is the best healer," they said.

In early February, I returned to Florida, rented an apartment and occupied my days with tennis and golf. I rotated my atmosphere, alternating every other week between Florida and Brooklyn. I spent time with my children and grandchildren, and convinced myself that returning to work part time would be a positive diversion.

In early March, a friend who had been through a similar tragedy convinced me to open a new chapter in my life, saying that our religious beliefs demand it. A few days later, back in Florida, another friend introduced me to a beautiful lady I had not known before, even though she lived in our Sephardic community. When I learned of her name, Tunie, I interpreted this as a good omen.

Although Tunie Cheika Fallack was 23 years my junior, we found so much in common. We chattered incessantly in French and English. She was empathetic to my pain and soothed my grieving.

Tunie also had suffered loss in her life. When she was 39, her husband died, leaving her with four children. At 45, she lost her only son. After marrying at 19 and coming to America from Lebanon, Tunie brought her family, her parents and five sisters to America and our Brooklyn community. She looked after their well being until they could manage on their own.

We began dating in secret, then told our families when we decided to marry, setting a date in December 1997, after the one-year passing of my first Tunie. In time, I got to know my new Tunie's family, her sisters and their spouses, her mother Sophia and her father Jack. I met her three lovely daughters, her sons-in-law, her grandchildren; and she met my growing family. With my new Tunie, I could close a chapter and begin a new one.

Today, Tunie and I have harmoniously combined our two big families, our children and grandchildren. She and I spend our winters as snowbirds in Aventura, Florida, our summers at the shore in Deal, New Jersey, and the rest of the year in Brooklyn, New York. In all three places, we are surrounded with our community, the Sephardic Jews who are so deeply rooted into our lives.

We joined the Beit Edmund J. Safra Sephardic Synagogue in Aventura, a commanding structure funded by wealthy Syrian Jews from New York, New Jersey, Argentina, Brazil, Panama, Mexico, and Geneva. I am proud to be one of its founders and its first elected president for three consecutive years. To this day, I remain an active member of the board. Moreover, I am also associated with a second synagogue in Aventura, a synagogue in Brooklyn, and two synagogues in Deal.

My successful real estate business with my two sons keeps me busy and productive. My personal time with Tunie is occupied with tennis, golf, world travel, an active social life, and lavish family and religious events and milestones.

Tunie, I and our families keep to the orthodoxy of Sephardic Judaism, observe the rituals of the Sabbath and the Jewish holidays, and follow the dictates and interpretations decreed by the Rabbis in our community.

Tunie and me,
our wedding reception
December 4, 1997

Tunie and me

Tunie with her
three daughters

Partying with my brothers Ralph and Joe and our wives

Beit Edmond J. Safra Synagogue, Aventura, Florida

2004 official grand opening, Beit Edmond J. Safra Sephardic Synagogue
Aventura, Florida
As the congregation's first president, I served as master of ceremonies

Presenting an award to Mrs. Lily Safra

Presenting an award to David Braka, the synagogue's Chairman of the Board;
to the left, Jeffery Perlow, Mayor of Aventura

EPILOGUE

By 1999, after neglecting my business responsibilities for
so long and my brothers' patience wearing thin, something I could
not fault them for, the three of us went our separate ways. Joe
continued in the apparel business with his sons. Ralph established
a new company with his sons. And I launched Sutton Management
with my sons, pursuing real estate management and development in
New York and New Jersey.

* * *

My life story will continue to unfold until my final hour.
I remember my brother Saleh who showed so much promise.
Handsome, smart, uninhibited, gregarious, adventuresome. I cannot
understand why he chose to neglect his health, why Hashem took
him at such a young age.

I remember John Bialy, my Christian friend from Shanghai,
who opened his lush living quarters to me, inviting me to live in
his upscale residence in the French Quarter of the city. He shared
with me his food, his cook, his maid and his driver. We engaged
in long conversations, played tennis at the country club, and
went swimming every morning. John, who worked for a shipping
company headquartered in San Francisco, genuinely cared about
me. He worried about my well being and my stateless position when
the Communists took over Shanghai. If it were not for John Bialy
pulling strings to get me on a ship out of China, my life would have
followed a much different path. Many years ago, John flew from San

Francisco to visit me in Brooklyn. I never reciprocated, even when I had opportunities to do so. Now, too many years have passed and John may not even be alive. I regret not making efforts to see him, not telling him how grateful I am to him for saving my life.

Rahmo Sassoon, who recently passed away, became a close friend. He and his brother, Edmond, were Syrian Jews living in Tokyo when I arrived there from Shanghai. Edmond had allowed me to use his posh apartment in Shanghai's French Quarter for my extravagant parties; I also was an usher at his wedding. Rahmo and Edmond encouraged me to get a visitor's visa to the United States. They did not allow my uncertainties over my stateless position to interfere with their efforts. Continuing to pressure me, they only stopped when I finally had a visa in my hand. If it were not for Rahmo and Edmond, I may never have made it to America. Rahmo eventually became a client in our finance business, and years later when he retired to Manhattan, we experienced an unbroken bond in our friendship.

My Iraqi-Jewish friend, Johnny Elias, moved to Canada with his Russian wife Valia and her sister Luba—my beautiful Luba with whom I was in love but who would only be my friend.

Moise Dweck, who left Aleppo and traveled with Saleh and me to Shanghai, settled in Italy, married, then divorced, left Italy, moved to Brazil to be near his family, then married for a second time. He died in Brazil, leaving a wife, children, grandchildren, and great grandchildren.

My brother Mike, who helped me while I lived in Shanghai, made his home in the Washington, D.C. area where he became a successful businessman. Periodically, we keep in touch, but because of the geographical distance, our relationship over the years has not been a close one. I wish I had made more of an effort to nurture a stronger connection. I wish our families had been closer.

I think often of my first Tunie, the mother of my children, my 45 incredible years with her, how very much I have loved her, how very much I still miss her.

I believe G-d's meddling has been at work in my destiny. It is not mere coincidence that so many people have come in and out of my life to guide me, help me, support me, befriend me, and, yes, love me unconditionally. I would not be where I am today if it were not for them.

My wife, my second Tunie, enabled me to have a second chance. I cannot imagine how I could have coped without her. She brought me back into existence, rekindled my spirit, and revived my energy. Her younger years have expanded the horizons of our life together.

* * *

Today, as we cross the threshold into the second decade of the second millennium, my business, like so many others, has felt the bite from the recession; yet, I am fortunate that the economic downturn has not affected me as greatly as it has others. My sons, Sammy and Abie, essentially run my real estate business. Their perceptions and competence continue to amaze me and I am so very proud of them.

My children, my grandchildren, my great grandchildren— they are all a great source of immeasurable joy for me and I love them more they could know.

* * *